Navigating Media's Influence Through Childhood and Adolescence

Navigating Media's Influence Through Childhood and Adolescence moves through research and questions that are relevant to practicing pediatricians and therapists in their everyday practice. As we navigate post-pandemic life where screen time was unrestricted in most homes, this book has never been more important. Written by a pediatrician and a professor of media effects, this book is a vital resource for practicing mental health clinicians, counselors, psychologists, physicians, and students studying in those areas. Grounded in developmental theory, mass communication theory, current research, and acumen gained from years of clinical and teaching experience, this book gives professionals what they need to understand the colossal effect media is having on their patients. An aid to practitioners, this book is organized by developmental stage and matches specific questions related to media's effects with explicit research-based recommendations and explanations. It is intended to be a quick resource guide for the busy professional.

Kate S. Kurtin, PhD, is an associate professor of communication studies at California State University, Los Angeles. She studies the way young people use media, has an interest in the relationship people form with media, and is the author of three books.

Mary Ellen McCormick, MD, works exclusively as an outpatient general pediatrician in the Los Angeles area. The effects of media on children are an important part of her day-to-day discussions with patients and their parents.

"*Navigating Media's Influence Through Childhood and Adolescence* is impressive in its approach and scope and brings together theory, research, and wisdom from medicine, childhood development, media, and media effects. Professionals working with children and youth will find the book's unique blend of scientific insight and clinical savvy invaluable as they grapple with the many issues surrounding youths media use."

Kaveri Subrahmanyam, PhD, *professor of psychology and associate dean, College of Natural and Social Sciences, California State University Los Angeles*

"Parents ask pediatricians (and others that care for children, adolescents, and young adults) about growth, development, problem behaviors, school, and sometimes just to know if something is normal. The need to ask these questions has intensified with increased use of social media, increased isolation, increased anxiety, depression, and stress. The authors, a communication scholar and a pediatrician, use research and experience to answer questions about media and its impact on children and adolescents. This is a well-written, well-resourced guide to common concerns about the role of medial in our children's lives. It is a great resource for social workers, pediatricians, teachers, and parents."

Martin M. Anderson, MD, MPH, FAAP, FSAM, *professor of clinical pediatrics and adolescent medicine, Mattel Children's Hospital*

"This is the book pediatricians and mental health professionals have been waiting for. Kurtin and McCormick translate research findings on the effects of media upon children into practical advice for guiding professionals who are navigating this new frontier."

Gail Shak, PhD, *Department of Psychiatry affiliate, Mills Peninsula Medical Center*

"This book offers researched answers to timely questions about how to work with children of the COVID era who have been exposed to 'screen time' as a means of entertainment, communication, education, and, for many families, as a means of survival. It has pertinent information for me as both a speech-language pathologist and a parent of young children."

Deanna Gilman, MS, CCC-SLP

KATE S. KURTIN, PHD AND
MARY ELLEN MCCORMICK, MD

Navigating Media's Influence Through Childhood and Adolescence

A Question and Answer Guide for Professionals

Routledge
Taylor & Francis Group

NEW YORK AND LONDON

Cover image: Getty Images

First published 2023
by Routledge
605 Third Avenue, New York, NY 10158

and by Routledge
4 Park Square, Milton Park, Abingdon, Oxon, OX14 4RN

Routledge is an imprint of the Taylor & Francis Group, an informa business

Library of Congress Cataloging-in-Publication Data
Names: Kurtin, Kate S., author. | McCormick, Mary Ellen, author.
Title: Navigating media's influence through childhood and adolescence : a
    question and answer guide for professionals / Kate S. Kurtin, PhD &
    Mary Ellen McCormick, MD.
Description: New York, NY : Routledge, 2022. | Includes bibliographical
    references and index.
Identifiers: LCCN 2022010341 (print) | LCCN 2022010342 (ebook) |
    ISBN 9781032121697 (hardback) | ISBN 9781032121680 (paperback) |
    ISBN 9781003223412 (ebook)
Subjects: LCSH: Mass media and children. | Child psychology. | Mass media
    and teenagers. | Adolescent psychology.
Classification: LCC HQ784.M3 K87 2022 (print) | LCC HQ784.M3 (ebook) |
    DDC 302.23083—dc23/eng/20220613
LC record available at https://lccn.loc.gov/2022010341
LC ebook record available at https://lccn.loc.gov/2022010342

ISBN: 978-1-032-12169-7 (hbk)
ISBN: 978-1-032-12168-0 (pbk)
ISBN: 978-1-003-22341-2 (ebk)

DOI: 10.4324/9781003223412

Typeset in Joanna MT
by Apex CoVantage, LLC

This book is dedicated to Claire, Will, Luke,
and Griffin, who give our lives and
this research more meaning.

Contents

Preface   ix

1   **Foundations in Development and Theoretical Considerations**   1

2   **Foundations in Media Literacy and Understanding Children's Media Environments**   22

3   **Current Guidelines on Digital Media Use by the American Academy of Pediatrics**   36

4   **Effects of Media on the Developing Infant and Young Child**   43

5   **Growing Up in a Digital World**   59

6   **Internet Safety**   79

7   **Video Games**   93

8   **Tweens and Teenagers: Development and Media**   106

9   **Learning in the Digital Age**   124

10   **Media, the Body, and Disordered Eating**   139

11   **Media, Gender, and Sexuality**   155

12   Pornography   170

13   Risky Behaviors Around Sex, Drugs, and Alcohol   184

Index   199

Welcome to *Navigating Media's Influence Through Childhood and Adolescence: A Question and Answer Guide for Professionals*. Thank you for reading! This book has been in the works for some time, but never has it been more important than in the wake of the COVID-19 pandemic. The topics we discuss in this book have been relevant since the invention of modern media and will be for decades to come, but the effects of the media were exacerbated during the pandemic, and therefore research in this area has never been more prolific. For the first time in history all entertainment, education, and socialization were all on a screen. We have known for some time that restricting media is in the best interest of everyone, but in 2020 that became impossible and the trains fell off the track.

Early research on the effects of quarantine revealed disastrous results. In their research in the effects of quarantine, Tang et al. (2021) surveyed 4,343 primary and secondary school students from Shanghai, China, who were in quarantine due to COVID-19. Through their research the authors discovered an increase in anxiety for nearly a quarter of the respondents (25%), an increase in depression (20%), and increased stress levels (15%) from the students surveyed. In addition, the authors noted a strong positive correlation between the age of the student and their psychopathological symptoms, which were also negatively associated with life satisfaction. Talking about these issues with an adult were shown to have dramatically positive results (Tang et al., 2021).

Also looking into the early effects of quarantine on youth, Singh et al. (2020) conducted a narrative review on articles relating to the mental health of children and adolescents during the COVID-19 pandemic and lockdown. Their results mirrored those of Tang et al. and added in the additional variable of the media. Specifically, this review of the literature revealed that Internet gaming and social media use put children and adolescents at a higher risk for psychopathological symptoms. As the authors of this book, and people who spend time discussing media effects every day, we know that these consequences of media use have always been present but dealing with them is now everyone's responsibility. Also, while we were writing the book, the social media giant Facebook (now Meta) took some heat for leaked data insinuating that their Instagram platform was "bad for teenagers." Again, something we have known for some time, but now it is making headlines.

Not to take advantage of a global pandemic, but 2020 also brought to light something that media effects scholars have been saying for decades – the media affects everyone and everything! In this book we talk about the American Academy of Pediatrics and their recommendations for screen time (page 23), the developing infant and young child (page 43), learning in the digital age (page 124), body image (page 139), gender (page 155), sexuality (page 155), and sex, drugs, and rock n' roll (page 184), to name just a few topics. While 2020 highlighted the importance of understanding what increased screen access is doing to our children and adolescents, this information was critical before the lockdown and will be for generations after.

We are writing this book for people on the front lines. As a media effects professor and a pediatrician, we are well aware of the types of questions you are asked every day. We are also intimately aware of how much time it takes to research and analyze all of these issues. This book is our way of answering all of the big questions and providing you with the research, background, and theoretical understanding of how those answers came to be.

It is our intention that this book be an accessible resource to people who want their questions answered about how the media is affecting children today. We see ourselves being the conduit between the research and practice, and the advice that therapists and physicians are asked to give every day. Most therapists don't have time to analyze the research or spend hours talking with kids and their parents, but they are still frequently placed in a position of needing to give advice on these issues. This book will help. Additionally, parents ask pediatricians for help with media, or areas affected by media, every day, but in a 20-minute well-child visit there is no time to get into it. This book will help.

We have organized the book by theme and developmental age. At the start of the process, we solicited questions from parents, therapists, and physicians about issues they encounter surrounding media and children. We then grouped the questions by theme, organized them into chapters, and that's what you have here. The questions are listed at the top of each chapter so that you know what you are getting into before you start and also indicated in italics throughout the chapter. Along with the questions, in each chapter we introduce the research and theory that exists in each area that we used to inform our opinions. Hopefully the expertise we bring from our fields will offer you a unique vantage point and be helpful.

ABOUT THE AUTHORS

When talking to my family about this book at dinner one night, my seven-year-old suggested that there should be an "About the Authors" section. When pressed further he said it should say: "*This book was written by two mothers of two who have frequent playdates with each other.*" That just about sums it up.

If you want to know our credentials, they are below.

Kate S. Kurtin, PhD

Kate S. Kurtin, PhD, received her undergraduate degree from Occidental College after studying sociology with a particular interest in media effects. She continued her education at Boston University where she received her MA for her work in advertising and communication research. Delving deeper into the role of advertising and media in the lives of children, she received her PhD from the University of Connecticut in mass communication. Her dissertation focused on the relationships preschool children have with media characters (parasocial relationships) and begins to explain that this generation of America's youth is being shaped by the media in ways we have not seen before.

Dr. Kurtin is now an associate professor of communication studies at California State University, Los Angeles. Her continuing passion within communication studies is the media's effect on children and, to that end, Dr. Kurtin studies the evolving way that young people use media within this frame. She became an associate professor in 2019 and has published three books on the subjects of communication, public relations, and advertising.

Mary Ellen McCormick, MD

Mary Ellen McCormick, MD, received her undergraduate degree in communication studies with a mass media emphasis at the University of California, Los Angeles. She went on to pursue her career in medicine by obtaining her medical degree at the University of California, Davis. A natural interest in children's health drove her to continue her medical training at the UCLA Medical Center, where she completed her internship and residency in general pediatrics. Since completing her residency in 2007, she has worked exclusively as an outpatient general pediatrician in the Los Angeles area. The effects of media on children have been a consistent interest in her career stemming from her undergraduate experience to her day-to-day discussions with patients and their parents. As a pediatrician and mother of two, she is eager to facilitate the discussion from the most updated research to those providing direct care for children and adolescents.

REFERENCES

Singh, S., Roy, D., Sinha, K., Parveen, S., Sharma, G., & Joshi, G. (2020). Impact of COVID-19 and lockdown on mental health of children and adolescents: A narrative review with recommendations. *Psychiatry Research*, 293(113429), ISSN 0165–1781. https://doi.org/10.1016/j.psychres.2020.113429

Tang, S., Xiang, M., Cheung, T., & Xiang, Y. T. (2021). Mental health and its correlates among children and adolescents during COVID-19 school closure: The importance of parent-child discussion. *Journal of Affective Disorders*, 279, 353–360, ISSN 0165–0327. https://doi.org/10.1016/j.jad.2020.10.016

This book is intended for professionals currently working with children and teens on their health, safety, and development. We won't take up too much of your time on fundamentals, however, one of the important features of this book, and hopefully why you are reading it, is because we have different backgrounds and understanding of these issues than you do. Given our background in childhood development, pediatrics, communication studies, media literacy, and media effects, we want to start with a chapter on foundations to get everyone up to speed and also introduce some theories that have guided the research in hopes for more clarity. In this chapter we review child development from 0–21 years old and then introduce significant social science theories. These topics will be the foundation of the book and help guide us throughout the remaining chapters.

CHILD DEVELOPMENT

Health surveillance in children and adolescence is multifaceted. At each well visit many concerns are addressed, including, but certainly not limited to, diet, growth, sleep, and immunizations. Also fundamental to each visit is an assessment as to how the child is developing. Screenings evolve as a child grows from infant to adolescence as do the types of "milestones" anticipated physically, cognitively, and socially/emotionally. As stated in *Bright Futures: Guidelines for Health Supervision of Infants, Children, and Adolescents*, many of our developmental screenings of early childhood rely on more standardized developmental screening tests (Hagan et al., 2017). One tool commonly used is the ages and stages questionnaires (ASQ). Screening for autistic spectrum occurs at the 18-month and 24-month visits in which a common tool utilized is the Modified Checklist for Autism in Toddlers (M-CHAT). As we approach middle childhood and adolescence, there is not one comprehensive screening tool. Naturally, each pediatrician assesses youth

DOI: 10.4324/9781003223412-1

for risk behaviors in addition to checking for healthy emotional and physical behaviors. As stated in the Bright Futures material,

> these are the things youth need to say yes to as they move toward adulthood. The child or adolescent should 1. Demonstrate social and emotional competence (including self-regulation). 2. Exhibit resiliency when confronted with life stressors. 3. Use independent decision-making skills (including problem-solving skills). 4. Display a sense of self-confidence and hopefulness. 5. Form caring and supportive relationships with family members, other adults, and peers. 6. Engage in a positive way with the life of the community. 7. Exhibit compassion and empathy. 8. Engage in healthy nutrition and physical activity behaviors. 9. Choose safety (eg, bike helmets, seat belts, avoidance of alcohol and drugs).
>
> (p. 78)

INFANT DEVELOPMENT

As with developmental screenings at any age, the goal of screening infants is to identify areas in which there may be a concern and facilitate intervention (Hagan et al., 2017). The first year of life is the most dramatic period of growth in life. By one year of age the infant's birth weight has tripled as their height has increased by 50%. Brain weight has doubled and by age two, there are twice as many synapses as adulthood. In the Bright Futures report, Hagan, Shaw, and Duncan stress the importance of positive early experiences to optimize brain development. In practice, screening of this population focuses on gross motor skills, fine motor skills, communication skills, and social skills.

EARLY CHILDHOOD DEVELOPMENT (ONE TO FOUR YEARS OLD)

This next developmental period moves beyond a one-year-old's focus of the world being what can be seen, heard, and felt. As a child progresses through these next few years, there is less focus on the present and more use of "mental symbols" and fantasy. There is a bigger focus on exploration and increasing independence. Communication of thoughts and ideas is of fundamental importance (Hagan et al., 2017). In terms of pediatric practice, well-care screenings are performed at 15 months, 18 months, 24 months, 30 months, 36 months, and 48 months. As mentioned earlier, at 18 months and 24 months there is an emphasis on screening for autistic spectrum disorder, which allows for critical early intervention and therapies for those who demonstrate concerns.

In this section, we will break down relative to age, the developmental goals at each of these surveillance points with respect to the domains of gross motor, fine motor, language, and social skills. For the purposes of this book, we will focus on their discussions on socialization, literacy, and school readiness.

During the second year of life huge and noticeable developments are made. By 18 months, a child may walk up to two feet per step with a hand held and carry a toy while walking. They become more proficient at scribbling and throwing a ball. They develop more words (six to ten words) and identify body parts. The social development at this point is pronounced. One expects to see more engagement with others in play, dressing and undressing, pointing to pictures in a book, pointing to objects of interest to draw attention, seeking adult attention if confronted with something new, and scooping with a spoon (Hagan et al., 2017). The M-CHAT screening questionnaire given at this visit provides specific questions to parents with regard to their child's behavior and social engagement. A scoring system allows for providers to identify those at risk and initiate the referral process for services.

By the age of two, there is a significant uptick in speech. At this point, children are speaking in two-word phrases and have moved on to using 50 words which are hopefully 50% intelligible to strangers. In terms of social skills, they engage in parallel play, take off clothing, and scoop well with a spoon. They are able to jump with both feet, kick a ball, and run proficiently. They start stacking objects, turning book pages, and functionally using hands (turn knobs, lids, etc.). The M-CHAT is administered again at this age to hopefully identify any concerns and allow for referral. By 30 months, pronouns are being used correctly. Social skills include urinating in a toilet, pretend play, and proficient fork use (Hagan et al., 2017).

In terms of a three-year-old, one observes three-word sentences with words that are 75% intelligible to strangers. Socially, they can engage in cooperative play and sharing. They begin in imaginative play and eat independently. Gross motor-wise, they can pedal tricycles and jump forward. Their fine motor skills consist of drawing a circle, using scissors, and drawing a person with a head and one other body part. Four-year-olds, however, are proficient in drawing a person with three body parts, drawing a simple cross and an enhanced grip such that they grasp a pencil with a thumb and fingers instead of a fist. They are able to climb stairs with alternating feet without support and skip on one foot. They use four-word sentences and are for the most part 100% intelligible. One expects proficient potty training, dressing/undressing and well-developed imaginative play (Hagan et al., 2017).

In *Bright Futures*, the authors present discussions on several different "highlights" of this developmental period. While all of great importance, we will focus on a few particularly as they pertain to later discussion regarding the effects of media on children. The importance of socialization is discussed and the importance of providing opportunities for interpersonal relationships as they promote "comfort and competence with relationships later in life" (p. 95). They describe social competencies including "planning and decision-making with others, positive and appropriate interpersonal interactions, exposure to other cultures and ethnicities, behavioral resistance to inappropriate or dangerous behavior, and peaceful conflict resolution." In addition, the authors encourage opportunities for children to engage socially in either structured or unstructured environments (Hagan et al., 2017, p. 95).

During this age period, the authors also discuss the importance of fostering literacy skills, as it is a complex process necessitating a variety of different inputs. It relies on "good, consistent relationships with caring adults who provide one-on-one interactions and who support the development of oral language" (p. 98). This is a critical time for toddlers as they are evolving in their communication skills, becoming more imaginative and receptive to stories. The authors encourage health care professionals to inspire parents to engage their child with stories, books, and opportunities for imaginary play. They recommend discourse with the child with respect to their ideas and questions. Finally, the authors advocate for focused time each for interactive reading which can give parents "a way to help their children grow up associating books with positive parental attention" (p. 99).

The impact of play is of critical importance in this developmental period (this will be discussed in detail in Chapter 4 (page 43)). However, one last highlight presented in *Bright Futures* is with regard to school readiness. The authors list skills that will be challenged when a patient starts kindergarten:

- Language and speech or signing that is sufficient for communication and learning
- Cognitive abilities that are necessary for learning sound-letter associations, spatial relations, and number concepts
- Ability to separate from family and caregivers (especially for the child who has not already participated in preschool activities)
- Self-regulation with respect to behavior, emotions, attention, and motor movement
- Ability to make friends and get along with peers
- Ability to participate in group activities
- Ability to follow rules and directions
- Skills that others appreciate, such as singing or drawing

(p. 101–102)

The authors emphasize the importance of school readiness as it is connected to later academic success. School readiness relies on efforts by everyone involved in the care of the young child.

MIDDLE CHILDHOOD DEVELOPMENT (FIVE TO TEN YEARS)

As mentioned earlier, development surveillance in this age group relies less on formal developmental screening tools and is a period of transition as a child evolves into adolescence. As described in *Bright Futures*:

> Middle childhood is an important time for families to strengthen their ties and to help children consolidate and build on their cognitive and emotional attributes, such as communication skills, sensitivity to others, ability to form positive peer relationships, self-esteem and independence. These attributes help them cope with stresses and potential risks of adolescence.
>
> (Hagan, Shaw, & Duncan, p. 102–103)

From a practical standpoint, as a pediatrician doing well care, a shift occurs in these visits. As opposed to demonstrating or reporting specific milestones, there are more discussions on hobbies, physical activity, school performance, and peer relationships. With respect to gross and fine motor skills, strength and coordination increase during this time. With increased competence comes more participation in activities, such as sports, which can facilitate positive interactions and positive self-image, not to mention positive effects on physical health.

In their discussion of cognitive and communication development, Hagan et al. (2017) describe a progression from magical to more logical thinking with abilities to articulate thoughts of greater complexity and creativity. This may foster a grander understanding of the world and subsequently more independence. The authors mention the importance of "self-efficacy" in this age group which they describe as the "knowledge of what to do and the confidence and ability to do it" (p. 104). Finally, Hagan, Shaw, and Duncan stress the importance of encouraging self-efficacy as it facilitates school success and productive use of their intelligence. Success in school in turn has a ripple effect to self-esteem.

Social and emotional development is very important in this age group. With increased independence and initiative, children of this group develop their own sense of "personhood." Hagan et al. (2017) present key areas including self and self-esteem, family dynamics, friendships, school performance, and community connections. They describe this as a time when a child is assessing where they "fit in." (p. 104). I mentioned at the beginning of this section that the well-child visits in this age group focus more on hobbies, peer relationships, and school dynamics. The goal is to address any area of discord such that the child can be supported and limit the potential for longer term emotional consequences.

ADOLESCENT DEVELOPMENT (11–21 YEARS)

Adolescent development is quite the complex process. Not only is the adolescent experience very dynamic, but each adolescent may differ in the timing of their physical, social, and emotional maturity. Pediatricians tend to divide adolescence into separate phases, including 11–14 years, 15–17 years, and 18–21 years, with each stage manifesting its own physiological, psychological, and social development. It is during adolescent visits that pediatricians have an opportunity to chat with patient's one-on-one and perform a home, education, activities, drugs (substances), sexuality, and suicidality (HEADSS) assessment.

Early adolescence refers to the 11–14-year-old age group. Physiologically, it includes the onset of puberty with growth spurt and menarche for girls. From a psychological standpoint, this includes a new reliance on concrete thought with a preoccupation on rapid body changes, sexual identity, questioning, and independence (Hagan et al., 2017). Socially, teens in this age group are searching for same gender affiliations, good parental relationships, and other adults as role models. With middle school comes more extracurricular activities as well as sensitivity to home culture and outside cultures for the first time.

Middle adolescence includes adolescents who are 15 to 17 years of age. Physically, young women are ovulating while young men are going through growth spurts. In terms of psychological manifestations, Hagan, Shaw, and Duncan describe "competence in abstract and future thought, idealism, sense of invincibility or narcissism, sexual identity, beginning of cognitive capacity to provide legal consent" (p. 107). Socially, teens in this group describe emotional emancipation and peer groups become more powerful as parental conflicts increase. Teens in this age group become more interested in sexual relationships, driving, and risk-taking behaviors. As with early adolescence, teens in this group have enhanced involvement in extracurricular activities and in addition, more potential culture conflicts between home life and outside culture.

Lastly, late adolescence is described as comprising adults aged 18 to 21 years of age. Growth is completed at this time. Psychologically, Hagan, Shaw, and Duncan list "future orientation; emotional independence; capacity for empathy, intimacy, reciprocity in interpersonal relationships; self-identity" as indicators of this group (p. 107). Socially, adults in this age group describe individual over peer relationships with a transition in parent relationship and transition out of home and into career development.

THEORETICAL EXPLANATIONS

This book comprises two different fields – medicine and childhood development with media and media effects. We just finished the childhood development portion of this chapter, and now we move into media effects. As you know, in the academic social sciences we understand things first through a theoretical framework. This section outlines two primary theories used to explain how media messages are attended to, understood, stored, and imitated by developing children and teens. We will refer back to these theories with regularity throughout the book.

SOCIAL LEARNING THEORY

Primary to research on media effects is social learning theory (SLT), which explains that viewers learn from what they see (Bandura, 2009). Social learning theory, and later social cognitive theory, describes individuals, including adolescents and children, as often emulating or using media as bases for decision-making and judgments. While the theory was originally drafted to explain how children model behavior they witness from adults (e.g., the Bobo doll experiment),[1] for decades it has been applied with mirrored results to media and mediated characters as a perfect replacement for adults in the original experiments. SLT proposes that individuals learn from monitoring the behaviors, attitudes, and reactions of others, including media characters, and puts forward the idea that individuals are more likely to model a behavior if it results in a rewarded or favored outcome (Bandura, 2009). While many of you may be familiar with the theory from psychological research, since the introduction of television, SLT has been applied to media effects and we see the exact same responses from mediated interactions as we see from interpersonal ones. Here the television world can create social norms and expectations, which can persuade behavior in a number of different contexts, including social norms, attitudes, and behaviors.

---

1. In the 1960s there was a long-standing belief that watching violent or aggressive behavior drained the viewer of their aggressive drive. In order to test this theory, in 1961 Albert Bandura conducted an experiment now known as the "Bobo doll experiment" to demonstrate that children are able to learn social behavior such as aggression through the process of observational learning. In the experiment children watched adults kick and punch a Bobo blow-up doll in a lab. The children were then released into a room full of toys and their behavior was observed. Results illustrated that children not only mimicked the aggressive behavior, but often exacerbated the behavior toward the doll.

Two specific components of SLT, prevalence and motivation, provide more clarity as to how the media may foster the acquisition of new behaviors. Prevalence, in social learning theory, refers expressly to how frequently an image or message is shown. Naturally, increased prevalence amplifies the opportunity for behavior modeling. The more children and teens are exposed to an image, whether it be sex, drugs, violence, or even play, it becomes cemented into their minds as appropriate behavior. Considering the number of hours children and teens spend on social media, prevalence is significant. In this way, SLT may be even more rampant with mediated images than interpersonal ones because of more frequent exposure – a child may spend one hour a day monitoring the behavior of a parent and four hours a day consuming the behavior of a media character (see the next chapter for media use statistics).

Continuing on, motivation in SLT literature increases the impetus to execute the modeled behavior (Harrison & Hefner, 2006). This depends on a number of attributes, including what the assumed outcomes are. Using the example of food and childhood obesity, in marketing food to children, most advertisers choose to have attractive children laughing, playing, and having a great time eating their products. By observing this behavior, a child viewer is likely motivated to make the decision to imitate that behavior in order to achieve the same outcome. In addition, no food advertising to children ever shows the adverse effects of eating a high-sugar, high-calorie diet, and therefore the negative repercussions are not known to the viewer. We see this also in teen programming about sex and sexual advances. I conducted a study on the popular show *The Family Guy* a few years ago, looking specifically at sex and sexual innuendo. Through a content analysis we discovered that there was a reference to sex in over 90% of scenes from the show seasons one through seven. Meanwhile, less than five percent of those depictions included a negative repercussion of the advance. Examples of sexual references range from the blatant mentioning of sexual rhetoric to hitting a character on the butt. In nearly all of the scenes these advances were either met with implied sexual activity or nothing at all. Through a SLT lens, it is explained that viewers of the show are learning that these sexualized behaviors and references often end in sex and almost never (less than five percent of the time) were met with a negative response. Social learning theory would then posit that viewers of these shows are learning these behaviors as appropriate. Throughout this book we discuss current research on what children and teens are seeing in the media. In Chapter 13 (page 184) on risky behaviors such as sex, drugs, and alcohol, we uncover the truth that kids are bombarded with sex, drugs, and alcohol content in their feeds and most of it is sponsored content, not paid advertising. The messages they are being send hundreds of times a day is that drinking, doing drugs, and having sex is appropriate behavior that generates likes.

Of course, social learning theory is relevant to an array of observable behaviors (Eyal & Kunkel, 2008). Bleakley et al. (2008) explain that while all people are taught from media depictions, learning is most likely to be translated into behavior when:

- The role model closely resembles the viewer (e.g., gender, age, etc.);
- The behavior being observed is realistic;
- The role model is attractive; and
- The behavior is positively enforced.

It is important to note, however, that these behaviors are not always mimicked immediately, but instead stored in "scripts" for when an appropriate situation arises. These scripts are considered memory guides for our behavior that are stored as blueprints for how one should behave in response, and what the likely outcomes will be. It is because of these scripts that media portrayals have such a strong connection to their audience's behavior. Bandura (2009) demonstrates that contextual details associated with television memories are often so similar to memories from real events, that they are likely to be seen as relevant in social situations. These psychological mechanisms that influence behavior are central to understanding how social learning theory works. Practically speaking, this theoretical reasoning explains that media viewers are often unaware of where they learned a certain behavior or way of thinking because their observations of behavior, whether interpersonal or mediated, are all stored in the same way in their head. We might find ourselves saying "a friend told me this," and be unable to remember which friend and unable to ration that it actually came from a television program you were watching. This is especially true with young people who watch teen dramas or television shows – the situations they are watching on the screen are real, even if the viewer has not experienced it before. Watching the situation play out on the screen created the scripts for what that viewer can do if ever in that position. This occurs every day in myriad ways. How to dress for the first day of high school for example, or even more important, what prom is like, or how your first sexual encounter should go. We talk about this in the pornography chapter (page 170), but almost all kids see a sex scene play out before they ever find themselves in the position of protagonist. Those sex scenes are stored as scripts for them to know how to behave.

Shifting the focus to SLT and disordered eating for a moment, Robinson (1999) borrowed from social learning theory in his experiment measuring the effects of reducing time spent viewing media on obesity, physical activity, and dietary intake. Using 192 third and fourth grade students, Robinson randomly assigned students to partake in an 18-lesson, six-month classroom curriculum to reduce television, video, and video game use. Outcomes illustrated that compared to the control group, students in the experimental classroom activity of limited media exposure had significantly decreased body mass index levels, waist circumference, waist-to-hip ratio, and a significant drop in the number of meals reportedly eaten in front of the television. This indicates that reducing the time spent with media reduces the likelihood that children will imitate the actors in the food commercials, thus decreasing the incidence of childhood obesity. I chose to use a physical example of body size to demonstrate this point because if media exposure can contribute to something physical, just imagine what it is doing to mental processes.

Criticisms of social learning theory stem primarily from the mediating effects of individual differences. Specifically, Park and Villar (2011) suggest that "people of different ethnicities, socioeconomic statuses, geographies, and other categories may process TV content differently from other groups and that researchers who focus on social learning may disregard these differences in consumption processes" (p. 94). Based on identification and perceived realism, certain television commercials are likely to influence viewers differently. Park and Villar (2011) use the example of reality television as being more likely to influence perceptions of reality, or have more powerful effects, on viewers similar to the actors because the events appear to be real situations that one could possibly encounter. This simple fact increases identification with the characters, which increases likelihood of imitation (Bandura, 2009). That being said, if a child is unfamiliar with an image on the screen, or if they cannot identify with the actors on the screen, they are less likely to learn and imitate the behavior shown, thus reducing the persuasive nature of the media.

INFORMATION PROCESSING THEORY

Accounting for individual differences, information processing theory (IPT) at its core focuses on how individuals manage incoming information by developing skills in the areas of acquisition, encoding, organization, and retrieval of information (John, 1999). Since its introduction, there have been many proposed models of information processing. The most fundamental, developed by Hovland et al. (1953), put forward the idea that the final decision to change one's way of thinking follows a specific progression of events. The authors explain that once an individual has been exposed to a message, they must focus on it, understand its content, and finally appraise that content. Many information processing theorists argue that this evaluation process is the most important part, as it includes the examining of each component to the message, measuring it against existing information, and then, based on this appraisal, forming new beliefs and attitudes about the message. Due to children's limited lived experiences and limited existing information they lack contrasting information about most things. Thus, using this model in relation to media effects, children are more likely to change their attitude based on what they see on a screen more readily than an adult with more lived experiences.

PIAGET

When researching children, the different process models of IPT are increasingly important as many describe and evaluate the process by which children of all ages understand the media. The majority of literature written on children and IPT begins with a short description of Piagetian cognitive development as a prevailing explanation for age differences in reactions to television advertising (John, 1999; Roedder, 1981).

According to Piaget, differences in cognitive ability are described in stages that are classified by age. By using this process, Piaget illustrated that as a child moves through the stages of development, each phase operates with limitations on the ability of the child to internally understand and perceive information from the environment (Roedder, 1981). In this vein, the assumption of stages implies a child's readiness to comprehend the same set of stimuli differently depending on his or her age (Palmer & MacNeil, 1991).

Through observation and experiment, Piaget's research illustrates that as a child interacts with their environment, knowledge systems (or structures) develop (Palmer & MacNeil, 1991). This is similar to the scripts that are formed by observing media character behavior in social learning theory. Looking specifically at the stages and knowledge systems within each one, Piaget outlines four distinct phases of development from birth through age 15, when a child is presumed to develop adult information processing ability.

Although extremely useful in describing age-related abilities, unfortunately, Piaget's theory offers little insight specifically into children's cognitive processing. Additionally, ample methodological shortcomings have been noted, which limits the usability of the theory even further (Roedder, 1981). As a result of these concerns, the most promising explanation in the media effects literature for children's cognitive responses to advertising remains information processing theory.

PROCESS MODEL

According to IPT, learning new information involves a process. The first step in the stage model of information processing is to attend to a stimulus. As in any marketing campaign, all efforts are wasted if the viewer pays no attention. From here, there are three sub-processes that must occur. These are: encoding, storage, and retrieval (Lang, 2000). Encoding is the process of filtering a stimulus for further processing. Meanwhile, storage is defined as linking the newly perceived and encoded stimulus to previously stored information; this process occurs in the short-term memory (STM). Empirical evidence has shown that if stimuli are similar, it takes less effort to attend to them, and therefore, they are more likely to be encoded and stored. Finally, the retrieval sub-process involves recovering previously stored information from the long-term memory (LTM). This is the action stage that is of particular interest to marketers and effects researchers. The retrieval process will show if the stimuli, or message, made it through to storage, and whether it is currently affecting behavior. In concert, the three sub-processes account for the stage processes of information processing theory (Lang, 2000; Roedder, 1981).

According to this view, incoming information from television commercials is represented in the STM. There is a limited capacity of storage in the STM and therefore, it is able to hold only a small amount of information for a short period of time (Roedder, 1981; Lang, 2000). Given this limitation, information in the STM is likely to decay unless it is transferred for permanent storage in LTM. The methods by which stimulus information is moved between the short- and long-term memory are rehearsal and retrieval (Roedder, 1981). Permanent storage, or learned information, in the long-term memory is achieved through active rehearsal and elaboration of information presently in the short-term memory. This information stored in STM may also serve as a prompt that arouses the recovery of thoughts from LTM and results in their representation in STM. This is what happens when information is called upon for decision-making (Roedder, 1981).

Information processing theory has a long history of being used to evaluate media effects, particularly advertising effects. For example, consumer socialization of children (John, 1999); advertising exposure, loyalty, and brand purchasing (Tellis, 1988); and age differences in children's responses to TV advertising (Roedder, 1981; Te'eni-Harari et al., 2007).

Tellis (1988) used IPT to explore advertising exposure, loyalty, and brand purchasing. Here the author proposed a non-linear approach to advertising effects, and explained that advertising reinforces brand preference rather than encourages brand switching. This helps to support the claim that advertising to children will create consumers for life. This also defends the choices of the big advertisers to keep creating commercials targeted at children. The exact same principles can be applied today to social media, YouTubers, TikTok stars, etc. It is also important to note the changes social media has demanded of advertisers – banner ads don't work anymore. Teens are "too smart" to be persuaded by something marked "paid content." Instead, advertisers work through "influencers" – defined as people with a lot of followers on a social media platform who are now paid for their social media content. Just like young children are deceived by commercials during their cartoons, teens are deceived by influencers who they "trust."

SCRIPTS

Also interested in how children evaluate media messages, Huesmann (1998) developed an information processing model to evaluate long-term effects of media violence on children. Huesmann's model focused on attitude change through the method of forming scripts for behavior. Similar to social learning theory research on scripts, Huesmann explained that in IPT, these scripts are a form of mental routine, or keys to proper behavior that are stored in the long-term memory. According to the author, a child who is exposed to a great deal of violence, either through the media or in real life, is likely to develop scripts that encourage aggressive action. These scripts for behavior are then called upon when each situation arises. Huesmann (1998) explains that because of this, if a child is continuously exposed to media violence, they will develop a solid set of scripts that are easy to recover when needed. The same can be said for a host of other behaviors, even for obese children and food preferences. If a child is continuously exposed to high-sugar and high-fat options in the media, when choosing what he or she wants for a meal, pre-existing scripts will be easy to retrieve. From here it is not a large mental leap to hypothesize the same is true for sex and promiscuous behavior. With these examples, it is easy to see how pervasive these processing models are in media effects research. The same process of creating a favorite brand can be seen in elevating violence levels, normalizing sexual acts, and forming dependencies on the content.

AGE EIGHT

Looking specifically at age differences and information processing, Te'eni-Harari et al. (2007) conducted in-depth interviews with children aged 2–7, 7–11, and 11–15. The authors reviewed previous research with children in these groups and revealed that considerable changes in the various levels of influence occur at the age of eight. The authors explain that until then, children have difficulty remembering specific advertisements. Furthermore, at and after age eight, children begin to have better recall and recognition of commercial advertisements (Te'eni-Harari et al., 2007). This research is paramount to understanding exactly when and how advertising has the greatest effect on children. This research also goes against social learning theory by illustrating that it takes more than simple exposure to effect long-term preferences and frequency of parental requests – the child must first be able to process the messages, and that requires recall and recognition of the brand.

The research on age differences and media is fascinating. Around age eight, research has shown, media affects children differently. Te'eni-Harari et al. (2007) contribute this to a change to how they process the material. Other research has also demonstrated that media influences how children play around this developmental milestone. In early years, media can help children use their imagination when the screen is off by providing characters and sets where players can fly or throw invisible lassos around their opponents. After age eight, the media is a hindrance on children's imaginary play having set the plot and solution to every situation. I saw this happen in my own home. When my older son was around eight and my younger son was six, I observed them in the playroom of our home. My younger son had arranged DC, Marvel, Ninjago, and Teenage Mutant Ninja Turtle characters all in their Ninjago City Lego building. All of these "good guys" were going after a set of "bad guys" from yet another Lego world. Meanwhile, my older son was on the other side of the room playing with Pokémon Legos. After everything was set, my younger son invited my older son to have his Pokémon characters join the "good guys" to take down the "bad guys." "No," explained my older son. "Pokémon are not in that universe," he stated matter-of-factly. And that was it. Games in the playroom were forever changed and since that day no two universes have crossed paths to take down evil (for my older son, the younger one still mixes and matches, but he is only seven). Even though I was expecting it from years of research, it was still alarming to see it happen. Even with my kids and their limited screen time, my older son was now being influenced by plots created by other people.

USING SLT AND IPT TOGETHER

As shown, social learning theory has a rich history in media effects research due to its ability to describe and explain the phenomena of consumers learning from and imitating the media as a model for behavior. At the same time, information processing theory has a strong theoretical base in marketing and persuasion research as it outlines the processes by which consumers understand a message and incorporate that understanding into their future behavior. It is for these reasons why they are the ideal theories to combine in order to further understand the overwhelming impact of media on children's behaviors.

Further identifying the similarities and uses of the two theories together, in his seminal article explaining social learning theory, Bandura (1969) describes the attention and retention processes also necessary in SLT. Here Bandura draws the similarities between the SLT and IPT even closer by explaining that "at the sensory registration level, it is exceedingly unlikely that a person could reproduce modeling stimuli if he did not attend to, recognize, and differentiate features of the model's responses" (p. 222). Furthermore, Bandura continues to explain that with children in particular, who often have difficulty distinguishing between complex and diverse messages, simple exposure to the modeled behavior is no guarantee that they will attend closely enough to learn the behavior. Here IPT is necessary to fill in the gaps of cognitive understanding and explain when and at what ages children are capable of attending to certain messages.

Looking at the exceptionally important issue of retention, Bandura (1969) again draws a correlation between SLT and IPT. Here he describes incidences and circumstances of retention are often ignored in behavior identification, but that these are paramount to observational learning. The author argues that retention is of special interest when observing behavior in children, as their patterns of learned behavior can be retained for extended periods of time. Further exploring this issue, Bandura discusses the processes of long-term retention, described in the long-term memory stages of information processing theories. Bandura goes on to describe, of the numerous retention processes, rehearsal operations as being the most effective in stabilizing and strengthening the learned behavior. This fact is a pillar in both theories – through continued observation and modeling, scripts for behavior are reinforced. Huesmann (1998) demonstrated this clearly in her longitudinal research on the media's effect on long-term aggression amongst children.

DIFFERENCES IN EXPLAINING BEHAVIOR

As shown through describing how the principal features of the two theories are similar, it is clear that both social learning theory and information processing theory make comparable predictions about the relationship between media exposure and a child's knowledge and reasoning. Both theories assert that after exposure, children attend to mediated messages, commit the messages to memory, and then model future behavior after what they remember from the ad. The difference between the two theories is based upon which variables each claim to have the greatest impact on future behavior. For example, social learning theory puts forward the condition of outcome importance. Here, if a behavior outcome is unfavorable, a consumer will choose not to emulate it. Similarly, SLT outlines model behavior that is most likely to be imitated. As Bleakley et al. (2008) recounts, if a model bears a resemblance to the consumer, they are more likely to identify with the behavior and process it more favorably. This is also true if the observed behavior is realistic, and if the model is attractive. This facet is missing in information processing literature as it is not based on the ability to process a message.

Contrasting these key variables from SLT with those of IPT, the path to memory retention and script formation looks quite different. IPT focuses on the process of attending to a message, organizing that information, and then storing it in long-term memory. In this process, the onus is placed on comprehending the messages as a key to retention, rather than on the features of the model leading to behavior change. Looking specifically at children's behavior formation, information processing theory makes a clear distinction between the process for children contrasted to adult processing. It explains that at various stages of development children develop skills that are necessary for understanding and catering to a message, and before a child reaches these stages, they are unlikely to be as persuaded by the message. This important feature is missing in social learning theory (page 5).

THE IMPORTANCE OF THEORY IN RESEARCH

As discussed, both social learning theory and information processing theory are useful in understanding and explaining the complex process of media effects on children and teens. While on their own, each theory describes the phenomenon of children modeling their behavior after media images, in this circumstance, however, they are most informative when used together. When used collectively, the key elements of both theories are highlighted as having the greatest effect on our understanding. Information processing theory teaches us at what ages and cognitive development stages children are first truly able to understand and be persuaded by mediated messages, while social learning theory explains what the ideal media message will look like to have the child identify with the message in the strongest way possible. Finally, both theories illustrate the power of repetition in cementing scripts and methods for behavior that are the strongest in predicting future behavior. In this way, the whole is clearly more than the sum of the parts. This is somewhat of a theme in the book – taking our collective and disparate knowledge and combining theory with practice.

NOW WHAT? WHAT DO WE DO WITH THIS INFORMATION AND HOW DO WE APPLY IT?

Ample research has used the social learning theory and/or information processing theory as foundational in understanding varying media effects. Simpson and Mazzeo (2017) used the lens of SLT to dive into "fitspiration" and the social media phenomenon of being "fit" and "skinny." Through a content analysis, the authors discovered that skinny is in fact, not enough. Specifically, results from the study showed that fitspiration messages were presented as encouraging; however, they also engender body dissatisfaction and compulsive exercise. Messages analyzed were presented as appearance, or health-related, and coded for social learning theory constructs: standards, behaviors, and outcome expectancies. Findings illustrated that the coded messages encouraged appearance-related body image standards and weight management practices more frequently than health-related standards and behaviors. Results of the content analysis also emphasized attractiveness as motivation to partake in such active behaviors (Simpson & Mazzeo, 2017). Results also indicated that fitspiration messages include a comparable amount of fit praise (e.g., emphasis on toned/defined muscles) and thin praise (e.g., emphasis on slenderness), suggesting that women are not only supposed to be thin but also fit. Considering the negative outcomes associated with both exposure to idealized body images and exercising for appearance reasons, the authors suggested that fitspiration messages are problematic, especially for viewers with high risk of eating disorders and related issues. Given this information, we can now openly discuss the images that our teens are seeing online, even those veiled as fitspiration, and break down the messages, and messaging, to create more body positive lessons.

In another example, Van Ouytsel et al. (2017) used social learning theory to investigate teen sexting behaviors. The results of the survey (n = 357) indicated that adolescents held positive attitudes towards sexting because they perceive that their peers approve of sexting. Findings also showed that teens engaged in sexting both within and outside of a romantic relationship. Further, sexting outside of a romantic relationship was also influenced by the thrill that young people get out of engaging in this behavior.

These are just two examples of how frequent media messages are interpreted, coded, stored, believed, and acted upon. We can use the foundations of social learning theory and information processing for all messages that children and teens are absorbing through the media. In the words of Brene Brown, we need to "reality check" the media with teens. Child development and cognitive development theories have demonstrated that kids lack the experiences and the processing abilities of adults and yet the media still shows them desirable content. This foundation in theory allows us to understand the process they are going through to be able to help.

REFERENCES

Bandura, A. (1969). Social-learning theory of identificatory processes. In D. A. Goslin (Ed.), *Handbook of socialization theory and research* (pp. 213–262). Rand McNally.

Bandura, A. (2009). Social cognitive theory of mass communication. In J. Bryant & M. B. Oliver (Eds.), *Media effects: Advances in theory and research* (pp. 94–124). Routledge.

Bleakley, A., Hennessy, M., Fishbein, M., & Jordan, A. (2008). It works both ways: The relationship between exposure to sexual content in the media and adolescent sexual behavior. *Media Psychology, 11,* 443–461.

Hagan, J. F., Shaw, J. S., & Duncan, P. M. (Eds.). (2017). *Guidelines for health supervision of infants, children, and adolescents* (4th ed.). Bright Futures/American Academy of Pediatrics.

Harrison, Kristen, & Hefner, Veronica. (2006). Media exposure, current and future body ideals, and disordered eating among preadolescent girls: A longitudinal panel study. *Journal of Youth and Adolescence, 35,* 146–156. https://doi.org/10.1007/s10964-005-9008-3.

Hovland, C., Janis, I., & Kelly, H. (1953). *Communication and persuasion.* Yale University Press.

Huesmann, L. R. (1998). The role of social information processing and cognitive schema in the acquisition and maintenance of habitual aggressive behavior. In R. G. Green & E. Donnerstein (Eds.), *Human aggression: Theories, research, and implications for social policy* (pp. 73–103). Academic Press.

John, D. R. (1999). Consumer socialization of children: A retrospective look at twenty-five years of research. *Journal of Consumer Research, 26*(3), 183–213.

Lang, A. (2000). The limited capacity model of mediated message processing. *Journal of Communication, 50*(1), 46–70.

Palmer, E. L., & MacNeil, M. (1991). Children's comprehension processes: From Piaget to public policy. In J. Bryant & D. Zillman (Eds.), *Responses to the screen: Reception and reaction processes*. Longman.

Park, D. J., & Villar, M. E. (2011). 'I want to be like people on TV': Effect of perceived realism, character admiration and frequency of sitcom and reality TV viewing among African-American students. *American Journal of Media Psychology, 4*(4), 80–100.

Robinson, T. N. (1999). Reducing children's television viewing to prevent obesity. *Journal of the American Medical Association, 282*(15), 1561–1567.

Roedder, D. L. (1981). Age differences in children's responses to television advertising: An information-processing approach. *Journal of Consumer Research, 8*(2), 144–153.

Simpson, C. C., & Mazzeo, S. E. (2017). Skinny is not enough: A content analysis of fitspiration on Pinterest. *Health Communication, 32*(5), 560–567. https://doi.org/10.1080/10410236.2016.1140273

Te'eni-Harari, T., Lampert, S. I., & Lehman-Wilzig, S. (2007). Information processing of advertising among young people: The elaboration likelihood model as applied to youth. *Journal of Advertising Research, 47*(3), 326–340.

Tellis, G. J. (1988). Advertising exposure, loyalty, and brand purchase: A two-stage model of choice. *Journal of Marketing Research, 25*, 134–144.

Van Ouytsel, J., Ponnet, K., Walrave, M., & d'Haenens, H. L. (2017). Adolescent sexting from a social learning perspective. *Telematics & Informatics, 34*(1), 287–298. https://doi.org/10.1016/j.tele.2016.05.009

Foundations in Media Literacy and Understanding Children's Media Environments

2

In March 2020, the way I do my job as a media effects professor and the advice I give all changed. Prior to 2020 I was the poster child for the American Academy of Pediatrics' (AAP) restrictive screen time policy (see page 36). I kept screens away from my own children and I would speak at events and give lectures explaining the same – no screen time until age two and then no more than one hour a day after that. I would talk about the screen as a babysitter and how that is important to working parents, but to never lose sight of what it is doing and that it should be avoided when possible. After years of this, parents became afraid to tell me the truth behind the actual amount of time their kids spent in front of the television and I started giving my students extra credit for reducing their hours (which when you counted each of the screens they use separately, often added to 20 hours or more per day!). That being said, we have always had an anti-dote to when screen time is allowed and that is what I preach now: media literacy. In this chapter we answer the questions: *What is media literacy and why is it important?* And *Somewhere a line was crossed from connecting with friends and being inspired to scrolling and even envy of the "perfect lives" some friends portray. How do we dial down this exposure without having our children feel disconnected from their classmates? What are some useful ways to talk to our young children in lower elementary grades to help them navigate the feelings of envy and self-esteem issues that come from imagining that some of their friends have the "perfect life?"*

Media literacy is the way that we, as consumers, combat media effects. By understanding what is happening and why, we can avoid the pitfalls of screen time. I still recommend that parents and caregivers limit screen time, but I spend most of my time discussing media literacy. What 2020 taught me is that avoiding screen time is no longer possible. In the following chapter we tell you everything we think you need to know about media literacy and the media environments that children and adolescents are living in. Those of you reading

DOI: 10.4324/9781003223412-2

these words are the defense team. The children and adolescents you are talking to are deep in their mediated world. They see the images, watch the videos, and are consumed by likes and followers. For some reason that is lost to us, it is necessary to compulsively follow your friend's geotags on Snapchat and watch people making strange food concoctions on TikTok.

Teaching media literacy takes time, just like teaching reading and math. It is a discussion that needs to be added to every dinner table along with "How was your day?" As outsiders in the lives of children and teens, those of us reading this book have an opportunity to have kids and teens open up to us because we aren't their parents. Practicing media literacy is helping children to "reality check" what they are seeing on the screens, asking them what they think about it, and understanding how they internalize those messages. We know that the media is influencing their lives, but they don't understand that to the level that we can. Being media literate is removing the curtain to help them see how they are affected by what they see and who they follow.

In this chapter we will review definitions of media literacy, see media literacy in action, highlight media use statistics so we can see how much screens are a part of young people's lives, and answer the question: *What is media literacy and why is it important?*

According to the Centers for Disease Control and Prevention, children between the ages of eight and 18 spend, on average, 7.5 hours in front of a screen for entertainment per day. When calculated together, the hours add up to 114 full days out of a year! When you write it like that, it really puts things into perspective. For example, kids around the country celebrate the first 100 days in school and the average school year in America averages to only 180 days. Kids and teens are spending nearly as much time in front of a screen as they do in school in a year! "Screen" here is used to be any technology device – a television, computer, phone, tablet, gaming system, etc. In the literature all screens are considered equal, it is the content that is not. The AAP has always directed us to limit screen time, and we are both in support of that, but when limiting screen use is not possible, or not within our control, an actual solution to combat the negative effects of all of this screen time is understanding the content through media literacy.

IMPORTANCE OF MEDIA LITERACY

What is media literacy and why is it important?

Common Sense Media defines media literacy as the "ability to identify different types of media and understand the messages they're sending" (np). This includes television, movies, radio, newspapers, social media, video games, and advertising. Media literacy is an essential skill for young people, who by nature have difficulty separating facts from fiction and real news from an advertisement. In their research into media accuracy awareness, Wineburg (2016) explained that 80% of middle schoolers could not tell sponsored content on a website apart from an article or a news story. As adults we take for granted the ability to recognize paid content but children and adolescents need to be taught this, and they need to practice this awareness over and over. Media literacy is a key concept throughout this book, in the previous chapter we discussed (page 8) specific theories that inform our understanding of cognitive development and media effects, and in all subsequent chapters we talk about themes and areas of life where young people are most affected by the media. It is imperative to maintain these media literacy fundamentals to those subjects as well.

FAKE NEWS

When children are getting a lot of their information from the media, understanding the difference between real and fake, and programming and commercial/advertisement is crucial. Reports have shown that one in five teenagers between the ages of 12 to 15 believe information they find on Google is accurate, and one in five can't identify paid ads on Google, even when it has the wording "ad" attached to it (OfCom, 2018). More importantly, research by Baker (2018) into media literate teenagers discovered that young consumers are not even stopping to ask the questions: "Is this real?" "If this is real, is it the truth?" or "Is someone trying to fool me?" Considering that anyone can set up a website and be discovered by the Google search engine, it becomes problematic if a child can't tell how to recognize if the information is trustworthy. Teaching a child to become more media literate helps them navigate these types of obstacles online.

Also of note, when we say "information," we mean pretty much anything. Children are learning everything from how to play a hard level of a video game, how to tie a tie, how to flirt, how to define their sexuality, and how to build a bomb all online every single day. I have run experiments in classrooms with middle schoolers where we visit different websites and I ask the students to identify if the information is real or fake. We usually go with funny stories or watch animals performing daring acts and the students are ready with "that's fake!" In my experience, students are able to discern real from fake when the issues are trivial or not personal. This becomes important, however, with those personal issues. If a 13-year-old is on Instagram seeing an image of another 13-year-old but their body in a bathing suit looks like Kim Kardashian, that is a perfect time for a media literacy "reality check" conversation. On a deep level, the teen viewing the picture knows that that is not what the model in the image looks like, but before they can process those thoughts, they think about themselves and how they definitely do not look like Kim Kardashian. Adults do this as well, and arguably American adults are no better at deciphering fake news than kids, but we have years of experience and a different lens to see these things.

CO-VIEWING

Somewhere a line was crossed from connecting with friends and being inspired to scrolling and even envy of the "perfect lives" some friends portray. How do we dial down this exposure without having our children feel disconnected from their classmates? What are some useful ways to talk to our young children in lower elementary grades to help them navigate the feelings of envy and self-esteem issues that come from imagining that some of their friends have the "perfect life?"

We now know the definitions and we know that fake news needs to be stopped, but what does media literacy look like in a practical sense? We have a few approaches when it comes to media and the most basic is restriction. When media is restricted, children and teens are simply not allowed to have screen time. This may be a toddler who doesn't get their one hour a day, or a teenager who is specifically cut off from social media. There are great reasons for this, including, if we see a change in the toddler's behavior after an hour of cartoons and if we are worried about a teen's body image after doom scrolling. Restriction will absolutely reduce the exposure and harmful effects to the screen, but it is not media literacy. In order to practice media literacy, there first needs to be media to digest.

In order for media literacy to be successful there needs to be communication. In the field we call this "active co-viewing." Active co-viewing means actually sitting with the child or teen and consuming media with them with the intent to discuss what they are seeing. While watching a teen drama with a teen in your life, active co-viewing means discussing the clothing of the teens in the show, or the sexual promiscuity, or the age of the actors, and "reality checking" it, or checking in to see how the child or teen is interpreting the plot line. They might be comments such as, "Do kids at your school dress like that?" or "I read that the actor in this scene is really 27 years old." This can also be applied to social media use when children are caught staring at their friends in their "perfect clothes" and "perfect friends" and ask them "Do you think this person is wearing makeup?" or "Do you think they edited the photo before uploading it?" and "What do you think the poster is trying to convey by posting? Do you think they are proud? Or maybe attention seeking?" This process involves pausing the show or the scrolling and asking more probing questions about how the teen watching feels about what is happening, or "What would you do in that situation?" When doom scrolling on Instagram or watching TikTok the same conversions need to be happening. All of this is an attempt to help the child understand how removed from real life their programming is. As I am sure you have realized, active co-viewing takes time, work, and a willingness for the child or teen to participate. These relationships of trust need to be built in order for co-viewing to have its necessary and positive effect.

The final method, in opposition to restriction and active co-viewing, is free-range. Free-range is when the kids get to watch whatever they want, whenever they want. It is also considered free-range when a parent is watching a show/social media with their child and not saying anything. Specifically, we call this "endorsement." If an adult in the child's life is watching the teen drama play out and not reality checking the content, research shows that the child or teen interprets this as endorsement. For example, a teen might be thinking: "Well, Mom is watching this with me and she didn't comment on the actor, so I guess all 16-year-olds look like that and I am just ugly/fat/slow to develop" or "Dad didn't say anything, so I guess you really are supposed to drink and make out with people at high school parties." As hopefully you can see, it is critical to talk to children and teens while they are engaging with media so that they don't think everything they see on the screen is "real" and "perfect."

THEORETICAL CONSIDERATIONS

Media literacy is a process between the child and hopefully a trusted adult figure to discuss the daily messages that kids are seeing online and process them. To have a better understanding of the type of content children are consuming on YouTube, Neumann and Herodotou's (2020) conducted a content analysis of the biggest genres of children aged zero to eight content on YouTube and organized them to create a rubric to help parents and guardians assess content before letting their children consume it. The four key criteria used in evaluation were: age appropriateness, content quality, design features, and learning objectives. The authors explain that through YouTube, children watch the behavior of others. This behavior then has the potential to impact them positively or negatively, depending on the quality of videos, images presented on the screen, and repercussions to bad behavior. Using social learning theory (page 8) and cultivation theory, the authors were able to show children change their perception based on the content of the media consumed.

Cultivation theory explains that over time exposure to media subtly "cultivates" viewers' perceptions of reality. Specifically, in their seminal research on the subject, Gerbner et al. (1986) explain, "television is a medium of the socialization of most people into standardized roles and behaviors. Its function is in a word, enculturation" (p. 175). In other words, this means that whether or not a teenager sees their own life as being portrayed on the television screen, they will believe that the media represents an accurate depiction of teenage life because of the effects of this media exposure. This theory also explains that continued exposure creates and supports a view of reality even if this "reality" is different to one's own lived experiences – if you see something enough, then it must be true or real. For example, in every teenage drama on television or in movies there is a big party with lots of drinking. If a teenager sees enough of these images, they will believe this scenario to be true regardless of their own lived experiences.

These images will then be placed in schema folders (page 156) and when the teen is in a similar situation, they will recall the scripts they learned from the media. This is even more prevalent with "real" media such as Instagram and TikTok, where the consumer is more familiar with the creator.

In addition, cultivation theory proposes a concept called "resonance" where if a viewer sees something in the media that relates to their lived experiences, or "resonates" with something they have experienced, their trust in the media grows. This is seen regularly with sex, drugs, and alcohol. It is unlikely that a teenager today would have never seen or heard someone talking about or engaging in one of these behaviors. Therefore, the expectation of this behavior is enforced regularly in the media. For example, if a young teen has an older sibling who goes to a high school party and the next morning recounts their tales of drinking, when the younger teen then watches a scene on television of kids drinking at a party, it will be reinforced as accurate. Further, the older teen who has now had that experience will be further convinced about the accuracy of the portrayal on the screen because it resonates with their lived experience. You can see now how this is a cycle.

Relying on Bandura's well-known Bobo doll experiment (page 20) and social learning theory, Neumann and Herodotou based their study on the premise that children who observed aggressive behavior (e.g., an adult uses a hammer to hit a Bobo doll) will initiate more aggressive behaviors than a group of children who observed non-aggressive behavior (Bandura, 1986). Follow-up studies examining the impact of media on children have further established Bandura's findings; repeated exposure to violent and aggressive video content had a greater influence on children's behavior, cognition, and emotions than infrequent exposure. This has been shown with non-aggressive behaviors as well. Meanwhile, the authors also employed cultivation theory to explain how viewing YouTube videos creates a viewpoint of reality that is based on the screen and not reality. Ultimately, the analysis of YouTube effects on zero to eight- year-olds suggests that given the popularity of the selected videos, children are more likely to be exposed to both high- and low-quality YouTube video content. This content will inform their views of the environments around them, and lead to behavior expectations. Neumann and Herodotou concluded that "having non-screen time periods, creating rules, monitoring what children watch online, turning off search functions, and providing opportunities for a wide range of digital and non-digital play activities" (p. 4427), is the best way to ensure your child's positive development. In other words, ensuring that one is a diligent parent that enforces limitations to their children's use of YouTube is the best way for both child and caretaker to be media literate.

MEDIA CONTENT

Carrying over the premise set by Neumann and Herodotou's work, Buzzi (2011) analyzed the type of videos that were being watched by the youngest demographics and how easily it is for adult content to be mistaken as children's content because of its lack of regulated rating systems that television and film have. For example, Buzzi noted a reposted version of Disney's *Snow White and the Seven Dwarfs* posted to YouTube that "was dubbed with porno-audio content (p. 130). While this specific video was categorized as "comedy" on YouTube and not "child," it was still easily found using "Snow White and Seven Dwarfs" keywords. Because there is little control on YouTube age-appropriate rating options available on the platforms, it is entirely possible that children can stumble upon potentially harmful adult content. While these studies point more to an elimination of screen time for our youngest kids, when that is not possible, media literacy comes in.

BEHAVIOR OUTCOMES

When looking at aggression, if you have a four-year-old who watches YouTube videos that demonstrate aggression, social learning theory does not say that the four-year-old will become violent, but it does say that that a four-year old witnessing the aggressive act will potentially learn from that behavior. The theory explains that without a punishment on the screen, the four-year-old viewer is likely to imitate that aggressive act. Using media literacy, an adult in the room can issue the statement: "Ouch! That must have really hurt to get hit like that!" or "We use our words, we don't hit" or maybe "What would happen if you did that in preschool?" Thus, creating a punishment of sorts for the behavior is key. Engaging in this conversation helps the child to understand that aggressive acts are not encouraged and the behavior is less likely to be imitated. This is also true if the viewer is 14 or 24 years old, but with elevated language to convey the punishment.

MEDIA LITERACY IN ACTION

For older children, Canada's Center for Media Literacy has mapped out a helpful process when becoming media literate. The center explains that when looking at messages in the media, it is essential to understand who created the message and why. Was it an individual or a company, and did they make it to inform others, change their minds, or buy something? As adults we ask these questions automatically — when LeBron James wears Nike from head to toe, we know that he is endorsed by the brand and not wearing it simply for its athletic quality. Without an adult to tell them these things, teenagers don't recognize that their favorite celebrities are walking billboards. Due to their attraction and familiarity, viewers are more likely to learn from and copy the behaviors of celebrities without asking who created the image, what is the intent of the image, and is it an endorsement.

It is important to look at the source critically and consider all the different sides. It is also essential to think about who is the target audience and what techniques or sources were used to make the message credible. Finally, one should consider if there was information that was left out and why. Looking at messaging critically will help to understand the meanings and reasoning that might not be obvious at first glance. As the educational requirements for media literacy have not reached schools nationwide, parents can help their children critically analyze the messages they are receiving online and become media literate (Canada's Center for Digital and Media Literacy).

EFFECTS OF EXCESSIVE SCREEN TIME

Adolescents today are known as digital natives. Holton (2019) explains, "digital native" is a term used to describe a group of individuals who have grown up during a time of "ubiquitous technology" and consider the Internet as an essential tool within their lives. With the Internet being a vital source of technology that digital natives find an absolute necessity for everyday life, the amount of time they spend on the Internet can come with risks. Cross (2020) describes, with half of younger adolescents owning a tablet by the age of eight and spending an average of 2.25 hours a day behind the screen, it has a significant impact on the child's development. Additionally, with excessive screen time, adolescents can develop what is known as "tunnel vision" (Cross, 2020). "Tunnel vision" can be dangerous because instead of children learning, observing, and experiencing their environment, they focus their entire attention on their device (Cross, 2020). This tunnel vision affects the child's ability to interact, learn, and develop their language skills (Cross, 2020) (page 43). Further, Morin (2020) states that excessive screen time can also cause behavioral, relational, and educational problems, as well as cause obesity, violence, and sleep problems (page 68). Altogether, younger adolescents who spend more time online risk hindering their cognitive development. To make matters worse, longitudinal research has demonstrated that the long hours spent online can also increase obesity, raise natural aggression levels encouraging violent acts or beliefs, and cause a lack of sleep. Although these factors are more physical based, the results of these problems expand to affect the adolescent's cognitive and emotional development, as well as their mental health. All of these will be addressed in the following chapters.

As adolescents transition to teen years, time spent on digital screens only increases. Common Sense Media (2019) found tweens ages 10 to 12 spend an average of five hours online, while teens 13 to 18 spend approximately seven hours online (Rideout et al., 2022). This data only includes entertainment use, and with digital screens integrating into the educational system, the amount of time spent continues to increase. As adolescents continue to grow and spend more time online, their mental health can also be affected. With high screen time, middle and older adolescents have lower self-esteem and struggle with anxiety, depression, and loneliness (Rosen, 2020). Twenge and Campbell (2018) found that adolescents who spent more than seven hours a day online were twice as likely to suffer from depression, anxiety, seek treatment with a mental health professional, or reported taking medication "for a psychological or behavioral issue." It is because of this data that we were unsurprised to read the staggering statistics of depressed teens during the COVID-19 quarantine (page ix). These findings show that excessive screen time has critical effects on an adolescent's mental health and holds the impact to cause adolescents to seek help from a mental health professional or medication. With digital screens being used for educational and entertainment use, the amount of time spent looking at a screen can also decrease focus and motivation within the adolescent's mind (Dunckley, 2015). This lack of motivation and focus can impact adolescents' mental health because it can cause them to fall behind or have difficulty academically, building relationships, and in their overall development (Dunckley, 2015). We believe that this is why many of you are reading this book – you have seen the effects of excessive screen time first hand and you want to help correct the course. The direct correlation between screen time and depreciating mental and physical health shows the link screen time carries regarding the severe risks that follows when adolescents spend extended time online.

MODELING BEHAVIOR

Before we let adults off the hook completely, screen dependency can also be a learned behavior. Research into parental use of screens found that one-third of children reported feeling unimportant when their parents looked at their smartphones during meals or when playing together. Additionally, when questioned, over 50% of the children felt that their parents checked their devices too often, but their biggest grievance, when given a list of possible bad device habits, was that their parents allowed themselves to be distracted by their device during conversations, leaving the child to feel unimportant. Taking the social learning theory approach once more, adults are modeling that being on a device is appropriate and a good use of our time. This is one of the first generations of kids needing to deal with this. I remember growing up my mother was a physician and always wore her pager. I knew as a very young child that when that pager went off, it would take precedence. My mother was responding to a sick kid, meanwhile, my texts from Amazon saying my delivery is on the way gets my attention away from my kids in 2021. We are doing a terrible job of setting priorities for the next generation and training them that what is on the screen is rarely as important as what is in front of them.

WHAT ARE THEY SEEING? 2021 MEDIA ENVIRONMENT

Now that we have covered what all this screen time is doing to our kids, we need a solid foundation and understanding of what they are seeing when they are spending their lives in front of a screen. Starting with the positive, the media today is much more diverse and inclusive than ever before. In mainstream children's programming audience members see characters of diverse gender, sex, race, ethnicity, and age.

You name it, you can find it. With the wide range of screen options available today, children and teens have instant access to any content they want. They can watch the biggest teen drama on primetime television, on their phone, on YouTube, alone, or in a group viewing party. Kids can also find programs that meet their unique taste levels. For example, anime is widely available, or a documentary series on Russian oligarchs. Mediated programming also deals with a range of subjects not seen in generations past. When Ellen DeGeneres was first broadcast on television, she was the only lesbian on primetime. Her show was canceled quickly but many in the queer community credited her with giving them a name for what they were also experiencing or a voice to come out to their families.

When I went to search for content analyses on race and gender representation to be able to present you with actual facts and figures of who children and teens were seeing in their 7.5 hours per day, the latest comprehensive research I could find was from 2008. I will spare you the now completely antiquated data and just say that if a kid wants to see something on their screen, they can. This can be extremely positive, being able to see someone who looks like you or acts like you or loves like you on a screen is powerful. If you are the only person of color in your friendship circle, being able to see someone who looks like you on a screen is comforting. The same can be said if you are the only queer person in your social circle, or the only athlete, etc. Once again we visit the teachings of social learning theory, which explains that consumers learn from what they see on television (Bandura, 1986). In this context social learning theory describes individuals, including adolescents and children, as often emulating or using media as bases for decision-making and judgments, which includes how they identify and define themselves, but also how they understand and treat others. In his later research, Bandura (2001) noted that television representations of social realities could lead to tangible conceptions of reality. Children are watching programs or seeing images on social media and taking them as tangible conceptions of reality. Research into cultivation theory talks about how racism and sexism is a product of the media cultivating a racist and sexist society. If you only see people of color as villains, then you will come to believe that is real. Since the beginning of the media, it has perpetuated terrible stereotypes of all people, but in 2021 we are starting to see a change. In recent years females of color in the television show *Grey's Anatomy* are running hospitals, gay men are adopting babies, and girls can play football.

In the following chapters we explore this through different themes but I do want to leave you with one thought. At the end of the movie, the couple is always happily in love, the once disapproving family opens their heart, and the bully sees the errors of their ways. It is incredibly great that there is more representation in what we see on the screen, but the messages are still lies that need to be reality checked. Young viewers experiencing some of the harshness of the real world might assume there is something wrong with them when their reality doesn't line up. These same individuals lack the media literacy training to see through the commercial and the intentions of the TikTok phenomenon to recognize the truth.

REFERENCES

Baker, F. (2018). Using pop culture to teach media literacy. *MiddleWeb*. www.middleweb. com/37592/using-pop-culture-to-teach-media-literacy/

Bandura, A. (1986). *Social foundations of thought and action: A social cognitive theory*. Prentice Hall.

Bandura, A. (2001). Social cognitive theory of mass communication. *Media Psychology*, 3, 265–299.

Buzzi, M. (2011). *Children and YouTube: Access to safe content. Proceedings of the 9th ACM SIGCHI Italian Chapter International Conference on computer-human interaction facing complexity* (pp. 125–131). https://doi.org10.1145/2037296.2037328.

Canada's Center for Digital and Media Literacy. (2017, January 19). Media literacy fundamentals. *MediaSmarts*. mediasmarts.ca/digital-media-literacy/

Common Sense Media: Ratings, Reviews, and Advice. (2019). *What is media literacy, and why is it important?* www.commonsensemedia.org/news-and-media-literacy/what-is-media-literacy-and-why-is-it-important

Cross, J. (2020, October 6). *What does too much screen time do to children's brains?* New York-Presbyterian. https://healthmatters.nyp.org/what-does-too-much-screen-time-do-to-childrens-brains/

Dunckley, V. (2015, August 18). Screentime is making kids moody, crazy, and lazy. *Psychology Today*. www.psychologytoday.com/us/blog/mental- wealth/201508/screentime-is-making-kids-moody-crazy-and-lazy

Holton, C. (2019, July 15). Digital native definition. *Investopedia*. www.investopedia. com/terms/d/digital-native.asp

Morin, A. (2020, September 17). How too much screen time can hurt kids and their families. *Verywell Family*. www.verywellfamily.com/the-negative-effects-of-too- much-screen-time-1094877

Neumann, M. M., & Herodotou, C. (2020). Evaluating YouTube videos for young children. *Education and Information Technologies*, 25(5), 4459–475. http://doi.org/doi:10.1007/s10639-020-10183-7

OfCom. (2018, August 6). *Children and parents: Media use and attitudes report 2015.* www.ofcom.
    org.uk/research-and-data/media-literacy-research/childrens/children-parents-
    nOv-15.

Rideout, V., Peebles, A., Mann, S., & Robb, M. B. (2022). *Common Sense census: Media use by
    tweens and teens, 2021.* Common Sense.

Rosen, A. (2020, January 20). How much is too much? Technology, screen time,
    and your mental health. *The Center for Treatment of Anxiety and Mood Disorders.* https://
    centerforanxietydisorders.com/how-much-is-too-much-technology-screen-time-
    and-your-mental-health/

Twenge, J. M., & Campbell, W. K. (2018). Associations between screen time and
    lower psychological well-being among children and adolescents: Evidence from
    a population-based study. *Preventive Medicine Reports, 12,* 271–283. https://doi.org/
    10.1016/j.pmedr.2018.10.003

Wineburg, S. (2016, November 2). Evaluating information: The cornerstone of civic
    online reasoning. *Stanford Digital Repository.* purl.stanford.edu/fv751yt5934

Current Guidelines on Digital Media Use by the American Academy of Pediatrics

3

In 2016, the American Academy of Pediatrics (AAP) released its guidelines on screen use for children and adolescents. This chapter will briefly summarize the recommendations presented. It does beg the questions: *What is the American Academy of Pediatrics?* and *Why are the recommendations so important in pediatric practice?* To start to answer these questions, the AAP was founded in 1930 and is composed of "67,000 pediatricians committed to the optimal physical, mental, and social health and well-being for all infants, children, adolescents, and young adults" (aap.org). As discussed on the AAP parenting website, the AAP has many facets, including advocacy, continued medical education, community involvement, and online resources for parents (healthychildren.org). As a pediatrician, their policy statements are critical resources in terms of providing clear guidelines for practice incorporating up-to-date research as well as commentary by experts in the field. Their policy statements regarding screen use in children in 2016 have provided a framework for pediatricians counseling families. As the dependence on screens has been dramatically affected by the pandemic, it is anticipated that the policies will continue to evolve with our changing times.

A snapshot of the recommendations presented in 2016 with regard to screen use in children include:

- For children younger than 18 months, avoid use of screen media other than video-chatting. Parents of children 18 to 24 months of age who want to introduce digital media should choose high-quality programming, and watch it with their children to help them understand what they're seeing.
- For children ages two to five years, limit screen use to one hour per day of high-quality programs. Parents should co-view media

DOI: 10.4324/9781003223412-3

with children to help them understand what they are seeing and apply it to the world around them.

- For children ages six and older, place consistent limits on the time spent using media, and the types of media, and make sure media does not take the place of adequate sleep, physical activity, and other behaviors essential to health.
- Designate media-free times together, such as dinner or driving, as well as media-free locations at home, such as bedrooms.
- Have ongoing communication about online citizenship and safety, including treating others with respect online and off.

AAP Newsroom (2016)

We will now break down their recommendations and justifications relative to infants and toddlers, preschoolers, and school-aged children and adolescents.

INFANTS AND TODDLERS

As stated above, the current recommendation for children younger than 18 months of age is avoid use of screen media with the exception of video chatting. In its 2016 AAP policy statement, "Media and Young Minds," the Council on Communications and Media (2016a) assert that infants and young toddlers are not equipped to actually learn from digital media given "immature symbolic, memory and attentional skills" (p. 1). The authors stress the importance of "hands-on" experiences and social interactions with caregivers as fundamental means to developing cognitive, language, motor, and social-emotional skills. To best facilitate learning via media, it is critical that the caregiver is watching with the child and reteaching content (we discuss this co-viewing further (page 25). With respect to video chatting, while it isn't discouraged in children under two, as it can enhance social relationships, the authors encourage parents to engage their child during the sessions to help provide context.

In children 18 to 24 months of age, it is recommended by the council that if digital media is introduced in this age group, it should be of high-quality educational content. They refer to Common Sense Media, *Sesame Street*, and PBS Kids as good resources. Again, they stress the importance of programming being interactive with the caregiver as it facilitates more optimal learning. In turn, solo media use in this age group is discouraged. After two years of age, it is recommended to keep screen time to one hour or less each day. At two years of age, there is some research to support that children are able to learn words from live video chatting or from an interactive touchscreen interface. However, parents should not feel pressured to push technology early as children easily pick up the skill sets very quickly once exposed in home or school.

In the next chapter we will be exploring more thoroughly the positive and negative impacts of digital media use in infants and young children. The authors in this policy statement do present some concerns in this age group. Specifically, obesity is a concern as they cite research with two-year-old children that body mass index (BMI) increases for every hour per week of screen time. Sleep can also be affected as infants exposed to screen media at night have demonstrated significantly shorter night time sleep duration. In terms of child development, the authors express concern that research continues to demonstrate "associations between excessive television viewing in early childhood and cognitive, language, and social/emotional delays, likely secondary to decreases in parent – child interaction when the television is on and poorer family functioning in households with high media use" (p. 2). The report explores the notion of media being used more excessively in children with more difficult temperaments and the use of screens to calm can lead to poor emotional regulation. Ambient media exposure, background television, and parental mobile device use is a concern in that it may limit crucial parent-child interactions and play. We discuss all of these issues in more detail in Chapter 4 (page 43).

PRESCHOOLERS

After two years of age, it is advised that screen time in preschool-aged children be limited to one hour a day. Moreover, it is again emphasized that media use in this population should be interactive with the caregiver which allows for context, discussion, and advanced learning. Screens should be off one hour prior to bedtime and devices out of the bedroom. Mealtimes should be screen free as should be parent-child designated play time. While these are all fairly basic and logical guidelines, they are difficult in practice. We discuss the necessity of these recommendations in Chapter 4 (page 43).

Content is critical in this population. The authors discuss how well-designed programs such as *Sesame Street*, "can improve cognitive, literacy, and social outcomes for children 3 to 5 years of age and continue to create programming that addresses evolving child health and developmental needs" (p. 2). This type of programming has also been demonstrated to enhance literacy skills in preschool-aged children. However, they do warn that many apps though touted "educational" have not been fully vetted for efficacy. As learned through research by Shaheen, 2014):

> It is important to emphasize to parents that the higher-order thinking skills and executive functions essential for school success, such as task persistence, impulse control, emotion regulation, and creative, flexible thinking, are best taught through unstructured and social (not digital) play, as well as responsive parent – child interactions.
>
> (p. 2)

Digital books often with visual enhancements may be a distraction and limit comprehension such that the authors recommend parental interaction as if reading a print book (we discuss this again in more detail in Chapter 9 on page 124).

As with infants and young toddlers, we will be discussing in the next chapter the potential negative effects of media use in this population (page 43). Heavy media use during preschool years is associated with significant increases in BMI and potentially set the foundation for weight gain later in childhood. Furthermore, exposure to media in the bedroom in early childhood has been associated with less sleep duration (page 67). From a child development standpoint, research from Nathanson et al. (2014), and the findings referenced in the AAP report, introduces the idea that earlier age of media use, more cumulative hours of use, as well as non-PBS content, have predicted poor executive functioning in preschoolers.

SCHOOL-AGED CHILDREN AND ADOLESCENTS

The most recent policy statement with respect to this age group was published by the Council on Communications and Media (2016b). It focused specifically on media use in school-aged children and adolescents. Historically the AAP had put a limit on two hours a day, however, its most recent policy focuses less on quantitative restrictions with more a focus on family developing a more consistent plan and routine. The "family media use plan," available to parents on the AAP website, provides an interactive road map that helps families achieve a consistent routine integrating optimal lifestyle choices. In addition, the authors in this policy emphasize the importance of addressing the type and quantity of media as well as appropriate media behaviors while placing consistent limits on time and modality. For example, it is encouraged that children get one hour of physical activity each day. In addition, sleep is also a priority, with a goal that each child gets 8 to 12 hours each day. Designated meal media-free times (family dinner) and media-free locations (bedrooms), along with avoiding devices one hour before bed and while doing homework. Furthermore, the Council on Communications and Media encourages the promotion of "activities that are likely to facilitate development and health, including positive parenting activities, such as reading, teaching, talking, and playing together" (p. 4). As with infants and younger children, caregiver co-viewing is encouraged, especially in ways that can foster learning. Caregivers are encouraged to facilitate discussions of "online citizenship," respectful behavior and avoidance of communications compromise safety and privacy. In turn, recruiting trustworthy adults can be helpful with supervision on social media and navigation through challenges (We discuss and define co-viewing on page (page 25). In summary, the focus of media use in this population is consistency with priority on healthy lifestyle choices (sleep, exercise, family time), as well as safe and appropriate engagement.

In this policy statement, the Council on Communications and Media also addresses some of the benefits of media for his population. They describe traditional and social media as helpful in providing exposure and awareness of current events and issues. It can provide an interactive venue to engage one's community. They mention how media can foster collaboration as well as connections with people who are not close geographically. Media allows those with disabilities or illnesses to form support networks, and in turn, social inclusion for those who feel more isolated. Lastly, digital media has the opportunity to educate and encourage healthy lifestyle- healthy diet, smoking cessation, etc. We address each of these items in the following chapters.

Meanwhile, the risks of media addressed in this age range from physical, mental, and safety concerns. Again, these topics will be addressed more extensively over the course of this book. However, the following discussion is focused on the most recent policy statement. As we discussed with the young children, obesity is a fundamental concern as the report presented a study finding the odds of being overweight were five times greater in adolescents who watch more than five hours of television each day (Gortmaker, 1996). Possible contributors to these phenomena include increased calorie intake as well as suggestive advertising for higher calorie foods. As with the other age groups, the council describes multiple ways in which sleep can be disrupted by media use. Gaming disorders are addressed such that children and adolescents can become preoccupied with video games allowing for addiction type behaviors (cannot cut down on time, withdrawal), and decreasing interest in real social relationships. We discuss video game effects in more detail in Chapter 7 (page 93). Furthermore, media allows exposure to alcohol use, tobacco use and sexual behaviors, and the potential for earlier interest in these things (discussed in Chapter 13 (page 184). Cyberbullying in its anonymity, as well as the ability to quickly spread information, are also tremendous concerns (discussed in Chapter 6 (page 79). Mental health is discussed in this policy and in particular, one study that found that passive uses of social media prompted decline in life satisfaction (discussed in Chapters 8 and 10 (pages 106 & 139). Lastly, the council express concerns about caregiver engagement in social media as a distraction from meaningful experiences and discourse with their child which are fundamentally important in a child's social and emotional development (discussed in Chapter 9 (page 124).

In their policy statements, the AAP not only provides recommendations for screen use but also some of the justifications for these guidelines. It is imperative to have these expert recommendations and analyses available as they provide a framework for screen time discussion in the clinic. Indeed, as we continue to forge through the pandemic and an unprecedented reliance on media for learning and social engagement, new guidelines, research, and commentary will continue to be greatly anticipated. In the meantime, this book will serve as further justification and recommendations for media use. In the following chapters we will explain the current state of the research and offer analysis for how to practically understand and use it.

REFERENCES

AAP Council on Communications and Media. (2016a). Media and young minds. *Pediatrics*, 138(5), e20162591.

AAP Council on Communications and Media. (2016b). Media use in school-aged children and adolescents. *Pediatrics*, 138(5), e20162592.

AAP Newsroom. (2016, October 21). *American academy of pediatrics announces new recommendations for children's media use.* www.aap.org/en/news-room/news-releases/aap/2016/aap-announces-new-recommendations-for-media-use/

AAP Parenting Website. https://healthychildren.org/English/Pages/default.aspx

American Academy of Pediatrics. (2021). www.aap.org

Family Media Use Plan. www.healthychildren.org/mediauseplan

Gortmaker, S. L., Must, A., Sobol, A. M., Peterson, K., Colditz, G. A., & Dietz, W. H. (1996). Television viewing as a cause of increasing obesity among children in the United States, 1986–1990. *Archives of Pediatrics and Adolescent Medicine*, 150(4), 356–362.

Nathanson, A. I., Aladé, F., Sharp, M. L., Rasmussen, E. E., & Christy, K. (2014). The relation between television exposure and executive function among preschoolers. *Developmental Psychology*, 50(5), 1497–1506.

Shaheen, S. (2014). How child's play impacts executive function – related behaviors. *Applied Neuropsychology: Child*, 3(3), 182–187.

Effects of Media on the Developing Infant and Young Child

4

The focus of this chapter of the book is on how media impacts the infant and young child. We will explore the best means in which to enhance and optimize a child's development. As discussed in the previous chapter (page 36), the American Academy of Pediatrics (AAP) has discouraged digital media use in children under 18 months of age with the exception of video chatting. In the 18–24-month-old age group, the AAP indicates that if parents chose to allow screen time to ensure it is of high content quality and in a context where the caregiver is engaged with the child with respect to the content, this is called "co-viewing" and we review this in the chapter on media literacy (page 25). In the preschooler set, it is recommended that screen time be limited to 1 hour a day and that the same "high quality" content be shown.

In this chapter, we will discuss the impact of media exposure on development and possible untoward consequences. With respect to preschool aged children, we will explore some of the potential benefits of screen time and also the potential negative consequences, particularly of excessive screen time on a child's general health and well-being. The question-and-answer portion at the end of this chapter addresses more specific concerns with respect to children's media use including the use of tablets and discussing "educational" applications and programming. The questions were plentiful and include: *A question I get asked all the time is about toddlers using tablets at the dinner table. What should I be saying to these parents? What about apps that teach toddlers to "talk" or their letters?" How do I take the screen away when they always want it, and it's the only thing that calms them down? Are there programs via media that help children's cognitive or language development? What about background TV? Is it ok to leave it on? Do the producers of such media have any standards to uphold to protect our youngest population from the negative effects? and What's more important: quality or quantity?*

DOI: 10.4324/9781003223412-4

OPTIMIZING CHILD AND INFANT DEVELOPMENT
THROUGH PLAY

We want to start this conversation by quoting Mr. Rogers: "Play is often talked about as if it were a relief from serious learning. But for children, play is serious learning. Play is really the work of childhood" (Fred Rogers Center).

It goes without saying that the best way to enhance a child's development is by consistent engagement. Many of our concerns regarding screen time and the effects of screen time stem from the passivity of screen use. As a pediatrician, I get asked on a pretty regular basis with respect to a child's development, "What are the best toys?" "What are the best games?" or "What are the best books?" Routinely, my response to these questions is pretty simple. Talk to your baby all the time, during diaper changes, bathing, and feedings. Go outside for walks and talk to them about clouds and sounds you hear. Play music and dance. Make reading time a priority. Outside of our limitations most recently with the pandemic, I encourage park dates, playdates, and experiences with other children. The focus is keeping your child engaged with a variety of inputs. You don't need to invest in the newest and greatest gadget. Later in the chapter, we will briefly address media products in the past such as Baby Einstein, which were advertised as "educational" to parents of infants and young children yet were encouraging passive screen time at very young ages. The fundamentals of optimizing a child's development are frequent active engagement and, as will now be discussed, the critical importance of play. Nowhere is screen time listed as critical to an infant or toddler's development.

PLAY

In 2007, Ginsburg and the Committees on Communications and Psychosocial Aspects of Child and Family published a piece titled "The Importance of Play in Promoting Healthy Child Development and Maintaining Strong Parent-Child Bonds." In this research, the authors clearly discuss how essential play is to the cognitive, physical, social and emotional well-being of children and youth. This piece wasn't as much focused on how play could be hindered by digital media use, though it provides a clear argument as to why play is critical.

As a pediatrician, I find that their discussion regarding the benefits of play encompasses all the complexities of why active play is so very important to the developing child. Specifically, the research explains,

Play allows children to use their creativity while developing their imagination, dexterity, and physical, cognitive, and emotional strength. Play is important to healthy brain development. It is through play that children at a very early age engage and interact in the world around them. Play allows children to create and explore a world they can master, conquering their fears while practicing adult roles, sometimes in conjunction with other children or adult caregivers. As they master their world, play helps children develop new competencies that lead to enhanced confidence and the resiliency they will need to face future challenges. Undirected play allows children to learn how to work in groups, to share, to negotiate, to resolve conflicts, and to learn self-advocacy skills. When play is allowed to be child driven, children practice decision-making skills, move at their own pace, discover their own areas of interest, and ultimately engage fully in the passions they wish to pursue. Ideally, much of play involves adults, but when play is controlled by adults, children acquiesce to adult rules and concerns and lose some of the benefits play offers them, particularly in developing creativity, leadership, and group skills. In contrast to passive entertainment, play builds active, healthy bodies. In fact, it has been suggested that encouraging unstructured play may be an exceptional way to increase physical activity levels in children, which is one important strategy in the resolution of the obesity epidemic. Perhaps above all, play is a simple joy that is a cherished part of childhood.

(p. 183)

In Ginsburg's research there was some discussion of the role of digital media with respect to play and essentially encouraging parents to not passively accept media, particularly media that purport being a more valuable resource in promoting success and happiness in children than "the tried, trusted, and traditional methods of play and family togetherness" (p. 187).

Later in 2018, Yogman et al. published a piece and policy statement discussing the critical importance of play, and in particular how play enhances brain structure and function and promotes executive function. While difficult to truly define, the authors describe play as "an activity that is intrinsically motivated, entails active engagement and results of joyful discovery" (p. 2). The authors went on to explain that play is voluntary, fun, and spontaneous, with no commanding goals. Children of all ages are seen engaging in play and these acts help develop executive functioning skills and even contribute to school readiness. Through decades of ethnographic research, scholars have gleaned that play creates an imaginative reality, and using your imagination is critical to further cognitive development. In the article, Yogman et al. express the importance of play as it helps build a pro-social brain that can interact effectively with others. They also describe play as critical in developing skill sets in problem solving, collaboration and creativity. Finally, Yogman et al. also describe the critical importance of play and nurturing relationships especially in an environment of adversity, as play and nurturing relationships help limit the effect of "toxic stresses" that can very much disrupt optimal cognitive and behavioral development.

Clearly, there are multitudes of factors that are critical when it comes to optimizing a child's development. However, for the purposes and discussion in this book, a major negative impact with respect to the effects of digital media and especially excessive media use is its ability to divert children from play. Prioritizing play time and consistent positive interactions with others is fundamental.

MEDIA IMPACTS ON INFANTS

As stated previously, the AAP in its policy statements has discouraged the use of digital screen media in children under the age of 18 months with exception of video chatting. We've already discussed the critical importance of engagement and play for the developing mind. In this next segment, we will discuss some of the downsides of digital media in this age group.

As a pediatrician and mother, I am often reminded of how exhausting that first two years of parenthood are. The sleepless nights, constant worry, frequent feedings and this is all before a little nine-month-old becomes mobile. After mobility comes the frequent chasing and protecting from falls, hazards, and ingestions. It is not a surprise that screen time can be embraced as a window of time for rest, getting dinner started, and finishing the laundry. Moreover, we are in a tech savvy culture. Being technologically competent is a big priority in our society. In my experience, I have observed parents taking pride in their young child being able to operate their parent's smartphones and tablets. It does make me question, however, how much time have they spent with these devices to become so skilled?

In 2011, the Council on Communications and Media published their research on media use by children younger than two years old. While the research was able to demonstrate some benefits of high-quality programs in children older than two, the research primarily asserted that media only has a positive benefit because this age group is able to understand the content and sustain attention long enough to reap any benefits. Children younger than 12 months "do not follow sequential screen shots or a program's dialogue" (p. 1041). In studies using noncommercial videos, a "video deficit" is described where young children have difficulty distinguishing video events from live events. In addition, children aged 12 to 18 months are more likely to learn from live presentations versus a televised one.

More recently, in 2017, Anderson, Subrahmanyam, and the Cognitive Impacts of Digital Workgroup, looked specifically into the effects of digital screen media and cognitive development. In the discussion regarding the impact of digital screen media on infants, the authors assert that for children less than two years of age, the impact of screen media is negative, particularly for language and executive function. Programming is often geared for adults and attention in this age group is limited. Essentially, programming is being relegated to "background television" which "has been shown to disrupt 12- and 24-month-old children's sustained toy play and reduce the quality of parent-child interactions compared with when the television is not on" (p. S58). The authors recommend clinicians being consistent in educating parents on their own use of smartphones and tablets as it affects their engagement with their infants and young toddlers as these behaviors are likely to overlap.

MEDIA IMPACTS ON TODDLERS

Continuing this research trajectory, Hish et al. (2021) presented their research on the impact of infant television watching their patterns as toddlers. For this research, the authors used longitudinal data from infants enrolled in a control group of Greenlight, a cluster randomized multi-site trial to prevent childhood obesity in pediatric residency clinics. Parents were asked about active screen time at scheduled well-child visits between 2 to 24 months. When the study concluded, results confirmed that infants who watched television became toddlers who watched more television. It does seem to be inversely related to the age at which television was introduced – such that the later the screen was introduced, the less the child watched as they aged and the earlier the screen was introduced to the infant, the more that child watched as a toddler.

In summary, screen time in infants does not appear to have any positive benefit, and in fact, is detrimental. Infants and toddlers 0–24 months are not at a developmental level to glean anything beneficial from the content. Furthermore, screen time takes away from play and meaningful engagements. We now know that the earlier we start television the more television in the preschool age which we will now discuss those impacts.

MEDIA EFFECTS ON PRESCHOOL-AGE CHILDREN

In their official policy statement in 2016, the American Academy of Pediatrics recommended restricting children ages two through five to one hour total of screen time a day and recommended that the content be "of high quality." In their work, Anderson and Subrahmanyam et al. (2017) explain that even though children around the age of two are able to understand and comprehend what is happening on the screen, this understanding continues to increase until around the age of 12. Until children can understand the intent behind the media messages, the media is their main source of knowledge. The authors explain, "once comprehension is established, television begins to influence child knowledge and, therefore, cognitive development more generally" (p. S59). In this next segment, we will explore both the possible benefits and negative impacts of screen time in this age group, especially when in excess, not only on child development but also on general health including obesity, sleep, and behavior.

SESAME STREET

In terms of benefits, the discussion naturally focuses on the gold standard in educational programming which is *Sesame Street*. In the

2016 policy statement, the Council on Communications and Media, explained that well designed programming such as *Sesame Street* "can improve cognitive, literacy, and social outcomes for children 3 to 5 years of age and continue to create programming that addresses evolving child health and developmental needs (eg, obesity prevention, resilience)" (p. 2). In addition, evaluations of both Sesame Workshop and the Public Broadcasting Service (PBS) online and mobile apps have also shown positive outcomes in terms of preschooler literacy skills.

Looking further into this, Anderson et al. (2001) published the results of a ten-year longitudinal study tracking the television viewing of preschool-age children through to high school. In brief, the children in the study who watched *Sesame Street* had larger vocabularies in high school, even relative to those with no television exposure. Further, kids of lower incomes were more prepared for school and children demonstrated higher grades in their courses, had a higher GPA, read more books, and ultimately, placed a higher value on achievement and were even rated as "more creative" in relation to their peers. In 2012, Goldman assessed Anderson et al.'s research and specifically noted how the behavioral findings of this study were especially interesting. In his report, Goldman asserted that boys who watched *Sesame Street* were "rated as less aggressive and girls more likely to participate in extra-curricular art classes" (np). The study followed children who watched programming other than *Sesame Street* and reported that similar effects were seen from teenagers who watched *Mister Rogers* as children, but not for any teenagers who watched other non-educational television programs while in preschool.

Much of the benefit provided by *Sesame Street* stems from extensive efforts put forth. Rich (2020) clearly sums this up:

> The genius of *Sesame Street* is simple: education scholars conducted formative research to design programming that was pedagogically sound, and once the shows were made and shown, they conducted summative research to evaluate how effectively the programming met intended goals.
>
> (p. 145)

Rich also alludes to the fact that *Sesame Street* as a resource is universally available to all children. What is also unique about *Sesame Street* is the interactive nature and the ways in which the show promotes dialogue off screen. While these results seem very positive and we should throw all children in front of *Sesame Street*, it is not without work from parents, caregivers, and the preschool all who reinforce the lessons of *Sesame Street* regularly. These are media literacy practices that we discuss in Chapter 2 (page 22).

Indeed, content is critical. Television can provide positive learning experiences to so many and *Sesame Street*, as one example, has been meticulously crafted to do so. Unfortunately, not all programs and applications on the market geared towards this age group are of this caliber. It will continue to be more and more important that parents and providers are educated on what qualifies as high-quality programming so the benefits of this media exposure is optimized.

SCREEN TIME

As content is an important consideration, clearly the duration of time spent engaging in watching television or using devices is fundamental. When considering some of the negative impacts of digital media on this population, it does appear that excessive use of screen time can negatively affect children cognitively, behaviorally, and physically. This is further complicated by the fact that parents may often have an inaccurate estimate of the amount of time spent watching media each day. This particularly applies to smartphones and tablets. In 2020, Radesky et al. analyzed data from 346 parents of children three to five years with programs that track device usage. One-third of parents in the study underestimated the amount of time spent on the device and typically underestimated by about an hour, which is significant in a population where it is encouraged to limit media to one hour.

LITERACY

One way in which excessive digital media use in this population in terms of cognitive development is with respect to literacy. In 2021, McArthur et al. explored the longitudinal associations between screen use and reading in preschool-age children. The objective of the research was to use a prospective birth cohort to examine reading and screen use at 24, 36, and 60 months in order to assess a direct association between screen use and reading. What they concluded was that greater screen use at 24 months was associated with lower reading and

26 months. In addition, lower reading at 36 months was associated with greater screen use at 60 months. In their commentary on this research, Radesky (2021) noted that in our evolving digital world and the easy accessibility children have to their favorite programs on demand, many of which have low educational value. She praises books in their capacity to "challenge readers' minds to stretch their attention span, pause and contemplate, and take others' perspective" (p. 1). In continued response to McArthur et al.'s research, Radesky commented that the results of the study are a "key window" with respect to choosing media over reading as a daily activity which sets the stage for more screen use around kindergarten entry. Clearly more research will evolve. However, this association of screen time with literacy is significant and it further supports the notion that children should have reading be part of their routine and in turn, being cognizant of time spent on digital media (further effects of this research are discussed in Chapter 9 (page 124).

BEHAVIOR

In my pediatric practice, I am always intrigued by the effects digital media, particularly in excess, may have on children's behavior. Of course, a pediatric office can be a place of distress for the young child and it is not uncommon that a tantruming toddler is soothed reflexively by grabbing a tablet or a parent's phone. As mentioned earlier, this often-subconscious move to soothe a young child with a screen may be contributory to possibly underestimating the cumulative screen time a child is exposed to each day. Moreover, what is the impact using media and screens as a means of consoling a child? In 2021, Coyne et al. published their research with regard to tantrums, toddlers, and technology. The authors' objective was to examine how using media to regulate children's difficult emotions may be related to problematic media use in childhood. Using questionnaires and observational data, Coyne's analyses revealed that children who needed greater amounts of emotional regulation were positively correlated to more extreme behavior when technology was removed. In a discussion of their research with a local media outlet, Coyne expressed concern that children don't learn to deal with boredom or negative emotions which in turn can lead to addiction. Giving the screen to the child does not allow an opportunity to engage the child, and moreover, a chance to problem solve (Collins, 2021). In the end, the multifaceted effects of using a tablet to calm a child are concerning particularly in missed opportunities to learn more functional ways to manage emotions and also concern for evolving media addiction.

CHILDHOOD OBESITY

As probably one of the prime examples of the effects of excessive screen time on physical health, childhood obesity is at the forefront. It is not a surprise that habits and routines established in early childhood may lay the groundwork for lifestyle choices as children grow older. In its policy statement in *Pediatrics,* the Council on Communications and Media (2016) distinctly addresses obesity with respect to limiting screen time in this age. In the report, the council cites a study of 2-year-olds and found that the children's body mass index (BMI) increased for every hour per week of media consumed. Thus, showing a causal relationship between media consumption and childhood obesity.

Along these same lines, in 2017, Robinson et al. outlined possible mechanisms in which screen time may propagate obesity. These included decreasing physical activity, increased caloric intake while viewing, and reducing sleep. While intuitive, previous studies had yet to establish a strong link between the substitution of screen time for physical activity, but the others suggest that this is a function of difficulty with measurements. What has been supported by evidence is the increase in caloric intake relative to screen time. Robinson et al. (2017) describes

laboratory-based experimental studies that revealed that screen media exposure can lead to incremental energy consumption without increased feelings of hunger or compensation by lower intake during the rest of the day. Screen time reduction interventions also documented reductions in dietary intake compared with controls.

(p. S99)

With this in mind, Robinson et al. (2017) also addressed the extent to which food advertising contributes to this seismic issue. As discussed throughout this book, young children are not able to recognize persuasive content and are therefore, much more easily persuaded by it (page 8). Think of the image at the end of breakfast cereal commercials where it says, "as part of a balanced meal" and there is the bowl of cereal surrounded by a glass of milk, a glass of juice, and a glass of water, with fruit and toast nestled in there as well. These are messages that commercials are sending to children who do not know any better. Lastly, the authors address the effects of screen exposure on inadequate sleep. Robinson et al. (2017) cite research that associates sleep deprivation with increased obesity in children between ages three to seven years old. Sleep deprivation lends itself to hormonal aberrations that limit satiety. Less sleep time lends itself to consuming more calories and increased snacking time (we discuss more about this in Chapter 5 page 59).

CONCLUSION

We cannot complete this chapter without circling back to the critical importance of play. As we look at infants, it is abundantly clear that screen time has very little positive impact and in fact, detracts from what is most important, interpersonal engagement and exploration. As we enter the preschool age, there are clear positive impacts as discussed with respect to *Sesame Street* and high-quality programming, but that should not be taken for granted. Collaborative screen time with the child and the caregiver allows for explanation, context and discussion (see co-viewing and media literacy pages 22–25). However, the effects of using screen time in excess has demonstrated cognitive, behavioral, and physical concerns. A focus on playtime lends itself obviously to the developmental benefits as discussed but also less time to be consumed by screens. As quoted at the beginning of this chapter, "Play is really the work of childhood."

Without further ado, we enter the question-and-answer portion of this chapter:

QUESTIONS

A question I get asked all the time is about toddlers using tablets at the dinner table. What should I be saying to these parents?

As a pediatrician, I have been told countless times that a child will only settle down to eat if able to have a tablet or screen. As based on our discussion above, my most immediate concerns are two-fold: the need for consistent and focused interpersonal engagement and in addition, optimizing the child's health and well-being. In terms of engagement, we discussed above the importance of play and the importance of engaging children to optimize their development. Mealtimes are critical opportunities where the focus can be on the interpersonal relationship, the perfect time to discuss experiences and feelings. It cannot be emphasized enough that raising a child in a nurturing environment surrounded with positive parent-child/parent-family experiences are fundamental. Mealtimes allow these experiences to be part of the daily routine.

The other main concern is the association of excessive TV watching and the potential for obesity. As discussed above, laboratory studies have shown that there is increased consumption without increased feelings of hunger. Robinson et al. (2017) explains, children eat an unreasonable large portion of their daily calories while sitting in front of a screen. In one such study, nearly one-third of daily energy intake and half of the participating children's meals were consumed in front of a screen. These meals in front of the screen were met with longer duration of eating, and the children being too distracted with what was on the screen to notice their own physical signs of being full. Clearly, we are inclined to eat more and be less attuned to feeling full when we are distracted by the screen.

What about apps that teach toddlers to "talk" or their letters?

We discussed at length above that there can be cognitive benefits to screen time if it is high quality and limited to an hour day (for older than 18 months). We also discussed above the "recontact study" (Anderson et al., 2001) in which ten years of longitudinal data collected from children age three to five who watched *Sesame Street* had larger vocabularies in high school than those who watched other television programming, or even no television at all. The effect of this research could not be explained by gender, family size, or parents' education. Preschoolers from lower income neighborhoods, in particular, who watched *Sesame Street* were more prepared for school than their peers who did not watch *Sesame Street*. All that being said, not all programming geared toward children may have this desired effect as stated in the previous discussion.

One specific example came from when the AAP supported consumers who questioned the educational validity of Baby Einstein and forced a recall in 2009. This was again demonstrated in 2014 with the Federal Trade Commission complaint against the program Your Baby Can Read, as

> defendants failed to have competent and reliable scientific evidence
> that babies can learn to read using the Your Baby Can Read program,
> or that children who used the program can read books such as
> *Charlotte's Web* or *Harry Potter* by age three or four.
>
> (Katz, 2014, np)

Clearly, there is an opportunity for media in terms of learning, however, ensuring the quality is fundamental. Early research into the effects of Baby Einstein, and all early childhood development programming showed that for every hour of screen time, babies actually acquired fewer words than their screen-free counterparts!

With respect to applications, as a pediatrician, I am eagerly anticipating further research in regard to their potential to be a legitimate adjunct to learning. In 2020, Griffith et al. researched whether children under the age of six can learn from interactive applications. In their studies, children under the age of six played with an interactive game while their academic, cognitive, and social emotional outcomes were measured. The authors were able to demonstrate "learning benefit of interactive app use for early academic skills across multiple studies, particularly for early mathematics learning in typically developing children" (p. 1). Again, there is now an opportunity for quality applications to play a role in enhancing learning

How do I take the screen away when they always want it and that is the only thing that calms them down?

As discussed earlier in the chapter, removing devices from children is a major challenge for parents in a digital age. It becomes reflexive to grab a phone or a tablet when your young child is acting up and in addition, it only gets harder and harder to separate the child from their device. In a 2020 piece for the *New York Times*, Petersen presented a discussion with various psychologists and researchers on strategies to help control the screen use in these situations. The interactivity of apps and games is very "gratifying" such that one touches a screen and something happens. Moreover, rewards are often a big part of apps and games which in turn are "monetizing our children's attention." Dr. Dimitri Christakis of the Seattle Children's Research Institute, was on the panel and described the role of dopamine which "sends a signal to the prefrontal cortex, the part of the brain involved in planning and organizing tasks. The message is 'do that again, get more of that'" (Petersen, np). This in turn can happen with screen time and when taken away, dopamine levels drop with subsequent potential for painful withdrawal.

In terms of how to take away a device, we agree with many of the strategies mentioned in this article:

> One key way to decrease the risk for outbursts is to "make screen time scheduled and predictable" which was supported by a study at University of Washington which enrolled 28 families with children less than 5 years of age. Transitions were better when the screen time was planned. Another manner to assist the transition from the device is to make a plan to do something fun when screen time is over with reminders of the positive activity planned afterward. In my experience, what can be tricky is the notion of reminders. Dr. Hiniker at University of Washington expressed concerns as warning can "spur a power struggle" and "could remind the child who is in charge and that they don't have a way" She suggests letting the child determine when they will get the warning (10 minutes or 5 minutes).
>
> (Petersen, np)

The next strategy was to avoid cutting the screen time in the middle of a show or game. The panel suggested instead to consider shutting off auto-play functions on some applications to avoid the next game/program to commence. Next, the panel suggested that you avoid screen time sessions that are too short as it leads to frustration. Per Paul Donahue, "It takes a while for kids to transition in and focus on what they are doing," he says. "If you say, 'You can have it for five minutes, then I'm going to take it out of your hands,' that is creating too much frustration." He recommends sessions of 30 to 45 minutes.

One other critical suggestion that is a common thread in parenting is doing your best to be consistent and not giving in. As per Radesky, "If you're intermittently rewarding your children's request for prolonged media time and they know Mom might say 'yes,' further transitions are likely to be rockier" (Petersen, np).

One last consideration is the notion of consequences. Donahue mentioned what to do if persistent tantrums with respect to digital media and more drastic measures. He suggested removing the device temporarily and setting the tone that these are privileges. After a few days of no device, hopefully this concept is better understood by the child and can transition back to devices with a "trial basis."

We really feel that all of these suggestions can be helpful and surely best when streamlined to the disposition of the child. Setting clear expectations while keeping a firm ground with respect to behavior and consequences are critical in minimizing difficult transitions off the device.

REFERENCES

Anderson, D. R., Huston, A. C., Schmitt, K. L., Linebarger, D. L., & Wright, J. C. (2001). Early childhood television viewing and adolescent behavior: The recontact study. *Monographs of the Society for Research in Child Development, 66*(1), I–147.

Anderson, D. R., Subrahmanyam, K., & On Behalf of the Cognitive Impacts of Digital Media Workgroup. (2017). Digital screen media and cognitive development. *Pediatrics, 140*(Suppl 2), S57–S61. http://doi.org/10.1542/peds.2016-1758C

Collins, L. M. (2021, May 26). Toddler pitching a fit in public? *Deseret News.* www.deseret.com/2021/5/26/22444589/toddler-tantrums-byu-study-says-screens-bad-tool-for-emotional-regulation-screen-time-for-kids

Council on Communications and Media. (2011). Media use by children younger than 2 years. *Pediatrics, 128*(5), 1040–1045. http://doi.org/10.1542/peds.2011-1753

Council on Communications and Media. (2016). Media and young minds. *Pediatrics, 138*(5), e20162591. https://doi.org/10.1542/peds.2016-2591

Coyne, S. M. (2021). Tantrums, toddlers and technology: Temperament, media emotion regulation, and problematic media use in early childhood. *Computers in Human Behavior* [e-Journal], 120. https://doi.org/10.1016/j.chb.2021.106762

Ginsburg, K. R., The Committee on Communications, & The Committee on Psychosocial Aspects of Child and Family Health. (2007). The importance of play in promoting healthy child development and maintaining strong parent-child bonds. *Pediatrics, 119*(1), 182–191. https://doi.org/10.1542/peds.2006-2697

Goldman, J. G. (2012). Sesame street and child development. *Scientific American.* https://blogs.scientificamerican.com/thoughtful-animal/baby-tv-sesame-street-and-child-development/

Griffith, S. F., Hagan, M. B., Heymann, P., Heflin, B. H., & Bagner, D. M. (2020). Apps as learning tools: A systematic review. *Pediatrics, 145*(1), e20191579. https://doi.org/10.1542/peds.2019-1579

Hish, A. J., Wood, C. T., Howard, J. B., Flower, K. B., Yin, H. S., Rothman, R. L., Delamater, A. M., Sanders, L. M., Bian, A., Schildcrout, J. S., & Perrin, E. M. (2021). Infant television watching predicts toddler television watching in a low-income population. *Academic Pediatrics*, 21(6), 988–995. http://doi.org/10.1016/j.acap.2020.11.002

Katz, M. J. (2014). Defendants settle FTC charges related to 'your baby can read' program. *Federal Trade Commission*. www.ftc.gov/news-events/press-releases/2014/08/defendants-settle-ftc-charges-related-your-baby-can-read-program

McArthur, B. A., Browne, D., McDonald, S., Tough, S., & Madigan, S. (2021). Longitudinal associations between screen use and reading in preschool-aged children. *Pediatrics*, 147(6), e2020011429. https://doi.org/10.1542/peds.2020-011429

Radesky, J. S. (2021). Establishing early literacy habits in a profit-driven digital world. *Pediatrics*, 147(6), e2020047472. https://doi.org/10.1542/peds.2020-047472

Radesky, J. S., Weeks, H. M., Ball, R., Schaller, A., Eo, S., Durnez, J., Tamayo-Rios, M., Epstein, M., Kirkorian, H., Coyne, S., & Barr, R. (2020). Young children's use of smartphones and tablets. *Pediatrics*, 146(1), e20193518. https://doi.org/10.1542/peds.2019-3518

Rich, M. (2020). Can smartphones make smart kids? *Pediatrics*, 145(1), e20193503. https://doi.org/10.1542/peds.2019-3503

Robinson, T. N., Banda, J. A., Hale, L., Shirong Lu, A., Fleming-Milici, F., Calvert, S. L., & Wartella, E. (2017). Screen media exposure and obesity in children and adolescents. *Pediatrics*, 140(Suppl 2), S97–S101. https://doi.org/10.1542/peds.2016-1758K

Yogman, M., Garner, A., Hutchinson, J., Hirsh-Pasek, K., & Michnick Golinkoff, R. (2018). Committee on psychological aspecials of child and family heath and Council on Communications and Media. *Pediatrics*, 142(3), e20182058. https://doi.org/10.1542/peds.2018-2058

This next chapter explores the effects of media on what is often referred to as "middle childhood" (children six–ten years of age). Historically, as introduced by Hagan and Shaw (2020), pediatricians had referred to his period of time as a "latency phase" suggesting that not much physical and mental development occurs during these few years of a child's life. However, Parasuraman et al. (2020) explored the epidemiological profile of health and behaviors in middle childhood and determined:

> Middle childhood is a developmental period marked by profound changes as children transition from early childhood to adolescence. Typically initiated when children begin school, cognitive and social capabilities expand as relationships with families, peers, and communities shift. Although past work has described the health and influencing factors associated with early childhood and adolescence, little corresponding research exists for middle childhood. This disparity in evidence could be due to the perception that this population is generally healthy but may also be related to the fact that these children have aged out of the intensive period of developmental monitoring associated with early childhood yet do not warrant the attention on health-risk behaviors and incident chronic disease associated with adolescence. Behaviors and habits that develop during this time influence outcomes that manifest during adolescence and adulthood, such as health-promoting or health-risk behaviors and chronic disease incidence. Research has revealed associations between heavy media use in childhood and increased obesity risk as children age and adverse associations with sleep habits in adolescence . . . Emerging evidence has also revealed the rate of bullying victimization to be higher among those in middle childhood compared with adolescents. Finally, several learning, behavioral, and

DOI: 10.4324/9781003223412-5

developmental conditions are typically first diagnosed during middle childhood.

(p. 2)

While overall children in middle childhood are generally doing well, research has described a "fragility" in this developmental period such that this is a critical time where health promotion and health-risk behaviors evolve. In this chapter, we will explore the effects of media in this age group and the potential impacts on physical health, mental health, sleep, and cognition. We will also discuss the media's role in race and ethnicity development, which is seen in this time period. Throughout the chapter we answer questions that practitioners had regarding this age group. Specific questions include: *How is bedtime affected by screens? How do screens affect sleep? What are your thoughts on Messenger Kids for children in the elementary grade levels in regards to benefits of connecting with friends in a controlled environment?* and *What should I say about the change in what is on television now versus when they were growing up?*

Even though this age group is seen to be doing well, they are at an important precipice of change.

MEDIA AND MIDDLE CHILDHOOD

As we discussed in Chapter 3 (page 36), the American Academy of Pediatrics (AAP) has started focusing less on the quantitative amount of time children spend with media, and more on quality of time in its most recent recommendations for monitoring screen time use. Whereas in the past there was a recommendation to limit screen time to two hours a day, the focus now is more on ensuring healthy daily lifestyle choices. In the "family media use plan" available online, parents and children can construct a daily schedule that integrates screen time with an emphasis on healthy goals. For example, when a family prioritizes 8–12 hours of sleep each day, no screens for an hour before bed, no screens during mealtimes, screen-less homework time, and one hour of physical activity each day, it does really limit the available screen time for a child, particularly on a regular school day. As a pediatrician during the annual wellness checks, a patient's growth, school performance, diet, sleep, activity, and screen time are all typically reviewed. What is interesting to me, however, is the inter-connectedness of all these foci and most especially, how media use can affect all these parameters in a child's current and future health.

COGNITIVE DEVELOPMENT IN MIDDLE CHILDHOOD

We will start our discussion with the effects of media on cognition. In 2017, Anderson et al. presented a discussion on digital screen media and cognitive development. The authors agree with previous literature that around two and a half years old, children are able to comprehend age-appropriate content on television. However, they offered a new revelation that children's comprehension of more complex programming continues to develop to at least up to 12 years old. The authors explain that, once children can comprehend what they are watching on television, the content of the media begins to influence their knowledge, and as a result, their cognitive development. In their discussion, Anderson et al. acknowledge that beyond the preschool years, most television is entertainment based, and as a result, there is increasing exposure to more adult content. Indeed, using this argument, it is via content that media may have its biggest influence, and it is the middle years that we start to see its effects. By the time a child is seven or eight years old, their vocabulary and ability to function as a person has grown exponentially from their preschool years. Given this, it is easy to forget there are still, as Piaget explains, limitations on the ability of the child to internally understand and perceive information from the environment (page 12). In their research, Anderson et al. (2017) explore both the negative potential effects but also address some of the potential positive effects of digital media use using their framework. In this chapter we divided the discussion between cognitive outcomes, mental health outcomes, and physical outcomes. We will discuss both the positive and negative outcomes of each area because there are many. It is important to remember, however, that media is a variable, but so is media literacy, and social support. The child can be both positively and negatively influenced by the media during middle childhood, just like they can be positively or negatively affected by their peer group.

NEGATIVE OUTCOMES

COGNITIVE

This area of content and the media's harmful effects on middle aged children is seen frequently in the literature. As stated above, and explained through uses and gratifications theory (page 80), elementary-school age children spend most of their screen time on entertainment. Circling back to Anderson et al. (2017), the authors presented that, while the data is inconsistent in confirming if watching adult entertainment programming has an overall positive or negative effect on a developing mind, the authors were quick to point out that clear evidence does exist to argue that violent content influences antisocial and aggressive behavior. Anderson et al. then made the final argument in connecting the dots and explained that the effect of viewing violent content on antisocial and aggressive behavior may account for negative associations of viewing violent content with school achievement. We discuss this again in the video game chapter (page 93). With respect to the use of interactive digital media, the authors are also unforgiving. They explain that similar to existing findings on the effects of television, the authors also found evidence that violent and aggressive computer games can influence antisocial and aggressive behavior. Clearly, it is critical in this age group that not only the cumulative screen time should be monitored, but the caregivers should also closely monitor the content presented to this age group. Children in the middle age group are starting to enjoy more independence. They no longer have to be watched all the time, they understand how the remotes work, and they can read and discuss the latest games and movies with their friends. Violent and aggressive themed media is attractive, and with their new independence, most kids will find it.

With respect to additional negative cognitive outcomes of screen time on the middle-age child, Anderson et al. explain that "at least since the advent of the dime novel, there have been claims that mass media for children foster a laxness of thought, reduced cognitive competencies, and compete with more developmentally productive activities" (p. S58). In one discussion, the authors address a theory that a negative side effect pertains to the notion that particularly excessive time viewing media may displace other more developmentally enriching activities, such as reading. There is evidence here to suggest that television viewing in the middle age group may be associated with decreased reading achievement in this critical time of learning how to read. While research has been equivocal, there has been considerable concern that television may negatively influence young children's executive function, especially the ability to focus and sustain attention in task situations (page 50). The research is very clear on this point – increased screen time comes with decreased other skills, like reading and executive function.

Furthermore, in 2018, Ruest et al. presented the results of their study on media exposure in school-aged children and found a correlation between increased media use and decreasing frequency of homework completion. In their cross-sectional study, Ruest et al. examined digital media exposure (not school-work related) among 6- to 17-year-old children and parental perception of frequency as a means of "flourishing." The authors describe childhood flourishing, or overall positive well-being, as evaluated by various markers. Diligence, initiative, task completion, and interpersonal relationships were all included as markers. What the authors were able to discover was a dose-dependent relationship between hours of media consumed and homework completion, such that children with less access to screen time completed their homework at a higher rate and were more prepared for academic success.

MEDIA EFFECTS ON MENTAL HEALTH

As a related topic, and another area where increased screen time has shown to have detrimental effects, we would now like to segue to the effects of media with respect to mental health in this population. In 2021, Nigg et al. published their results of an 11-year longitudinal study evaluating the role of physical activity, screen time, and mental health during childhood, pre-adolescence, and adolescence. Organized by respondent's gender, the authors followed the relationships of physical activity and screen time with respect to mental health. The mental health challenges they described were emotional symptoms, conduct problems, hyperactivity/inattention, peer relationship problems, prosocial behavior and overall strengths and difficulties. Nigg et al.'s findings support the understanding that increased physical activity time predicted less television/video time in females and less television/video/PC/Internet use in both genders. In such, the authors report that for females, increased media time correlated to higher mental health challenges overtime. Next, Nigg et al. also described preadolescent males with mental health challenges were more inclined to increased screen time as adolescents. Finally, the authors support our overall claim that we need to explore more unique effective ways to reduce childhood screen time. This is especially true, given the results for their research, for tweens and teens with early signs of mental health issues.

PHYSICAL HEALTH

When the average child is now spending nearly eight hours a day in front of some kind of screen, many of their opinions and preferences are being shaped by the marketing campaigns you all create. And that's where the problem comes in . . . And I'm here today with one simple request – and that is to do even more, and move even faster to market responsibly to our kids.

Michelle Obama during White House Convening
on Food Marketing to Children (2013)

Unfortunately much research has pointed to media use and its effect on obesity beginning in early childhood and extending to children in this age group. Reid Chassiakos et al. (2016) provided a discussion on the link between media use and obesity and the connection of high levels of media use and obesity and cardiovascular risk throughout one's life course. Starting in preschool, research has shown small, yet noteworthy increases in body mass index (BMI) in children with heavy media use. Throughout the study, increases in BMI occurred every hour per week of media consumed. With respect to the middle childhood population, Gortmaker et al. (1996) evaluated five–ten year olds and the effects of heavy media use. It was found that the odds of being overweight were nearly five times greater for youth watching more than five hours of television per day compared to those limited to under two hours per day. Another study from de Jong et al. (2013), showed that particularly in children four to nine years of age that over 1.5 hours per day of media use was linked to obesity. That same year Braithwaite et al. (2013) ran a large international study with 300,000 children enrolled and found that watching between one and three hours of television per day resulted in a 10 to 30% increase in obesity. Clearly, media use, particularly in excess, can very much negatively impact physical health.

In 2017, Robinson et al. published their research on media exposure and obesity in children and adolescents. In their report the authors describe multiple manners in which screen time can lead to obesity.

In particular, they describe the impact media may have on reducing physical activity, increasing food intake, and reducing sleep (we will review effects of media on sleep later in the chapter). The data is also sound with regards to the effects of screen time on energy/calorie intake. Robinson et al. described children who spend more time with media as also consuming fewer fruits and veggies and being prone to consuming suboptimal choices (calorie-dense drinks and foods, fast foods, etc.). The authors also describe studies that have shown children consume up to one-third of their daily calories while on a screen. Satiety may also be impacted as the authors explain that as kids engage with screens, they consume more calories without more feelings of hunger or even compensating with fewer calories throughout the day. The effects of food advertising on this population are also of great concern. As a pediatrician, I assumed a strong link between screen time and obesity as a fundamental cause.

Meanwhile, Story and French (2004) reported that American children view an estimated 20,000–40,000 commercials each year and that food advertising alone accounts for over 50% of all ads targeting children. The authors explain that, at this rate, children watch approximately one food commercial for every five minutes of television viewing time and may see as many as three hours of food commercials each week.

LINKING WATCHING FOOD COMMERCIALS WITH OBESITY

In light of these findings, the World Health Organization (WHO), the Institute of Medicine (IOM), and the British Food Commission, have completed assessments of academic research that indicate a link between child-targeted marketing and childhood obesity. The 2006 seminal report released by the IOM found that "for younger and older children, the evidence clearly supports the finding that television advertising influences their food and beverage purchase requests" (McGinnis et al., 2006, p. 21). It was in response to these reports and the rising obesity rates for children that the AAP issued its, now extremely well known, and since updated, guidelines that television and video game time be limited to no more than two hours per day for children (Council on Communications and Media, 2011).

In addition, Robinson et al. explain that children are now exposed to food advertising in new media, including food company-sponsored websites, apps, and advergames, as well as on mobile devices and social media. This new marketing is interactive and often disguised as entertainment or messages from friends. As we know from cognitive development theories (page 12), children in this age group are not yet capable of recognizing food marketing as persuasive content. Additionally, research has shown that food advertising impacts children's food preference and food intake. For example, Robinson et al. (2017) ran randomized controlled trials of food commercials that were embedded into animated programs and revealed that advertising increases automatic eating for foods not being advertised. Even more compelling is that results from Borzekowski and Robinson's (2001) study revealed that even a single 30-second commercial has the ability to impact brand food preferences. Finally, a randomized controlled trial also revealed that fast food branding altered young children's actual taste perceptions in side-by-side taste tests (Robinson et al., 2017).

Ultimately, there are multifactorial causes in terms of decreased satiety and increased consumption being combined with often suboptimal food choices being actively presented to this population. However, Reid Chassiakos et al. (2016) allude to the possibility that this influence may be evolving because children watch more videos from streaming services such as Netflix and Hulu, which do not contain the same amount of commercials. While the current research is in agreement that there is no silver bullet connection such that watching television will make children obese, the overall sum of these findings clearly suggests that some real relationship does exist (Vandewater & Cummings, 2008). Like so many of the topics in this book, this issue too can be helped by media literacy. If we understand that screen time is leading to decreased activity and increased caloric intake and suggestions from commercials, we can suggest to parents and caregivers that they reduce the screen time of their children in middle childhood and adopt the AAP position on prioritizing other daily activities. We can also talk directly to the children about the persuasive influence of screen time on daily snacking and food choices.

With respect to the effects of reducing screen time and its effect on obesity, Robinson et al. (2017) provided a discussion on experimental trials testing media exposure and weight gain. One study was a seven-month randomized controlled study of third and fourth grade children. Results from screen-time reduction curriculum, behavior change skills lessons, an electronic television time manager, and educational parent newsletters targeted reducing time spent watching television, playing sedentary video games, and using computers were extremely positive. At the end of the seven-month study, children who received the screen-time reduction curriculum significantly reduced their television viewing, video game use, and number of meals eaten in front of the television. These students also reported a slower BMI gain, lower triceps skinfold thickness, waist circumference, and waist-to-hip ratio. This study is one great indicator that reducing screen time can have real and physical implications to children's health. Finally, Reid Chassiakos et al. (2016) also present the effects of television in the bedroom as an independent risk factor for obesity. We can assume that removing the television from the bedroom and reduction of that screen time would have a positive physical effect.

SLEEP

How is bedtime affected by screens? and How do screens affect sleep?

The last negative effect we will discuss is the media's impact on children's weight with respect to sleep. We were discussing the contributory mechanisms linking media and obesity and a critical factor to weight gain is inadequate sleep. Robinson et al. (2017) describe a literature review of screen time and sleep and found that the majority of studies demonstrate links between screen time and poor sleep measured by later bedtimes and less total sleep time. In three to seven year old children, it was found that obesity and weight gain were associated with poor sleep and three possible mechanisms have been suggested: sleep deprivation causes changes in the appetite-regulating hormones ghrelin and leptin to increase hunger and decrease satiety, short sleep duration can affect children's choices to consume more calories and fewer nutritionally-dense foods, and shorter sleep duration may lead to increased snacking and eating outside of normal mealtimes, including during the night.

In 2017, LeBourgeois contributed to our understanding with their research on media and sleep in children and adolescence where they describe the underlying mechanisms in which screen-based media use may affect sleep health with respect to delayed bedtimes and decreased duration of sleep. The authors describe time displacement (screen replacing time spent sleeping), psychological stimulation and lastly, the effects of light emitted from devices on circadian timing, sleep physiology and alertness. In their review of the literature, LeBourgeois et al. describe the one study that to date by Higuchi et al. (2014) that was able to quantify the amount of melatonin suppressed by a light stimulus of 580 lux (typical indoor light levels) in children was nearly two times higher than that of adults. Moreover, with larger pupillary diameter compared to adults, children are more affected by light. LeBourgeois et al. also explain that "prepubertal children in comparison to post pubertal adolescents, have greater melatonin suppression to low (15 lux) moderate (150 lux) and bright (5000 lux) light exposure in the evening hours before bedtime" (p. S94).

Poor sleep can also have significant effects on behavioral health. In 2019, Guerrero et al. published their research on screen time and problem behaviors in children and explored the mediating role of sleep duration. In their study, nine- and ten-year-old children and their parents self-reported their child's "emotional and behavioral syndromes" in addition to sleep duration. Meanwhile, children self-reported their screen time behaviors (types and content). The results explained that increased screen time was associated with increased problem behaviors while more sleep time was associated with fewer problematic behavior. Ultimately, sleep duration "mediated the effects of screen time on problem behaviors" (p. 1).

While we are all sufficiently concerned about the amount of screen time the children in our lives and in our practice are getting. Let's take some time to discuss the positive effects that the media can have on children in the middle age group.

POSITIVE OUTCOMES COGNITIVE

Switching gears now to discuss more positive topics involving the media. We started this conversation in the last chapter when we introduced the benefits of higher educational content (i.e., *Sesame Street*) on younger children, and we can see some of that with middle childhood as well. In its policy statement in 2016, the Council on Communications and Media presented a discussion on media use in school aged children. In the report, the authors describe the benefits of traditional and social media in providing exposure to new ideas and information. In addition, the council reported that screen time in children in the middle-age group makes them more aware of current events and issues, and finally, that it has the ability to promote community and civic engagement. These are all things that children would largely be unaware of if it were not for the media. When discussing social media specifically, the report supports the use of it as a means to facilitate collaboration and communication, as well as enhance support networks, especially for those children who may feel excluded or socially isolated. We discuss social media effects throughout the book and it is important to keep in mind the different effects are largely dependent on the age and cognitive maturity of the child. As with everything, including the *Sesame Street* studies – the positive outcomes of media effects on children are most often seen when accompanied by adult intervention. When co-viewing is in effect and adults are actively endorsing the prosocial messages and breaking down the negative messages, screen time is seen to have a positive effect on young users.

Another manner in which interactive digital media may have a positive impact is with video gaming. Anderson and Subrahmanyam (2017) investigated digital screen media and cognitive development and introduced the idea that there are short-term benefits and increases in cognitive skills from playing interactive, logic-based video games that often encourage players to read, problem-solve, and work together to solve challenging issues. The authors also described cognitive gains when assessing skills immediately after the completion and training and after a lapse of time. We discuss this further in the chapter on video games (page 93), and while much of the evaluations were geared towards older children and adults, there is still a potential for positive effects, in the correct circumstances, and with the right media. If media is geared toward children in the middle age range, is interactive, and the material is age appropriate and easily comprehended, then we are able to see some positive effects of screen time in this age group.

MENTAL HEALTH

What are your thoughts on Messenger Kids for children in the elementary grade levels in regards to benefits of connecting with friends in a controlled environment?

Just as there are ways in which the media can have positive effects on cognition in the middle-aged child, it may also enhance and provide positive mental health effects. In fact, the AAP has always had a caveat for video chat, even for the youngest kids because of the connection that children can foster through video chat. Communication across distances as well as chatting with family and friends separated geographically clearly has benefits. Specifically, Reid Chassiakos et al. (2016) discuss some of the ways media can support health particularly via social media. The authors describe the use of social media as a way to create and maintain peer connections among patients who might elsewhere feel excluded. The data also illustrates that for respondents with mental illness, social media allows for greater connectedness and feelings of belonging due to the fact that these individuals are able to find like-minded people, share personal stories and strategies for coping with challenges. The advantages are clear: Connecting via social media for ostracized children includes avoiding bullying and stigma, enhancing their social community and networks, and sharing resources with peers. With all certainty, volumes will be written about the effects of digital media and reliance on digital media with respect to children in the context of the COVID-19 pandemic. Aside from using media as a means to learn (page 124), it was the avenue for children to socialize and engage each other via gaming, google classrooms, zoom, etc. In what clearly has been a challenging and confusing time for children of all age groups, media provided the means to commiserate, socialize, play and ideally decrease feelings of isolation and those positive effects were seen for this age group more than the younger kids.

RACE AND ETHNICITY

In addition to new found independence and cognitive abilities, another issue that is now salient for children in the middle age group is race – their race, their friend's race, and the race of the people in the media. In many Western societies, including the United States, an individual's exposure to races and ethnicities that are different from one's own is a near certainty. It is, however, also true that these cross-cultural encounters may be limited in information and, therefore, may manifest prejudices and biases based on limited information and interaction. Mass media has the ability to reach thousands to millions of people instantaneously. This ability to reach millions provides the media a unique advantage to showcase the perceptions and prejudices of the individuals who write and produce media characters, and how characters are stereotyped based on racial stereotypes, which may affect viewers. As Helms (1995) notes, "A person internalizes the racial societal messages that are available to him/her and process them in the manner that the ego (and society) permits" (p. 188). Social realities are raced, generated, and perpetuated by mass media, and could therefore presumptively affect the parasocial relationships in which individuals create and engage, including interracial relationships (Helms, 1995).

For their research on race in the media, Monk-Turner et al. (2010), revealed that the media portrayals of race remained unchanged from 2000 to 2010. The authors reported that over 70% of all actors on television were White. The remaining 30% consisted of 15% African American, five percent Latin American, and less than two percent Asian (Monk-Turner et al., 2010). It is evident through these findings that the media portrayal of racially-diverse characters is not yet an accurate portrayal of present U.S. racial demographics. White and African American populations are overrepresented, while Latin Americans and Asian Americans remain underrepresented in media (Monk-Turner et al., 2010). In 2021, Common Sense Media continued this research and found that representation of diverse races and ethnicities is still lacking. Specifically, the report found that

> people of color are underrepresented in movie and TV roles, and when they are represented, they're often stereotyped. Meanwhile, parents and caregivers have reported that they want to use media as a tool to help kids not just see themselves reflected back, but also to inspire acceptance and inclusion in general.
>
> (np)

While we can say confidently that with the increase of media outlets and social media communities and influencers, the racial breakdown of media characters has changed, in mainstream media and the areas of media where our middle-aged children are, the actors on the screen are still significantly lopsided.

STEREOTYPES

One of the main issues of the media portrayal of race and ethnicity not being accurate is the proliferation of stereotypes. Media portrayal statistics quantify the number of times each character race is depicted, but stereotypes allow researchers to qualify that evidence. Stereotypes describe the expectations and beliefs of social norms, as well as connect assumed characteristics and attributes to a group (Verkuyten, 2005). Bandura (2001) notes that television representations of social realities could lead to tangible conceptions of reality. The stereotypes portrayed by television characters have been found to have material effects and consequences on the continued, or cultivated, belief of a racial group (Punyanunt-Carter, 2008). Research has demonstrated that unfavorable portrayals of African Americans not only influenced White perceptions of African Americans, but also the self-perception of African Americans (Punyanunt-Carter, 2008). While undeniable, the effects stereotypical portrayals have on viewer's perceptions do vary by individual social identity association. For example, Pornsakulvanich (2007) reported that if an individual strongly identifies with their racial group, they are less likely to be influenced by the media, conversely, if one less strongly identifies they will be more likely to be influenced by the media.

Reid Chassiakos et al. (2016) addressed this in their longitudinal research into media effects on self-esteem. The authors describe a longitudinal study of 396 White and Black pre-adolescent boys and girls and found that the effects on esteem were either positively or negatively influenced by demographics. In the study, it was found that greater television exposure resulted in decreased self-esteem for White girls, Black girls, and Black boys, however interestingly, the study found that greater television exposure increased self-esteem in White boys. These findings support the notion that most television content reinforce both racial and gender role stereotypes. Findings from the study showed that these stereotypes are positive for White boys, but not other groups. The authors suggest that from media exposure, Black children and White girls internalize "social norms" portrayed on the screen and, unfortunately, have been known to use these lessons from the screen for self-evaluation and reduced self-esteem. These findings further underscore a common theme with respect to media exposure in children and the critical role of the caregiver with respect to engagement and providing context.

RACIAL IDENTITY

Racial identity is central to understanding personal and group identity, as well as interracial relationships. According to Helms (1990), racial identity is defined as a collective identity based on one's perception of having a shared racial heritage with a particular racial group, while racial identity development is based on the evolution of belief systems that evolve due to reactions to "perceived differential racial-group membership" (p. 3). The variance within the behaviors, attitudes, and perceptions of racial groups may impact how individuals perceive their similarity to a racial group or groups. Race is a social construction that is historically, discursively, and materially constructed based on phenotypic characteristics such as skin color and hair texture (Omi & Winant, 1994). Although often used interchangeably in the vernacular, ethnicity and race are quite different. While race is often assumed based on phenotype, ethnicity is often inferred or assumed through social practices, rituals, behaviors, language (Phinney, 1995), or gender expression.

RACE, ETHNICITY, AND CHILDHOOD

In an attempt to understand and evaluate the age at which children develop stereotype consciousness, McKnown and Weinstein (2003) ran two ethnically and racially diverse samples of child aged six to ten in order to understand when children begin to stereotype based on race. The first study revealed that for these children their ability to infer an individual's stereotype increases dramatically with age. Meanwhile, the children's awareness of generally held stereotypes also increases with age. When looking at specific races in the study, McKnown and Weinstein indicated that African Americans and Latinos were more likely than children of other races to be aware of broadly held stereotypes. Research does suggest that racially and ethnically minority children report earlier awareness of stereotypes than White children because these cognitions are more predominant in their daily lives. That being said, the research by McKnown and Weinstein (2003) illustrates that by the ages of six to eight, all children are making surface-level stereotypical opinions associated with race and ethnicity.

Social learning theory (page 8) teaches us that children learn by watching. As we already covered, the media is notorious for relying on stereotypical images. Even more than that, the most successful characters on television have historically always been White, and the uneducated characters are people of color. Moreover, throughout this book we explain that children are spending more time with screens than with anyone else in their lives. Cultivation theory (page 278) explains that the media cultivates a reality, whether it is real or not. In particular, cultivation theory deals with generalizations and consistency across all mediated messages. In this way, it does not account for individual differences. When it comes to portraying different races, for example, all African Americans count the same. This is especially important when it comes to children between the ages of six to ten. Research shows that they are aware of stereotypes, they also have limited lived experiences and potentially limited interactions with people outside of their race. Without real life scripts to rely on, children in this age group are going to turn to the media to write their scripts for how people who don't look like them behave.

At the beginning of this chapter, it was mentioned that as pediatricians, there are critical foci that are addressed at each well-care check, including diet, exercise, sleep, weight/height, school performance, and physical activity. In review of the effects of digital media on this population, it is abundantly clear that screen time and content have global effects on children's health, well-being, and social interactions. We started an early section with a quotation from Michelle Obama encouraging food advertisers to appreciate their influence on children and their choices given the extent they are a captive audience. Indeed, this sentiment can be applied more broadly as we are aware of cognitive, behavioral, mental and physical impacts of digital media use.

FINAL QUESTIONS AND ANSWERS

I hear from parents all the time that they "had unlimited access to television when they were growing up and it wasn't so bad." They question the American Academy of Pediatrics limit on screen time constantly. What should I say about the change in what is on television now versus when they were growing up?

We both get asked this question a lot. To start, in 2021, collective media consumption continues its upward trajectory, and is set to be at the highest it's ever been. In addition, discrepancies in media use have a generational. For instance, older Americans like baby boomers still consume media routinely through television. Meanwhile, younger generations, like millennials and Gen Z more frequently consume more media through digital and mobile devices. So right there, things are different. Moving on, when we were growing up, shows had a set schedule and even if we had "unlimited access" the access was limited by the media available and times the shows were on. "Prime time" television, as we all remember fondly, was two hours in the evening. These scheduling restrictions no longer exist as entire seasons of shows are available to be streamed at any time. Another difference, just talking about quantity is what we would do while we were watching television. As we were growing up, when the television was on, we watched. For the majority of people, it wasn't possible to also play video games, scroll social media, and watch television at the same time until the 2000s with handheld devices became more popular. This level of multitasking is what current children and teenagers have come to expect.

According to the AAP, all screen time counts towards your total for the day. Calculated out, if you were to watch television while also scrolling through social media for two hours, that would be four hours of collective screen time. As we hope we have made clear, each form of media has effects and when we combine them, the effects are magnified.

Next, it is also important to note that the content of television programming has changed. In an attempt to capture the eyes and attention of viewers with decreasing attention spans and increasing media options, media visuals and plotlines have become more sensationalistic, more extreme, and more flashy. "Family programming" is no longer 30-minute sitcoms featuring single camera shots of funny family dynamics. Shows are now dealing with racier topics, more mature content at younger ages, and engaging in more complicated technology to keep the viewership up. Shows also need to all have unique plotlines and unique messages to compete with the million other programs that are available. This means that the need for media literacy is even higher as parents and caregivers need to break down and explain the topics to their children so that they are not learning the wrong things. With increased screen time, comes increased need for these conversations.

REFERENCES

Anderson, D. R., Subrahmanyam, K., & Cognitive Impacts of Digital Media Workgroup. (2017). Digital screen media and cognitive development. *Pediatrics*, 140(Suppl 2), S57–S61. https://doi.org/10.1542/peds.2016-1758C

Bandura, A. (2001). Social cognitive theory of mass communication. *Media Psychology*, 3, 265–299.

Borzekowski, D. L., & Robinson, T. N. (2001). The 30-second effect: An experiment revealing the impact of television commercials on food preferences of preschoolers. *Journal of the American Dietetic Association*, 101(1), 42–46.

Braithwaite, I., Stewart, A. W., Hancox, R. J., Beasley, R., Murphy, R., Mitchell, E. A., & ISAAC Phase Three Study Group. (2013). The worldwide association between television viewing and obesity in children and adolescents: Cross sectional study. *PLoS ONE*, 8(9), e74263.

Common Sense Media. (2021, November). *The inclusion imperative*. www.commonsensemedia. org/research/the-inclusion-imperative

Council on Communications and Media. (2011). Media use by children younger than 2 years. *Pediatrics*, 128, 1040–1045.

Council on Communications and Media. (2016). Media and young minds. *Pediatrics*, 138(5), e20162591. https://doi.org/10.1542/peds.2016-2591

de Jong, E., Visscher, T. L., HiraSing, R. A., Heymans, M. W., Seidell, J. C., & Renders, C. M. (2013). Association between TV viewing, computer use and overweight, determinants and competing activities of screen time in 4- to 13-year-old children. *International Journal of Obesity*, 37(1), 47–53.

Gortmaker, S. L., Must, A., Sobol, A. M., Peterson, K., Colditz, G. A., & Dietz, W. H. (1996). Television viewing as a cause of increasing obesity among children in the United States, 1986–1990. *Archives of Pediatrics and Adolescent Medicine*, 150(4), 356–362.

Guerrero, M. D., Barnes, J. D., Chaput, J. P., & Tremblay, M. S. (2019). Screen time and problem behaviors in children: Exploring the mediating role of sleep duration. *International Journal of Behavioral Nutrition and Physical Activity*, 16(1), 105. https://doi.org/10.1186/s12966-019-0862-x

Hagan, J. F., & Shaw, J. S. (2020). Is latency lost to screen time? *Pediatrics*, 145(6), e20200560. https://doi.org/10.1542/peds.2020-0560

Helms, J. E. (Ed.). (1990). *Black and White racial identity: Theory, research and practice*. Greenwood Press.

Helms, J. E. (1995). An update of Helms's White and people of color racial identity models. In J. G. Ponterotto, J. M. Casas, L. A. Suzuki, & C. M. Alexander (Eds.), *Handbook of multicultural counseling* (pp. 181–198). Sage.

Higuchi, S., Nagafuchi, Y., Lee, S. I., & Harada, T. (2014). Influence of light at night on melatonin suppression in children. *The Journal of Clinical Endocrinology and Metabolism*, 99(9), 3298–3303.

LeBourgeois, M. K., Hale, L., Chang, A. M., Akacem, L. D., Montgomery-Downs, H. E., & Buxton, O. M. (2017). Digital media and sleep in childhood and adolescence. *Pediatrics*, 140(Suppl 2), S92–S96. https://doi.org/10.1542/peds.2016-1758J

McGinnis, M. J., Gootman, J., & Kraak, V. I. (2006). *Food marketing to children and youth:Threat or opportunity?* Institute of Medicine of the National Academic.

McKnown, C., & Weinstein, R. S. (2003). The development and consequences of stereotype consciousness in middle childhood. *Child Development*, 74(2), 498–451.

Monk-Turner, E., Heiserman, M., Johnson, C., Cotton, V., & Jackson, M. (2010). The portrayal of racial minorities on prime time television: A replication of the Mastro and Greenberg study a decade later. *Studies in Popular Culture*, 32(2), 101–114. http://www.jstor.org/stable/23416158

Nigg, C. R., Wunsch, K., Nigg, C., Niessner, C., Jekauc, D., Schmidt, S. C. E., & Woll, A. (2021). Are physical activity, screen time, and mental health related during childhood, preadolescence, and adolescence? 11-year results from the German Motorik-Modul longitudinal study. *American Journal of Epidemiology*, 190(2), 220–229. https://doi.org/10.1093/aje/kwaa192

Obama, M. (2013, September 13). *Remarks during White House convening on food marketing to children.* obamawhitehouse.archives.gov

Omi, M., & Winant, H. (1994). *Racial formation in the United States: From the 1960s to the 1990s.* Routledge.

Parasuraman, S. R., Ghandour, R. M., & Kogan, M. D. (2020). Epidemiological profile of health and behaviors in middle childhood. *Pediatrics*, 145(6), e20192244. http://doi.org/10.1542/peds.2019-2244

Phinney, J. (1995). The multigroup ethnic identity measure: A new scale for use with adolescents and young adults from diverse groups. *Journal of Adolescent Research*, 7, 156–176.

Pornsakulvanich, V. (2007). Television portrayal of ethnic minorities in the United States: The analysis of individual differences, media use, and group identity and vitality. *ABAC Journal*, 27, 22–28.

Punyanunt-Carter, N. (2008). The perceived realism of African American portrayals on television. *The Howard Journal of Communications*, 19, 241–257.

Reid Chassiakos, Y. L., Radesky, J., Christakis, D., Moreno, M. A., Cross, C., & Council on Communications and Media. (2016). Children and adolescents and digital media. *Pediatrics*, 138(5), e20162593. https://doi.org/10.1542/peds.2016-2593

Robinson, T. N., Banda, J. A., Hale, L., Lu, A. S., Fleming-Milici, F., Calvert, S. L., & Wartella, E. (2017). Screen media exposure and obesity in children and adolescents. *Pediatrics*, 140(Suppl 2), S97–S101. https://doi.org/10.1542/peds.2016-1758K

Ruest, S., Gjelsvik, A., Rubinstein, M., & Amanullah, S. (2018). The inverse relationship between digital media exposure and childhood flourishing. *The Journal of Pediatrics*, 197, 268–274.e2. https://doi.org/10.1016/j.jpeds.2017.12.016

Story, M., & French, S. (2004). Food advertising and marketing directed at children and adolescents in the US. *International Journal of Behavioral Nutrition and Physical Activity*, 1, 3–17.

Vandewater, E. A., & Cummings, H. M. (2008). Media use and childhood obesity. In S. L. Calvert & B. J. Wilson (Eds.), *The handbook of children, media, and development* (pp. 355–380). Blackwell.

Verkuyten, M. (2005). *The social psychology of ethnic identity*. Psychology Press.

This chapter is one of the more difficult, and yet important, chapters in this book. We want this book to be a tool for professionals and people with children and teens in their life to help combat the often-harmful effects of the media, with that comes the harsh truth that the Internet is a big scary place. While the Internet has opened the doors to beautiful and diverse online communities where like-minded people can come together and share, it also created a new way for young people's innocence to be exploited and taken away. In this chapter we focus on the bad and the scary because within our expertise as authors, that is an area where we can shed some light. It is also where the questions directed us. In this chapter we review Internet safety, introduce uses and gratifications theory, and spend time discussing cyberbullying, grooming, and online predators. The questions we answer are: *What can we do to protect their children from cyber predators? I recently read about extremist groups targeting boys online. Is that still a large concern for Internet safety?* and *My clients are concerned about their son's safety on his phone. Over the summer they checked his text messages and learned that he was prostituting himself. The teenager (18) does not communicate about this part of his life with them,* and *What is the best way to talk to kids about Internet safety?*

Since the Internet has no filter or R-rating, there are no restrictions in showing children imagery that is not appropriate for them. As discussed throughout this book, and no doubt seen in your practice, the violent and pornographic content available online today can desensitize children (more on pornography in Chapter 12). The Internet has also brought us social media, and that is likely where most of the young people in your life are spending their time online. When children have access to platforms where they can continuously post and share personal information and opinion, full age groups of young people are caught in its trap and do not fully understand the consequences. Chief among the biggest fears of Internet safety are online bullying

DOI: 10.4324/9781003223412-6

and being in danger of online predators. The fact that things posted online are on the web permanently, even after you thought you might have deleted them, means a child might face embarrassment and potential damage later in life over things they posted at a young age.

In this chapter we are covering a number of less-than-pleasant topics. As adults we think of the Internet as both a tool and also a time vacuum where we can spend hours a day reading, observing, and escaping. While there is a place for this in our lives, we often over-look the developmental pitfalls of childhood and how children use the Internet differently. I like to say that "I keep my Facebook account to see who from my life has gotten a new job, pregnant, or married." I like the voyeurism of watching my acquaintances from the past have happy moments, but I am able to separate that from my daily reality and self-worth. The ability to separate takes practice, age, experience, and media literacy (page 22). Due to their development (page 12), children and adolescents are unable to separate online life from real life. Teenagers, especially, think that the whole world is watching them. By age 13 clothing and friends are very important because "everyone is watching and everyone cares." As adults, we know that this is just not true, we know that everyone in middle and high school is too concerned with their own clothes and friends to care about someone else's, but no matter what adults say, teens carry this same viewpoint online. As adults we can post a picture and appreciate the 30 "likes" and comments that we get. When a teen posts a picture. it is a representation of themselves and if they don't get a certain number (often in the hundreds or thousands) of likes in an hour the post must be deleted because something is wrong with them. In order to under-stand this, let's visit one of the oldest and most basic communication theories: uses and gratifications.

USES AND GRATIFICATIONS THEORY

Uses and gratifications theory is arguably the most tried and true of any mass communication theory. Like its name states, the theory explains that consumers have different uses for, and gain different gratifications from, the media they choose to use. The theory has been around since the first form of mass communication and explained the many uses people had for the printing press and the ways in which they were gratified by the published word. In practical terms, citizens needed to know about the happenings of the community and the daily newspaper provided that service to them, therefore they used the newspaper, as opposed to local gossip, to gratify their need for local news. The theory was then expanded when consumers had the choice between the newspaper and the radio, then television, cable television and so on. As a college professor, every semester I ask my students to explain why they need both Instagram and Snapchat. To me, they are both visual social media. I can clearly see the difference between Facebook and Instagram, and Twitter is in a world of its own as a text-based medium, but Instagram and Snapchat, or Snapchat and TikTok, are all too similar for me to objectively understand. When I pose this question, my students look at me as if I have just asked them to discuss the difference between an apple and a glass of milk! Sure, they can both be consumed in the morning, but other than that, they share no similarities. My students explain to me that Instagram is a curated art form saved for the special single photo where they intend to get many "likes," and Snapchat is for their close circle of friends (who are also on Instagram) but it is more content and less curated. Does this make sense to you? Maybe read it again, or maybe just understand that media has different uses and offers different gratifications for its users.

The uses and gratifications paradigm assumes that psychological motives drive people to use media in order to satisfy their needs and seek gratification. Audience activity is essential to any uses and gratifications research, and communication motives are predictive of audience activity – specifically, people's motivation to fulfill communication needs and ability to select media or other sources to allow them to accomplish their goals, or to gratify their needs. For my students, the use of one social media over another is as obvious of a decision as what goes in a glass – an apple or milk. However, while they are Snapchatting and TikToking, I will still be over on Facebook seeing who got a new job, who got married, and who got pregnant.

The uses and gratifications paradigm, which argues that some users have high surveillance needs (like my need to see who is now pregnant) and that those who seek more information about the world around them (like the early newspaper adopters) will do so because they have a greater objective interest in issues. In practice, those with high surveillance needs are believed to be higher consumers of all types of media, compared to their peers with lower surveillance needs.

Specifically, the interactivity of the Internet allows people to more actively engage in media use, particularly as they seek information. Media users who have a more internal orientation will, by contrast, be motivated to entertain themselves and divert their attention from stress and negative affect.

While on its face uses and gratifications theory doesn't offer much depth, it does help us to start a conversation with understanding why children and teens are making the media choices they are making. If we understand the gratification (e.g., to connect with friends, to feel good about oneself, to keep an eye on old friends, to learn a new skill), we can understand the role that it plays in the child's life. Taking from the previous chapter on media literacy (page 22), this is the place where I like to start the conversation on teen media use: "What do you do on Instagram?" or "What do your friends do?" If you can understand the use and gratification of the media tool, it is a good place to start understanding the importance of it in their life.

Now that we understand what brings children and teens to a specific media, let's explore the potential risks and concerns that may encounter.

CYBERBULLYING

Perhaps the most common risk kids face on the Internet is cyberbullying. With the advancements of technology, traditional face-to-face and at school bullying problems have started to go beyond the school setting (Lee et al., 2018). Unlike when we were kids and we could leave school for the sanctuary of our homes away from the mean kids at school, now the bullies follow you home on your phone and on your computer. Even though traditional school bullying, as expressed through verbal or physical bullying, is slightly decreasing, there has been an expansion of cyberbullying and victimization in recent years. Many studies point to the fact that cyberbullying is an international phenomenon and is increasing globally at an alarming rate (Chun et al., 2020).

As of now there is still a debate on how to define cyberbullying. Some researchers argue that cyberbullying is a version of bullying through technology and in an online setting. For example, Kowalski and Limber (2007) characterize cyberbullying as "bullying through email and instant messaging, in a chat room, on a website, or through a text message sent to a cell phone" (p. S22). Meanwhile, other researchers prefer to extend the traditional definition of bullying to cyberbullying. Along these lines, Hinduja and Patchin (2008) defined cyberbullying as "a willful and repeated harm inflicted through the use of computers, cell phones, and other electronic devices" (p. 129). Diving deeper, Smith et al. (2008) defined cyberbullying as "an aggressive, intentional act carried out by a group or individual, using electronic forms of contact, repeatedly and over time against a victim who cannot easily defend him or herself" (p. 376). Understanding the definition helps to understand both the action and also the medium. In a review of the definitions, it is clear that scholars in the field of cyberbullying note the action is intentional, repeated, and over a mediated channel. At this point we all know that cyberbullying can take place over email, text, social media, and video; essentially, any way that you can be communicated to, you can be cyberbullied. Furthermore, what we need to take note of is that teens are accessible 24-hours a day on a device. While school only lasts seven hours, the Internet is forever and kids are constantly checking. This can have horrible repercussions. There is no escaping the bully which makes it that much more real and monumental. When we were young our support figures could remind us that those were just one person's opinions and when they were said once we could believe them, now bullies can echo messages on all media channels and the messages take hold and feel real. We won't tell you about the effects of constant negative messaging because you are the experts, but we will discuss a bit more about the research into cyberbullying.

To start, in 2019 37% of young people between the ages of 12 and 17 had been bullied online, and 30% have had it happen more than once (Patchin, 2019). Furthermore, according to DoSomething. org, 23% of students reported that they've said or done something mean or cruel to another person online, and 27% have reported that they've experienced the same from someone else. On top of all of that, research dictates that girls are more likely than boys to be both victims and perpetrators of cyber bullying. Specifically, 15% of teen girls have been the target of at least four different kinds of abusive online behaviors, compared with six percent of boys (Marcum et al., 2012). In reports on cyberbullying, Instagram is the social media site where most young people report experiencing cyberbullying, with 42% of those surveyed experiencing harassment on the platform. Finally, also in the DoSomething report it was noted that at least 50% of students in the LGBTQIA+ community have experienced online harassment. Unfortunately, the research is screaming that cyberbullying is prevalent and the young people in our lives are all experiencing it.

Research examining the frequency of cyberbullying has primarily been conducted with middle school students. Very few studies have focused on cyberbullying victimization and perpetration among elementary school students. According to Kowalski et al. (2019), the few papers that have been published examining elementary school cyberbullying have illustrated that: (a) very young children are absolutely victims of cyberbullying, and (b) prevalence statistics are highly variable depending on the study and country within which the data were collected.

Since this book is about media, we won't explore the research on face-to-face bullying, however, we imagine that it is quite similar to cyberbullying. That being said, despite the similar features of cyberbullying and traditional bullying, it is important to note the distinctive features in the behaviors. To start, anonymity is one of the key ways in which cyberbullying and traditional bullying differ from one another (Kowalski et al., 2019). It is possible to be someone else while online. This can have positive elements in allowing teens to reinvent themselves, but it can also allow for a mask for bullies. This anonymity creates a space for teens to say things and do things online that they wouldn't dare to in real life. It can also allow for bullies to have multiple personas and repeat their messaging as "different people" without the victim ever knowing.

ONLINE PREDATORS

Cyberbullying is easier and more prevalent online, but unfortunately it is also the tamest danger of the Internet we are covering in this chapter. Next let's turn to online predators. There are many types of cyber predators online. Grammer (2020) states, cyber predators have a range of motives when communicating with others online. Motives include obtaining, trading, or showing inappropriate photos of children or themselves, wanting to meet in person and engage in sexual activities, wanting to create a sexual conversation, or to receive financial benefits of some kind. Like with bullying, stalking and manipulating someone online is considerably easier and less risky than doing it in person. With children and adolescents using the Internet for both educational and entertainment use, there are many platforms in which the child may interact, as well as communicate, with online users they do not know. As explained in a website dedicated to online predators: 33% of adolescents are Facebook friends with individuals who they do not know offline (Statistics, 2018). This is a breeding ground for dangerous activity because children view the Internet as a trustworthy source of information, especially on a platform like Facebook, which is built on the idea of friendship. That being said, online predators are unfortunately not only on Facebook, but all other social media platforms including Twitter, Instagram, Snapchat, Omegle, TikTok, Reddit, and WhatsApp (Grammer, 2020). In their research on child predators, Grammer (2020) explains that when cyber predators do not achieve their motive from individuals on one site, they move onto another website and keep targeting the same victim. This means that the cycle for cyber predators to prey on children who unknowingly trust others online continues. It also helps the predators gain prevalence in the children's lives as they see them on more than one platform.

What can we do to protect their children from cyber predators?

Elgersma (2017) and Birdsong (2020) provide parents and caregivers with a list of strategies to protect their child(ren) from online attacks. First, Elgersma (2017) states that parents should advise their child(ren) to keep their private information private (e.g., phone number, address, location, etc.) and to monitor their child's online usage and what platforms they use in an effort to address how crucial it is to establish a positive digital footprint. Establishing a positive digital footprint is important because information that is shared and sent into the Internet cannot be erased, learning best practices early will keep children and adolescents safer. Next, Birdsong (2020) states that parents should have an open and honest dialog regarding suspicious activity their child may experience. This is important because one in five adolescents who use the Internet on a daily basis have admitted to receiving unwanted sexual solicitation. By creating an open and honest dialog, parents are able to identify if the child is in danger or is interacting with an individual who may be a cyber predator. Oftentimes, tweens and teenagers do not want to have these conversations with their parents. This can be out of embarrassment, fear, believing that their parents won't understand, or a host of other factors. According to Elgersma and Birdsong, it is critical, however, that these conversations happen with someone.

GROOMING

Because the Internet is oftentimes a void that children escape to with little to no parental knowledge, it is incredibly easy for a child to be taken advantage of by someone who is significantly older than them. Grooming is a specific act by an online predator. Specifically, in their research on Internet risks, Machimbarrena et al. (2018) define grooming as "the process by which an adult, using digital media, prepares a minor in order to obtain sexual material from him or her or to sexually abuse him or her" (p. 3). Additionally, online groomers use this information to foster abusive and unhealthy relationships that children then deem as "normal" and "mature." When looking specifically into understanding the role of trust and complimenting behavior in online grooming discussions, Lorenzo-Dus and Izura (2017) classified grooming in a series of five strategies that the abuser will take in order to take control of the victim. The strategies are as follows: praise, sociability, exchange of personal information, activities, and relationships. Obviously, it is important to be watchful of this happening to children, and be able to recognize signs of it happening to the children in one's life, and we will explore one example in the "worst case scenario" written below. These are key signs to look out for when a child is engaging with people online, but stopping grooming after the fact does not always halt the lasting effects that it has on one's mental health.

Grooming's long-term effects are documented to last well into adulthood. In recent research by Wood and Wheatcroft (2020), the researchers explore what young adults, both who have experienced grooming and who have not, and what they believe about themselves, their groomers, and the psychological impact of experiencing grooming. In addition to victims of grooming being more susceptible to depression, low self-esteem, and sexual dysfunction, most young adults stated that they felt that the concept of grooming was too vague to know exactly how they felt about it and how closely they associated with being groomed in their youth (Wood & Wheatcroft, 2020). Because of this, understanding and studying the long-term effects of grooming, especially on adults, is significantly more difficult.

WORST CASE SCENARIO

While I can understand this subject on a logical level, the true dangers of Internet grooming didn't sink in until I heard the story of Alicia Kozakiewicz while I was teaching a seminar on children and media. In 2001, Alicia was 13 years old and on New Year's Day she snuck out of her house to meet a "friend" she had met online and was abducted by a pedophile. You can read her story here, www.bbc.com/news/magazine-35730298. In essence, Alicia was groomed by an older man online. Alicia says,

> At that time the Internet was really just entering the home and my parents had thought that they had given my brother and me this wonderful gift. They had talked to me about 'stranger danger' but there is a difference between a stranger you meet on the street and the stranger you meet online. People online may be strangers at first, but then you learn about them, and soon they seem like friends."

As the story goes, Alicia met a "boy" online who liked the same things she liked and listened to the same music, so after a few weeks of talking online, he asked to meet up and she didn't think anything of it. On New Year's Day she slipped out of her house and into the arms of Scott Tyree who chained her up, raped, and abused her for four days before the FBI raided the home. While this story is unimaginably terrible, the worst part for me was actually when the parents were interviewed after the fact. In tears, Alicia's mother told the reporter that she thought she was doing everything right – her daughter was upstairs safe, not out at parties or driving through the streets. The Internet was there to improve their lives and instead it aided in her daughter being stolen from right under their noses. Thankfully, Alicia is now safe and is an advocate for Alicia's Law, which provides a dedicated steady stream of state-specific funding to the Internet Crimes Against Children (ICAC) Task Forces and Tyree was sentenced to 19 years in prison.

QUESTIONS AND ANSWERS

The questions we received about Internet safety run the gamut, which is a good representation of just how huge this topic is. Instead of trying to introduce each one, we'll just get right to answering:

What is the best way to talk to kids about Internet safety?

Thankfully the Internet is full of helpful suggestions for talking to kids about Internet safety. The most important variable is knowing that these conversations have to happen, and they need to happen early. Once again, this is where media literacy (page 22) comes in. As soon as a kid has access to their first device, whether it be an iPad or their parent's phone, the conversations start. These conversations are naturally going to vary by age, but the best conversations are frequent, open, and honest. Make sure to always remind kids of the most important lessons. For example, children should never share their full name or address with anyone who they don't know offline. Because of our overreliance on community video games and social networking it is unrealistic that children are not going to engage with people they don't know offline, but it is critical they understand the difference in these relationships. Additionally, using analogies can help children understand these more abstract concepts. For example, you can explain that sharing the password to your online account is akin to giving away the key to the door of your home. By making the connection to the real world and keeping the rules consistent for online and offline activities, it helps children to better understand the dangers of cybersecurity and physical security. Next, make these conversations interactive – show, don't just tell. It may be helpful to use demonstrations and examples to help them better understand how to stay safe online. One great activity could be to visit the kid's favorite website together and brainstorm with them how to respond to chat messages from strangers and also how to create strong passwords for the websites they are visiting. The most important thing is that kids never feel like they can't talk to you about their online activities and people they are meeting.

I recently read about extremist groups targeting boys online. is that still a large concern for Internet safety?

In 2019 a series of reports in mainstream media were published with first-hand accounts of extremist groups specifically targeting White teenage males. First, the *Washington Post* published an article written by Caitlin Gibson describing a story of "11- and 14-year-old boys . . . started asking questions about timely topics such as cultural appropriation and transgender rights." The article goes on to explain the boys got their information from social media and describes the barrage of racist, sexist, and homophobic memes that where all over the kid's social media accounts. These images had been presented as insulting and "edgy" humor meant to indoctrinate children into the world of alt-right extremism and White supremacy. Next, National Public Radio (NPR) ran a story about a father who stumbled upon his 15-year-old son's notorious neo-Nazi propaganda book explaining "the white culture's in trouble, we are under attack by Jews, blacks, every other minority" (Kamenetz, 2018). In the story we learn that John's son had been spending a lot of his time playing first-person shooter video games online. NPR explained that "games like these are multiplayer – you must form teams with friends or strangers. You can chat in the game, over voice or text, or in separate chat rooms. Some of these are hosted by sites like Discord that make it easy for anyone to create a private chat" (Kamenetz, 2018). You can see where this is going – extremist groomers targeted John's son and became his son's friends, just like the groomers and online predators discussed above. They would talk to him about problems at school, and after talking with his son about this, John learned that his son's new "online friends" had suggested some of his African American classmates as scapegoats for the problems in school. The online "friends" also keyed into his interest in history, especially military history, and in Nordic mythology. While they were busy sharing interests and playing online video games, these new online "friends" were also indoctrinating him into the thinking that white people are superior to all else.

One thing that was similar in both of these stories from the *Washington Post* and NPR, aside from the obvious, is that all of these boys came from educated and liberal backgrounds. In addition, the messages they were receiving online, whether it be social media or through video games, differed drastically from what they were learning from their parents.

Unfortunately, the answer to this problem does not lie with the media producers. According to NPR, the three biggest video game platforms – Microsoft, PlayStation, and Steam – host 48 million, 70 million and 130 million monthly active players respectively and so they rely on the players to moderate themselves and do not take responsibility for any discussion that happens during game play or in the chat. These boys were victims of online predators that had a singular motive and used the technology to achieve their indoctrination.

The question asked if this was still a concern for Internet safety and we can say unequivocally that the answer is yes! These teenagers are missing something socially or emotionally and so they are turning to online chat groups, online game communities, and people they don't know to gratify a need they have. Communication is the key to making sure no more kids are corrupted by extremist groups. As we discussed above in the previous question, Internet safety conversations need to include discussions of any new "friends" and interests of those friends.

My clients are concerned about their son's safety on his phone. Over the summer they checked his text messages and learned that he was prostituting himself. The teenager (18) does not communicate about this part of his life with them.

As a media effects professor with a PhD in communication, this really speaks to two things I find most important in this life – communication and the unending consequences of media. I suppose the quick answer to this question is: I agree, your client should be concerned about their son's safety on his phone. As we have covered in this chapter and with the horrific story of Alicia Kozakiewicz, if young people are not armed with tools (page 88), there are many places for them to get hurt online. Taking a step back to uses and gratifications (page 80) it is critical that we understand the use and gratification for the teens in our lives using media. Is it to stay connected with friends? Show off their body? Make new friends? Earn money? And why? If they are using the media to stay connected with friends, maybe they are lonely. If they are using media to show off their body then maybe their self-esteem is connected to the gratification they receive from likes and engagement. If they are using the media to earn money, why? Are they saving to buy a car? Or to buy drugs? With everything, the media is a band aid – it is a babysitter for young kids and it is a replacement for deeper issues as we all grow up. For the discussion on prostitution, we are not experts on that, but we do have a chapter on pornography that may be of interest (page 170). The important takeaway here is that fear and concern over media use is good and justified. They now need to come up with a plan to have this conversation with their child.

REFERENCES

BBC. (2016). *Kidnapped by a pedophile I met online.* Retrieved August 2021, from www.bbc.com/news/magazine-35730298

Birdsong, T. (2020, June 15). Reports of online predators on the rise. how to keep your kids safe. *McAfee Blogs.* www.mcafee.com/blogs/consumer/family-safety/reports-of-online-predator-on-the-rise-how-to-keep-your-kids-safe/

Chun, J. S., Lee, J., Kim, J., & Lee, S. (2020). An international systematic review of cyberbullying measurements. *Computers in Human Behavior, 113,* ISSN 0747–5632. https://doi.org/10.1016/j.chb.2020.106485

DoSomething.org. (2021). Retrieved August 2021, from www.dosomething.org/us/facts/11-facts-about-cyber-bullying#fnref3

Elgersma, C. (2017, August 3). Parents, here's the truth about online predators. *CNN.* Retrieved from https://edition.cnn.com/2017/08/03/health/online-predators-parents-partner/index.html

Gibson, C. (2019). Do you have teenage sons? *Listen Up.* Retrieved August 2021, from www.washingtonpost.com/lifestyle/on-parenting/do-you-have-white-teenage-sons-listen-up-how-white-supremacists-are-recruiting-boys-online/2019/09/17/f081e806-d3d5-11e9-9343-40db57cf6abd_story.html

Grammer, D. (2020, May 28). Child predators: Ultimate guide to protecting your child. *Bark.* www.bark.us/blog/protect-child-online-predators/

Hinduja, S., & Patchin, J. W. (2008). Cyberbullying: An exploratory analysis of factors related to offending and victimization. *Deviant Behavior, 29*(2), 129–156.

Kamenetz, A. (2018). *Right-wing hate groups are recruiting video gamers.* Retrieved August 2021, from www.npr.org/2018/11/05/660642531/right-wing-hate-groups-are-recruiting-video-gamers

Kowalski, R. M., & Limber, S. P. (2007). Electronic bullying among middle school students. *Journal of Adolescent Health, 41*(6), S22–S30. http://doi.org/10.1016/j.jadohealth.2007.08.017

Kowalski, R. M., Limber, S. P., & McCord, A. (2019). A developmental approach to cyberbullying: Prevalence and protective factors. *Aggression and Violent Behavior, 45,* 20–32, ISSN 1359–1789. https://doi.org/10.1016/j.avb.2018.02.009

Lee, J. M., Hong, J. S., Yoon, J., Peguero, A. A., & Seok, H. J. (2018). Correlates of adolescent cyberbullying in South Korea in multiple contexts: A review of the literature and implications for research and school practice. *Deviant Behavior, 39*(3), 293–308. http://doi.org/10.1080/01639625.2016.1269568

Lorenzo-Dus, N., & Izura, C. (2017). "Cause Ur Special": Understanding trust and complimenting behaviour in online grooming discourse. *Journal of Pragmatics*, 112, 68–82.

Machimbarrena, J. M., Calvete, E., Fernández-González, L., Álvarez-Bardón, A., Álvarez-Fernández, L., & González-Cabrera, J. (2018). Internet risks: An overview of victimization in cyberbullying, cyber dating abuse, sexting, online grooming and problematic Internet use. *International Journal of Environmental Research and Public Health*, 15(11), 2471.

Marcum, C. D., Higgins, G. E., Freibuger, T. L., & Ricketts, M. L. (2012). Battle of the sexes: An examination of male and female cyberbullying. *International Journal of Cyber Criminology*, 6(1), 904–911.

Online Predators – Statistics. (2018). *Pure Sight*. www.puresight.com/Pedophiles/Online-Predators/online-predators-statistics.html

Patchin, J. (2019). *2019 cyberbullying data*. Retrieved July 30, 2019, from https://cyberbullying.org/2019-cyberbullying-data

Smith, P. K., Mahdavi, J., Carvalho, M., Fisher, S., Russell, S., & Tippett, N. (2008). Cyberbullying: Its nature and impact in secondary school pupils. *Journal of Child Psychology and Psychiatry*, 49(4), 376–385. http://doi.org/10.1111/j.1469-7610.2007.01846.x

Wood, A. C., & Wheatcroft, J. M. (2020). Young adult perceptions of internet communications and the grooming concept. *SAGE Open*, 10(1). https://doi.org/10.1177/2158244020914573

7

This chapter we are talking about video games. This is a hot-button topic because, as the research shows, 90% of American kids and teens play video games. While the research is somewhat at odds over the effects, decades of longitudinal research has pointed to negative effects of playing violent video games, in particular, producing more aggressive tendencies for years to come. We discuss that research in addition to physical effects of video game play, video game addiction, and end with the benefits of video games. In this chapter we also answer the questions: *My client is concerned about her son's exposure to violence. What is the damage of introducing information about violence and weapons?* and *I have a client who stays up all night playing video games. It is wreaking havoc on him physically. What is going on? Are video games addicting?*

Over the years, the advancement of technology has rapidly expanded. Children are so focused on technology that they have largely replaced playing with dolls or action figures because they are entertained with video games. According to Barclay (2018), nearly all American children play video games and if possible, rates are only increasing. Since the COVID-19 outbreak, video game sales have increased by 37%, and 41% of video game users play more (Epstein, 2020). This is an unsurprising, and yet a very noteworthy statistic because research has shown that spending too much time playing video games can bring long term consequences. We think Wan et al. (2020) said it best when they explained: "the digital era has ensured that children shift their focus from physical playgrounds to digital virtual ones" (p. 188).

For context, 66% of children from ages 7–13 play video games for about three hours a day, every day, and these numbers are only increasing (Center of Media and Child Health, 2020). According to Milani et al. (2015), video game contents are often violent, requiring the player to overtly injure or kill "enemies" to progress in the game. While this is alarming and of course not preferred, the issue for

DOI: 10.4324/9781003223412-7

children comes from the fact that due to the fast and constant technological evolution of consoles and personal computers, these plot lines are often displayed with a very high degree of realism. As we know from developmental theories like Piaget (page 12), young children will have a very difficult, if not impossible time, discerning what is real from what is imaginary. With that being true, the young children will therefore believe what they are seeing on the screen as real at a vulnerable age. Children playing these video games will assume whatever it is they are witnessing on the screen actually happens in real life.

In college I used to tutor a young elementary school boy and help him with his homework. As a reward for finishing his work, he would get to play video games. The year I was with him his favorite game was a first-person shooter Vietnam War game. I remember so clearly seeing the Vietnamese soldiers in straw hats fighting his American soldiers in full combat gear. When I asked him about it, he said that Vietnam was a poor country and they couldn't afford combat gear so that is how the soldiers actually fought. When this kid wasn't playing video games, he was reading about wars. He loved war history and could tell you any detail about any war, including what the video game had rewritten about the Vietnamese soldiers in straw hats. Perhaps this is where my interest in media effects started.

By 2022, it is estimated that the video game industry will earn over $230 billion, and further estimate that more than half of the current top-selling video games on the market will contain violence (Coyne & Stockdale, 2021). A tremendous amount of research has been devoted to the effects of excessive digital play and found more negative than positive outcomes. Increase in aggressive behavior and unhealthy habits are among the few negative outcomes that have been found in studies. Although there is correlation between video games and negative effects, a few studies have found that video games can facilitate positive outcomes, such as enhance intrinsic motivation, foster healthy relationships, and boost cognitive development skills. Even with decades of research on the effects of violent video games on behavior, the effects of violent video games remain highly disputed. That being said, cross-sectional and longitudinal studies have repeatedly shown an association between playing violent video games with an increase in aggressive behavior and a decrease in prosocial behavior.

Additionally, some studies have found a link between playing violent video games and depression and anxiety (Coyne & Stockdale, 2021). As with all media choices, it is necessary to choose quality over quantity. When given the choice, a strategy video game will be much better for the well-being of the player compared to a first-person shooter game. That being said, just like *Sesame Street* produces prosocial effects (page 37) on its viewers, it does not hold the attention of its consumer forever. The same is true for video games. A few of the effects of video game play, both positive and negative, are discussed below. We will start with violent media because that seems to be the most prolific.

VIOLENCE

Violence and video games go hand-in-hand, and so does research on the topic. For decades researchers have been testing violence and aggression outcomes of video game play. One of the first longitudinal studies on the subject of media violence was published by Huesmann et al. (2003). In their research on media violence and childhood aggression, Huesmann et al. demonstrated long-term effects on children's aggressive behavior as a direct result of exposure to violent media. Specifically, the authors examined the longitudinal relationship between viewing violent media at ages six to ten, and adult aggressive behavior 15 years later. Through interviews and archival data, Huesmann et al. were able to demonstrate that exposure to violent media as a child predicted increased aggressive behavior in young adults for both males and females. Further details from the study reveal that, for children who identified with the aggressive character, and saw the character as more "real" was also a predictor for aggressive tendencies as a young adult. Finally, these findings persisted even when the research controlled for the effects of socioeconomic status, intellectual ability, and a variety of parenting factors. In a nutshell, Huesmann et al.'s research showed that media effects are not fleeting – they do not only take place at a cross section in time. The children in her study who demonstrated higher levels of aggression at testing, had even higher levels after engaging with violent media.

What does that mean for us now? Huesmann et al.'s research helps to predict that children who play violent and aggressive video games (think first-person shooter games) will likely have higher levels of aggression as teens and adults than they would have had they not played those video games as kids. It is important to note that just playing video games will not make a person violent or aggressive, but it will contribute to their current and natural levels, which, for young children especially, remain unknown in large part. We get asked this question a lot and so it is worth repeating – playing violent video games is not a single predictor to being a violent and aggressive person. Plenty of mild mannered and low-aggressive children play video games and they go on to be mild mannered and low-aggression adults. Where this is most important is with the children who are more aggressive by nature. These children are also more likely to be attracted to the violence in video games. These are the kids that we have to worry about 10–15 years later, especially given Huesmann et al.'s findings.

Continuing this research nearly two decades later, Prescott et al. (2018) completed a meta-analysis of all research studies relating to video game aggressive play and people being aggressive. In the end, results supported the claim that playing violent video games is associated with greater levels of overt physical aggression over time, after accounting for prior aggression. Furthermore, and perhaps the greatest contribution of the research, is that the results directly addressed the primary criticisms of scholars who combat the findings that video game play leads to aggressive behavior. Specially Prescott et al. (2018) demonstrated:

> (i) that violent video game play is associated with increases in measures of serious aggressive behavior (i.e., overt, physical aggression), (ii) that estimates of this effect are only slightly decreased by inclusion of statistical covariates, and (iii) by finding no evidence of publication bias.
>
> (p. 9887)

THEORY IN PRACTICE

My client is concerned about her son's exposure to violence. What is the damage of introducing information about violence and weapons?

Typically, when a child or teen plays a violent video game involving a gun or shooting others, the game rewards or gives them with more points to get to higher levels in the game. As a result, it can "lead to a learning behavior that prods children to become more self-centered and ready to release aggression upon the slightest provocation" (Wan et al. p. 189). This takes us back to our theoretical considerations of social learning theory and information processing theory (page 8). Chang and Bushman (2019) use this theoretical understanding to go one step further in their investigation into video games and firearms. The authors found that children who were exposed to violent video games had increased dangerous behavior around real firearms. Of the 222 children who were surveyed, 70% of them who played violent video games were more likely to both hold a weapon and pull the trigger according to the findings from the research (Chang & Bushman, 2019). One such explanation for the comfort children feel with firearms comes from the simulated violence in games making the children immune to violence. Wan et al. (2020) extend that if children become too comfortable with these storylines, they can start acting guided by the tendencies they see in the games. This relates directly to Bandura's original Bobo doll experiment (page 20). I have watched the videos of that experiment hundreds of times (I use them in my teaching material) and I am always less interested in the kids in the experimental condition who copy the adult's behavior exactly and more interested in the kids who don't. For example, some of the kids mimic the adult research assistants by knocking the Bobo doll down and sitting on it like the adults showed them to do. Conversely, the kids that alarm me are the ones who held the toy gun up to the Bobo doll when that behavior was never modeled or who used the tether ball to try to decapitate the doll. We learned from Chang and Bushman (2019), that the same thing is happening with video game modelling behavior – kids are both modeling the behavior of the game and also creating novel ways to play with firearms.

WEAPONS IN VIDEO GAMES

Also looking at the use of guns and video games, Farrar et al. (2017) focused on the context surrounding the video game play on elevated aggression. The authors report that in addition to individual risk factors, the study provided confirmation that the contextual features of games also contributed to increased outcome aggression. The author's specific study focused on the relationship between violent video game play and the use of gun controllers on both social norms related to aggression and real-life behavioral aggression. In the end, Farrar et al. discovered both violent video game play and gun controller use were positively related to behavioral aggression.

Once again, a really important note here with this research is that violent media, and aggressive video games are not going to make every child a violent serial killer. Video games don't have the power to turn a calm and sensitive kid into a sociopath, but as you know, there is so much we don't know about young children, and the media exacerbates everything that is already there. For example, many young people are drawn to video games because of a mental illness, but that illness has yet to be identified because the kid is five years old. Video games, and violent media in general, are attractive to a certain type of person. In most cases nothing will come of it, but in some, the violence on the screen overtakes the player and they can become aggressive adults. This research is useful to understand as a potential variable in explaining violent and aggressive behaviors in children and teens. To answer the question above explicitly, the danger of exposing children and teens to violence, aggression, and weapons, is desensitizing them to the devastation. Given their limited lived experiences and exposure to weapons in real life, the media creates the reality for them. First-person shooter games give the illusion that you are in command of the weapon and as the research shows, this makes children and teens less afraid of the weapon in real life and more likely to experiment with it, or assume they understand how it works.

PHYSICAL AND EMOTIONAL EFFECTS

A large subset of the video game research happening in communication studies today is about the physical, as well as emotional, outcomes of game play. For example, Gentile et al. (2017) conducted a study on the relationship between playing violent and non-violent video games and how game play connects to arousal and aggressive thoughts in children both male and female. The authors were able to demonstrate that playing violent video games increased male's cortisol and cardiovascular arousal more than did the equally exciting nonviolent game. In addition, playing the violent game also increased the accessibility of the player's aggressive thoughts. The cortisol findings in particular suggested that playing a violent video game may activate the sympathetic nervous system and elicit a fight-or-flight type response in children. This may cause a repeatable physical response in children when they are presented with a similar situation in real life.

DECREASED PHYSICAL ACTIVITY

We talked about this extensively in Chapter 3 on developing infants and toddlers (page 36) and again with the middle-age child (page 59) but the same is true for older kids and teens: one thing that we are constantly telling parents is that there are only so many hours in the day. Every hour spent playing video games is one less hour spent outside or doing something physical. Recent research by Wan et al. (2020) considered decreased physical play as one of the primary concerns of video game play. Through their research, the authors explain that children are spending less time in physical education and more time playing video games, which can result in children not developing correctly or becoming overweight. The authors explain some advantages and disadvantages of children playing video games, however, they spend more time discussing the negative and are quick to note that children experience more disadvantages, such as having lower grades, violent behavior, anti-social behavior, and social isolation the more video games they play.

VIDEO GAME ADDICTION

I have a client who stays up all night playing video games. It is wreaking havoc on him physically. What is going on? Are video games addicting?

Whether or not video game overuse is a pathological or mental disorder continues to be a heavily discussed and unfinished argument in the social sciences. With proposals to include "gaming disorder" in both the *Diagnostic and Statistical Manual* (DSM) and *International Compendium of Diseases* (ICD), the concept of video game addiction is a very popular topic (Bean, 2017). In their research on video game addiction, Stockdale and Coyne (2018) discovered that video game addicts had poorer mental health and cognitive functioning including poorer impulse control and attention deficit hyperactive symptoms compared to controls. In addition, the research exposed that addicts presented with elevated emotional problems including increased depression and anxiety. The authors also discussed that the video game addicts in their study felt more socially isolated, and were more likely to display internet pornography pathological use symptoms.

While the research is extremely compelling, both empirical data and scholarly opinions contrast in regard to the question of if gaming is an addiction and if thinking of it as one is the best frame by which to understand video game use (Ferguson & Colwel, 2020). In their most recent exploration, Ferguson and Colwell (2020) examined the status of scholarly opinions in a meta-analysis of 214 papers on the possible behavioral effects of games. Results indicated a wide variety of perspectives. Of the work examined, 60% of scholars agreed pathological gaming could be a mental health problem, and 30% were skeptical. Additionally, nearly 50% believed the DSM criteria for "internet gaming disorder" were valid, with around 50% in support of the World Health Organization (WHO) "gaming disorder" diagnosis. Unsurprisingly, a majority of scholars worried about both the DSM and WHO overpathologizing normal youth than those who were not worried about the same. In the end, Ferguson and Colwel (2020) described the belief in pathological gaming as being positively correlated to negative attitudes toward children and negatively by participants' experience with games. Due to continuing debate, many scholars in the field argue that the currently proposed categories of video game addiction disorders are premature.

In regards to the physical effects of video games, they have been documented to include carpal tunnel syndrome, migraines, sleep disturbances, back aches, eating irregularities, and lack of personal hygiene. While these are all important to look out and could signal that the child or teen is playing too much, the American Psychological Association has termed internet gaming disorder (IGD) as experiencing at least five of the following nine criteria over a 12-month period (Faust & Prochaska, 2018):

- Gaming preoccupation
- Withdrawal
- Tolerance
- Loss of interest in other activities
- Downplaying use

- Loss of relationship, educational, or career opportunities
- Gaming to escape or relieve anxiety, guilt, or other negative mood states
- Failure to control
- Continued gaming despite psychosocial problems

If five of these symptoms are experienced in a 12-month period it may be due to too much video game play.

BENEFITS

Now that we have spent the majority of this chapter discussing the negative effects of video game play, it is only fair to mention the benefits. It is also important to be realistic – as we mentioned in the beginning of the chapter, 90% of American children play video games, and therefore, we must learn to embrace them as inevitable, but always remember quality over quantity. The remainder of the chapter will help with those distinctions.

Aside from being entertaining and a fun pastime, playing video games can provide a way for children and teens to interact with each other as a virtual community. In many games players work together toward completing common tasks. It is well documented that our society suffers from an epidemic of loneliness and gaming can be one vehicle to connect people. In addition to social benefits, there are a few cognitive benefits including problem solving and increased cognition.

COMMUNITY BUILDING

Continuing this discussion, children who play video games can improve and exercise their interpersonal relationships. Certain game consoles have the opportunity to connect online where you can connect and interact with people globally during gameplay. This feature allows for children to practice their social skills with like-minded people who are also playing video games. Through their research, Halbrook et al. (2019) discussed how video games with a social component can support the psychological well-being of the player. In addition, when engaging in dialogue with another player, the video game itself can promote positive prosocial behavior, which the authors defined as a proxy for social well-being (Halbrook et al., 2019). Looking more closely at this issue, Wan et al. (2020) explained that for children who have difficulty making friends, *Pokémon Go* is a video game that helps with physical development. For instance, in the game *Pokémon Go*, players need to work in teams to build a strong defense, and the authors argue that players, specifically children, can learn to value the ability of cooperation through the game (Wan et al., 2020).

PROBLEM SOLVING

In order to win most video games children are presented with situations that require them to make decisions and solve problems. Not only that, children have to develop the skills of perseverance and determination while trying to beat certain levels or challenges during game play. According to Adachi and Willoughby (2017), just like aggressive behavior continues overtime, so do problem solving abilities. In their research, the authors explain that for subjects who played strategic video games, they were able to predict greater self-reported problem-solving skills over time and these, in turn, predicted higher academic grades over time (Adachi & Willoughby, 2017). Just like we can't assume all children who play violent video games will be more aggressive adults, we also can't extrapolate these findings to all children and teens, but this study does give further support to the conviction that video games can be beneficial to cognitive development of children. In the same study, Adachi and Willoughby (2017) reasoned that playing video games was correlated to enhanced visual-spatial abilities, executive control, memory, and attentional control. These all point to the positive effects of certain role-playing and logic video games as having valuable prosocial effects on the player.

In my classroom my students all know my feelings about video games and many who grew up playing are desperate to get me to see the positives. One student brought to life Adachi and Willoughby's results when he told me that playing video games was how he connected to his dad and brothers. He said that he learned how to read by playing strategy and logic games with them and he learned to problem solve and be useful at a young age in order to hang out with them. In this way, playing video games was how his family connected – it was a positive environment and he credits those games with his logic and reading abilities.

INCREASED COGNITION

Koves-Masfety's (2016) research focused on the association between the amount of time spent playing video games and children's mental health and cognitive and social skills. The findings might seem surprising to some, as they did to us. The study focused on children between 6 and 11 years old and found that playing certain video games can positively affect children. Children whose video game usage was described as "high" were associated with higher intellectual functioning and higher overall school competence. More video gaming was also associated with fewer problems with peers. This was explained by the researcher saying video gaming is a collaborative activity played with friends, so children who play video games might be more socially cohesive. This is undoubtedly positive information for parents worrying about their children's social skills. This study highlights the importance of knowing what video games kids are playing and with who. It is also important to keep in mind the Internet gaming disorder symptoms mentioned above and the point of decreased returns when children spend too much time with video games.

MODERATING EFFECTS

As mentioned briefly at the start, the field is somewhat divided by the actual severity of negative effects of video game violence. After reading thus far, you should know where we stand – the early data from Huessmann et al. and subsequent research on harmful effects of video game play is too compelling for us to look away. That being said, we have read both sides, hopefully given you information to consider and now leave you with one more explanation: moderating effects.

Prescott et al. (2018) meta-analysis on video games effects tested specially for moderators explained by the data. The authors' findings offer a possible alternative explanation for the differing conclusions reached by researchers on opposite sides of the debate. In fact, Prescott et al. (2018) found substantial evidence that the effects of video game violence on aggression as moderated by ethnicity, such that White participants showed the strongest effect, while Hispanic participants show no significant effects and Asian participants fell in between. This data was not extensive since a majority of academic research still fails to properly represent America's ethnic breakdown but it is a note worth making. There are numerous variables that play a role in video game effects on children and teens. One is aggression, but another is race and ethnicity leading to cultural understandings. We would also argue that media literacy plays a key role in determining the effects of video games on our youth.

REFERENCES

Adachi, P., & Willoughby, T. (2017, March 17). The link between playing video games and positive youth outcomes. *Child Development Perspectives*, 11(3), 202–206.

Barclay, R. (2018, October 20). *Do video games make kids saints or psychopaths (and why is it so).* Retrieved August 2021, from www.healthline.com/health-news/video-games-saints-or-psychopaths-082814

Bean, A. M., Nielsen, R. K. L., van Rooij, A. J., & Ferguson, C. J. (2017). Video game addiction: The push to pathologize video games. *Professional Psychology: Research and Practice*, 48(5), 378–389. https://doi.org/10.1037/pro0000150

Center on Media and Child Health. (2020, October 2). Retrieved November 20, 2020, from https://cmch.tv/

Chang, J. H., & Bushman, B. J. (2019). Effect of exposure to gun violence in video games on children's dangerous behavior with real guns: A randomized clinical trial. *JAMA Netw Open*, 2(5), e194319. https://doi.org/10.1001/jamanetworkopen.2019.4319

Coyne, S. M., & Stockdale, L. (2021). Growing up with grand theft auto: A 10-year study of longitudinal growth of violent video game play in Adolescents. *Cyberpsychology, Behavior, and Social Networking*, 24(1), 11–16. http://doi.org/10.1089/cyber.2020.0049

Epstein, A. (2020, September 28). *Game on: How COVID-19 became the perfect match for gamers.* Retrieved November 19, 2020, from www.weforum.org/agenda/2020/09/covid19-coronavirus-pandemic-video-games-entertainment-media/

Farrar, K. M., Lapierre, M. A., McGloin, R., & Fishlock, J. (2017). Ready, aim, fire! violent video game play and gun controller use: Effects on behavioral aggression and social norms concerning violence. *Communication Studies*, 68(4), 369–384. https://doi.org/10.1080/10510974.2017.1324889

Faust, K. A., & Prochaska, J. J. (2018). Internet gaming disorder: A sign of the times, or time for our attention? *Addictive Behavior*, 77, 272–274.

Ferguson, C. J., & Colwell, J. (2020). Lack of consensus among scholars on the issue of video game "addiction". *Psychology of Popular Media*, 9(3), 359–366. https://doi.org/10.1037/ppm0000243

Gentile, D. A., Bender, P. K., & Anderson, C. A. (2017). Violent video game effects on salivary cortisol, arousal, and aggressive thoughts in children. *Computers in Human Behavior*, 70, 39–43. https://doi.org/10.1016/j.chb.2016.12.045

Halbrook, Y., O'Donnell, A., & Msetfi, R. (2019). When and how video games can be good: A review of the positive effects of video games on well-being. *Perspectives on Psychological Science*, 14(6), 1096–1104. http://doi.org/10.1177/1745691619863807

Huesmann, L. R., Moise-Titus, J., Podolski, C. L., & Eron, L. D. (2003). Longitudinal relations between children's exposure to TV violence and their aggressive and violent behavior in young adulthood: 1977–1992. *Developmental Psychology*, 39(2), 201–221.

Kovess-Masfety, V., Keyes, K., Hamilton, A., Hanson, G., Bitfoi, A., Golitz, D., Koç, C., Kuijpers, R., Lesinskiene, S., Mihova, Z., Otten, R., Fermanian, C., & Pez, O. (2016). Is time spent playing video games associated with mental health, cognitive and social skills in young children? *Social Psychiatry and Psychiatric Epidemiology*, 51(3), 349–357. https://doi.org/10.1007/s00127-016-1179-6

Milani, L., Camisasca, E., Caravita, S. C. S., Ionio, C., Miragoli, S., & Di Blasio, P. (2015). Violent video games and children's aggressive behaviors: An Italian study. *SAGE Open* 5(3). http://doi.org/10.1177/2158244015599428

Prescott, A. T., Sargent, J. D., & Hul, J. G. L. (2018). Violent video games and aggression metaanalysis. *Proceedings of the National Academy of Sciences*, 115(40), 9882–9888. http://doi.org/10.1073/pnas.1611617114

Stockdale, L., & Coyne, S. M. (2018). Video game addiction in emerging adulthood: Cross-sectional evidence of pathology in video game addicts as compared to matched healthy controls. *Journal of Affective Disorders*, 225, 265–272, ISSN 0165-0327.

Wan, A., Yang, F., Liu, S., & Feng, W. (2020). Research on the influence of video games on children's growth in the era of new media. *Advances in Social Science. Education and Humanities Research*, 468. https://doi.org/10.2991/assehr.k.200901.037

Tweens and Teenagers: Development and Media

8

Pediatric well-care visits evolve dramatically as children transition into adolescence. Whereas early visits with younger children are fueled by parental report, the focus during teen visits is to engage the adolescent such that there is designated time to speak to the patient with and without the parent present. The goal is to provide a forum for open discussions of home life, peer-related issues, potential substance use, sexual activity, and mental health concerns. As a result, not only are we addressing physical health concerns (height, weight, growth, diet, etc.) but also getting a gauge as to how the patient is doing from an emotional and mental health standpoint. As part of each visit, it is important to address the extent of non-academic related screen time as this may have a ripple effect on so many areas of a patient's well-being.

By this point in the book, you have hopefully grown familiar with our style of inserting and answering questions. We received more questions for this chapter than any other. These included: *I am working with a 12-year-old who is on her phone for six hours a day. What is this doing to her? My client has screen time rules at home, but the kids are breaking them — excusing themselves from the dinner table to get water (meaning get on phone) or downloading an app to hide their search history, etc. My client's ten-year-old daughter spends a lot of time on Tik Tok and is learning about mature topics — she will talk about suicide, anxiety, depression, panic attacks, etc., and throw around these terms that she doesn't understand. The mom says this premature exposure is becoming a self-fulfilling prophecy. My clients often speak of a "push-pull" to respect versus protect their children from the media. It is causing internal turmoil. Does violence on television affect children's development?* and *What is a "normal" amount of screen time use for teenagers? When does media seem to cause the most impact?*

For this chapter, we want to begin with what is at the crux of this material:

> *I am working with a 12-year-old who is on her phone for six hours a day. What is this doing to her?"*

DOI: 10.4324/9781003223412-8

Clearly this question does not have a short or decisive answer. It is our hope that we can provide the content and discussion that will provide some guidance to the potential effects of digital media for kids age 11 and older. This chapter explores the effects of media use on tweens and teens in terms of their health and development. As presented in previous age groups, we will explore the effects on their physical and mental health, but we will start this discussion with the effects on the home dynamic.

DIGITAL MEDIA USAGE AND EFFECTS ON HOME LIFE

As we have discussed in previous chapters (page 36), the American Academy of Pediatrics (AAP), in its most recent policy statement regarding screen time and school-aged children and teens, veered farther away from strictly limiting screen hours and instead focused on creating a family plan that supports healthy lifestyle choices (sleep, screen free time, and physical activity). That said, it is without question that the pandemic created a reliance on media beyond entertainment and it became the fundamental means for learning and socialization. This has changed the dynamic between teens and technology without a doubt. You are likely seeing those effects now in your practice, and research will continue to study the effects for years to come.

What is a "normal" amount of screen time for teenagers?

In 2013, the AAP presented a policy statement where Strasburger et al. explored media as a dominant force in children's lives (Council on Communications and Media et al., 2013). The statement cites a study conducted by Rideout (2010) where it was discovered that the average eight- to ten-year-old spends nearly eight hours a day with media and older children and teenagers spent greater than 11 hours a day. Earlier in the book we have updated those with more recent figures (page 36). This is all worsened with television being available in the bedroom. The evolution of high-speed Internet and accessibility of cell phones has also been a game changer such that at the time this was written, 88% of teenagers were utilizing text messaging, and the council's policy statement cited Lenhart's (2013) work that discovered teenagers were sending an average of 3,364 text messages per month, with one-third of teenagers were cited as sending more than 100 text messages per day! These figures are widely out-of-date by today, but it is important to know the realities which caused the AAP to issue their statement in the first place, and then to understand how much farther we have come since then. The authors acknowledge a general lack of rules with respect to time spent with media in most households and the potential negative consequences. Regulation of content is compromised in this situation as is frequency after "lights out" time where a child will continue to use their phone after bedtime, lending themselves to fatigue particularly at school. While this policy predates the more recent AAP guidelines with respect to screen time, it urges pediatricians not only to ask about duration of leisure of screen time, but also presence of media devices in the bedroom. At that time, it was recommended to keep the total amount of total entertainment screen time to less than one to two hours a day and ideally with a caregiver monitoring of content and websites (page 25).

Following this report, in 2019, Common Sense Media published *The Common Sense Census: Media Use by Tweens and Teens* with respect to several key findings in this age group. For example, Rodeout and Robb, the authors of the report, found that on average, 8 to 12-year-old children use just under five hours of entertainment screen media per day whereas teens are more inclined to use around 7.5 hours of leisure screen time. Meanwhile, online viewing time had doubled from four years prior with a concomitant "large drop" of time spent watching television on a TV set. In addition to the online media surge, smartphone usage is significant such that by 12 years of age more than two-thirds of tweens reported having their own cell phones. When these technologies were created there was an assumption in the community that due to the creative capabilities of the devices, users would explore and become content creators in more creative ways. However, despite the potential outlets for creative content accessible through media, it is underutilized (Rideout & Robb, 2019). Finally, the report outlines that more than half of tween time was devoted to television or videos (53%), 31% to gaming, leaving two percent for video chat, two percent for e-reading, and just two percent for creating content. These trends were different for the teen population which had

39% television and video, 22% of their time went on gaming, and they reported 16% of their media time to social media, four percent to video chatting, three percent to creativity, and two percent to e-reading. These statistics illustrate that while it was intended to be used for content creation, tweens and teens are not using media in those productive ways.

Aligning with concerns addressed in the AAP report, authors from Common Sense Media do address concerns with respect to parent surveillance. Twenty-eight percent of tweens and 14% of teens reported that their parents use a device to track duration of screen time. Moreover, 50% of tweens and 26% of teens say that their parents use an app or tool to monitor the content. This shows us that it is now commonplace for parents to monitor and have some control and understanding of their tweens and teens media usage. This is a tool for media literacy (page 22) and should be utilized. Moreover, if a teen says that "they are the only ones" who have parents that check up on them, we now have the data to say that that is not true.

Circling back to the question about what is normal amount of screen time, the focus should not only be on duration but also content as well as time taken away from meaningful family and social experience. Referring back to the AAP family media plan (page 40), when one prioritizes a good night of sleep (eight to nine hours), regular physical activity, after school activities, family time, screen-less meal time, reading, chores/job in addition to time spent in school, the amount of time left for leisure screen use is limited. What is also of critical importance is caregiver supervision and to be aware of the amount of time spent with screens and especially the content being viewed. Common Sense Media states it clearly how online opportunities and more independent participation creates challenges for tracking and evaluating content in this population: "There is a such a wide array of content to select from, both high and low quality, from celebrity influencer videos to do-it -yourself maker videos to violent or sexual content and everything in between" (p. 25). We review many of these in the chapters to come in this book. In summary, a caregiver should be proactive, not only in how much time is devoted to media, but in addition, be engaged in what their child is viewing. There is no normal amount of screen time, and the data coming back about quantity is extremely high. As expressed continuously throughout the book is that we need to focus on quality of content, over quantity of time. This is especially relevant in the discussion of virtual learning (page 124).

> My client has screen-time rules at home, but the kids are breaking them – excusing themselves form the dinner table to get water (meaning get on phone) or downloading an app to hide their search history, etc.

Unfortunately, the parent in this scenario is not the only one. In 2020, D'angelo and Moreno explored the topic of problematic Internet use (PIU) and in particular, the role pediatricians can play in terms of screening. The authors asserted that 93% of adolescents and adults between 12 and 29 years of age go online, and up to 25% of teens describe themselves as "constantly connected" (p. S182). The authors explained potential consequences of such a high rate of usage as it may precipitate psychological, behavioral, physical, and attention issues. The concept of PIU is described as a separate entity from an addiction which would imply more symptoms of withdrawal and loss of control. PIU represents a broader array of concerns. To help define PIU, they refer to a concept mapping study that integrated data from researchers in adolescent health, addiction science, and technology, as well as from adolescents/young adults. Taking from Moreno et al. (2013), they were able to identify seven different constructs with respect to PIU: (1) psychosocial risk factors (i.e., anxiety) that increase because of PIU behavior, (2) physical impairment, (3) emotional impairment, (4) social and/or functional impairment, (5) risky Internet use, (6) impulsive Internet use, and (7) dependent Internet use. From this study's findings, PIU was defined as "Internet use that is risky, excessive, or impulsive in nature, leading to adverse life consequences, specifically physical, emotional, social, or functional impairment" (Moreno et al., 2013, p. 1885). What is interesting is that they surmise that one in ten adolescents suffer from PIU which is of incredible significance given the high association PIU has with other behavioral issues, such as fighting, depression, hyperactivity, difficultly concentrating, poor interpersonal skills, and even suicidal thoughts (D'angelo, 2020).

Per the authors, PIU is a relatively new phenomenon with much research needed in terms of prevention and management. They encourage pediatricians to try to identify those at risk:

Previous research supports that there are particular groups at increased risk, including males, those who experience depressive symptoms and use the Internet for relationships and mood regulation, adolescents with high levels of narcissism and the feeling of a need to belong, and those who experience fear of missing out. Family risk factors can also play a role, including adolescents who experience family dissatisfaction and adolescents who have parents with mental health issues.

(P. S183)

A screening tool can also be utilized when there are parental concerns regarding sleep and negative school performance. One tool, in particular, that can be used in the pediatric setting is the problematic and risky Internet use screening scale (PRIUSS) (Jelenchick et al., 2014). The larger scale is an 18-item questionnaire however one may start with the three-item PRIUSS as it screens for separation anxiety from the Internet, decreased motivation when on the Internet, and feelings of withdrawal. If participants score highly on the three-item pretest, then the full-scale questionnaire may be utilized.

In regards to the question posed at the beginning of this section about children breaking away from the table to access their devices, a paucity of research exists on intervention with respect to PIU. The author of the question indicated a problem with media use despite the fact that there are family rules in place. As we have discussed many times in the course of this book, one intervention that can be utilized in this population is the AAP family media use plan which can provide structure for family media use relative to their individual needs (page 40). The "media time calculator" facilitates ensuring Internet and media time do not supersede necessary activities such as sleep, homework, physical activity, social activities, etc. Utilizing this media use plan may give the tween or teen who feels compelled to "break the rules" for their phone confidence that they know when their next "scheduled" time to use it will be. Another tool is to "reality check" the need to use the device during dinner. We talk about this in the media literacy chapter (page 22). In this line of thinking, it helps to understand the uses and gratifications gained from the media (page 80). Indeed, more research is so important to help not only identify, but provide effective intervention, for problematic media use.

My clients often speak of a "push-pull" to respect versus protect their children from the media and it is causing Internal turmoil.

Without question these dynamics can be very challenging. It is natural for a child, especially an adolescent, to expect autonomy. That being said, it is the role of a caregiver to ensure the tween or teen is safe and not being exposed to harmful material. In their AAP Council on Communications and Media policy statement in 2013, Strasberger et al. describe that two-thirds of children and teenagers reported a lack of rules regarding time on media. Moreover, we know from previous chapters in this book that even younger children are exposed to inappropriate content. As mentioned earlier 60% of teenagers receive text messages after "lights out." Strasburger et al. cite the National Campaign to Prevent Teen and Unplanned Pregnancy where it was reported that 20% of adolescents either sent or received a sexually explicit image via Internet or cellphone. We review more about this in Chapter 12 (page 170). Clearly supervision and rules are critical.

Moving on, in 2018, Marres et al. explored parents working together with respect to setting boundaries with children's media use. In an online survey, one parent was questioned about the consistency and conflict between themselves and their partner with media restrictions. The study revealed that when "one parent was more restrictive than the other, participants reported more inter-parent conflict about media rules and more child exposure to media violence." (p. 177). Moreover, the authors explained that when parental conflict and exposure to mediated violence were both in effect, it predicted their child would be more likely to experience physical and relational aggression. Ultimately, Marres et al. discovered less conflict and less potential exposure to violence when both parents were restrictive on their children's exposure to media, thus temporizing the negative consequences mentioned above. This is something that we can advise parents to do – get on the same page in terms of adolescent screen use.

Returning to the question regarding "push and pull" challenges with caregivers and their child's media use, it is abundantly clear that boundaries and supervision are fundamentally important. Moreover, as discussed in the study above, consistency between caregivers in the household is significant. In the course of this book, even with the younger ages, we continue to stress the importance of parents being involved and engaged with their child with respect to media content (page 23). In advising pediatricians who work with parents, Strasberger et al. encourages co-viewing media with their children and using it as mechanism to discuss family values (page 25). Specifically, it is recommended that we encourage parents to model behavior and to establish a family media use plan for all family members. These rules should be reasonable, but unyielding, with respect to all media cell phones, Internet, etc.

DIGITAL MEDIA USE AND ITS EFFECTS ON MENTAL AND PHYSICAL HEALTH

Without question, this is a very expansive topic. Other chapters in this text cover more focused concerns including body image, identity, gaming, pornography, and risky behaviors (pages 139, 155, 170, and 184). The questions we received really drove the conversation to mental health concerns with media use, as well as potential effects on physical health. For example:

> My client's ten-year-old daughter spends a lot of time on Tik Tok and is learning about mature topics — she will talk about suicide, anxiety, depression, panic attacks, etc., and throw around these terms that she doesn't understand. The mom says this premature exposure is becoming a self-fulfilling prophecy.

In pondering this statement, it is obvious that children and adolescents are potentially exposed to emotional and mental health themes by virtue of the media, and particularly, social media. What is interesting however, is what role does the use of media play in facilitating symptoms of anxiety and depression? Looking specifically into media, anxiety, and depression in children, Hoge et al. (2016) introduced the topic by acknowledging early research that traditional media (e.g., television and movies) has impacted children's fears, resulting in anxiety and sleep disturbance. In this review, the authors explored the impact of new media (e.g., interactive media and social media) in terms of potentially propagating anxiety and depression. The foci they discuss include (1) anxiety and depression associated with technology-based negative social comparison, (2) anxiety resulting from lack of emotion-regulation skills because of substituted digital media use, (3) social anxiety from avoidance of social interaction because of substituted digital media use, (4) anxiety because of worries about being inadequately connected, and (5) anxiety, depression, and suicide as the result of cyberbullying and related behavior. In the discussion on the impact of traditional media on anxiety and depression, Hoge, Bickham, and Cantor discuss the potential impact of frightening content, as well as the impact of idealized characters. With respect to the child exposed to frightening material, they describe dramatic consequences such that "loss of sleep and heightened levels of unnecessary anxiety can cause physical, cognitive and emotional problems" (p. S77). Regulating for developmental age, children should be protected from disturbing content, which naturally changes as they grow up and mature. In addition, the authors describe how programming demonstrates "attractive people leading exciting and idealized lives in media programs" lending itself to social comparison and potential personal dissatisfaction (p. S77). Naturally, this extends to social media with opportunities for "technology-based negative social comparison" which may foster "negative self-regulation or anxiety about evaluation by others" (p. S77). We discuss this in detail in Chapter 11 (page 155).

Furthermore, we have seen an increase in anxiety from tweens and teens due to low emotion-regulation skills because these individuals have substituted digital media use as a distraction from underlying anxiety. Hoge et al. (2016) describe this as "behavioral avoidance of emotional experiences" (p. S77). The authors assert that it is of fundamental importance for a child to develop the skills necessary for emotional regulation. The concern expressed is that excessive internet use is a means to avoid feelings of depression and anxiety. Media is being used dysfunctionally to regulate emotions which is a problem as emotional regulation is "an essential component of mental health, and problems with it are a hallmark characteristic of a variety of psychopathological disorders, such as anxiety and depression" (p. S77).

Does social media affect interpersonal relationships?

In their discussion of social anxiety and depression from lack of social interaction because of substitute digital media, Hoge et al. describe how reliance on non-interpersonal communication (such as texting, emailing, etc.) exacerbate symptoms for people suffering from social anxiety as it fosters social avoidance. A tween or teen who suffers from social anxiety and fears of social humiliation may utilize these communications more frequently which may propagate more and more anxiety. It would be useful to discuss uses and gratifications with these individuals in order to have a clearer understanding for their behavior (page 80). This would get at the tween or teen's motivation in using the technology. As online interactions willfully replace interpersonal interactions, social impairments may intensify. Hoge et al. also address the impact of decreased interpersonal interactions and depression especially with mobile phone use. Here the authors assert that excessive use of mobile devices may further social isolation. In their research into the effects of mobile phone use on depression, Bickham et al. (2015) ran a longitudinal study that was able to link increased phone use with depression one year later.

In addition to depression, research has also connected increased mobile phone use with increased anxiety. Lu et al. (2014) were able to connect anxiety and fear of ostracization in tweens and teens specifically when text messages did not receive a rapid response. This immediate increase in anxiety points to a larger issue where tweens and teens place a tremendous amount of importance on text messaging and being dependent on that form of communication. When we were growing up, we would need to call our friends on their family landline. If no one picked up, or our friend wasn't home, it was disappointing, but rarely anxiety inducing. This rapid form of communication has made users dependent on it for instant satisfaction.

Finally, in their discussion of anxiety, depression, and suicide as a result of cyberbullying and other media use behaviors, Daine et al. (2013) mention cyberbullying in adolescents is extremely prevalent. They describe how those prone to bullying offline are likely to also be bullied online. We discuss this in detail in Chapter 6 (page 79). In their review of studies on the influence of internet on self-harm and suicide in young people, Diane et al. explained that victims of bullying may be more prone to mental health problems as many of the victims reported negative feelings that included embarrassment, worry, fear, depression, or loneliness, after being victims of cyberbullying. Unfortunately, it is also clear from the research that victims of cyberbullying are prone to suicidal ideation and self-harm. Hoge et al. (2016) describe how using the Internet

> exposes young people to stories and conversations about suicides, and such exposure especially in the form of discussion forums increases suicidal ideation. Furthermore, groups that congregate specifically to discuss issues related to suicide and self-injury provide any youth exploring the topic with details and potential support through normalization of the behavior. Youth who exhibit self-injurious behaviors use the Internet more and in ways that may expose them to high-risk situations. Youth who are cyberbullied are more likely than their peers to think about and attempt suicide.
>
> (p. S78)

However, the authors do acknowledge a positive role media can play in terms of therapeutic support via online support groups and also as a means to provide distractions, humor, peer connections, and wider social networks. We discuss this benefit of social media specifically in many chapters in the book (page 69). If tweens and teens have difficulty finding communities in person where they can truly express themselves, there are certainly enclaves online for them (page 40).

Returning back to the question about TikTok, as stated above, it is a legitimate concern that children are exposed to difficult mental health challenges facilitated often by social media and often in the context of cyberbullying. We have already discussed several of the ways that media exposure and usage may precipitate symptoms of anxiety and depression. Common threads discussed throughout this book resonate with these topics as well. For recommendations, pediatricians and clinicians should continue to integrate questions about media exposure most especially in patients that demonstrate symptoms of depression or anxiety. In addition, parents should be urged to monitor content and screen material content. Hoge et al. also make a special note that children with underlying social anxiety should be encouraged to engage in in-person activities and limit online engagement. Lastly, medical professionals working with children should encourage parents to establish rules for media use as the authors assert that media use rules have been associated with decreased levels of depression in this population. The concerned mother in that question is right to be concerned, but exposure alone does not prescribe a self-fulfilling prophecy. Make sure to engage in media literacy tactics and continue to have open and honest conversations (page 22).

VIOLENCE IN THE MEDIA

Does violence on television affect children's development?

In 2017 Anderson et al. published their latest article reviewing screen violence and youth behavior. In the research the authors discuss violence in media, which they defined as "depictions of characters (or players) trying to physically harm other characters (or players)" as pervasive in our society (p. S142). In a meta-analytical review of data spanning 60 years, the authors were able to accrue very strong evidence of both short and long-term effects of screen violence and youth behavior. Specifically, the authors note:

> The vast majority of laboratory-based experimental studies has revealed that violent media exposure causes increased aggressive thoughts, angry feelings, physiologic arousal, hostile appraisals, aggressive behavior, and desensitization to violence and decreased prosocial behavior (e.g. helping others) and empathy.
>
> (p. S142)

These findings are particularly compelling when combined with the knowledge that adolescents frequently spend nine hours a day consuming media, with some teenagers getting over 40 hours a week of screen time, making this research that much more critical. We review these topics in regards to violence, video games, body image, disordered eating, sex, and sexuality in the following chapters of the book. That being said, it is critical to mention that there is a need for more long-term assessments and in addition, the development of tools to help reduce these behaviors. In their discussion, Anderson et al. admit that not all video games are bad and not all violence results in negative behavior. They also contend that there is no one single risk factor with respect to one demonstrating aggressive or violent behavior as it is likely a composite of many risk factors. We discuss this further in Chapter 7 on video games (page 93), and also when writing about social learning theory on page 8. However, based on available research, it does appear that this particular media exposure is a legitimate concern.

Looking further into video games and the tween and teenage groups, Anderson et al. specifically looked into the impact of violent video games on one's aggression, desensitization, and potentially, attention. The authors defined aggression as "any action that is intended to cause harm to another who is motivated to avoid being harmed" whereas violence is referred to as "an extreme form of aggression that has the potential to produce severe physical harm, such as injury or death, to another" (p. S143). Here the distinction is made such that aggression does not equal violence, however, violence is aggression. Along these same lines, Anderson et al. presented a metaanalysis of 381 effects from violent video games studies involving 130,295 participants which demonstrated that video games "increase aggressive thoughts, angry feelings and physiological arousal which can explain aggressive behavior" (p. S142). Finally, the authors discussed the concept of violent media as a desensitizer for tweens and teens such that it is a gradual and subconscious process. Brockmyer (2015) added to this explaining that viewers are desensitized to violent media by being told it is necessary, justified, and fun.

PHYSICAL EFFECTS: SLEEP

At the beginning of this chapter, we presented one of the questions posed: *I am working with a 12-year old who is on her phone six hours a day. What is this doing to her?* We hope the above discussions have adequately demonstrated effects on mental health and family dynamics. We would be remiss if we didn't mention some of the ways excessive screen time may also affect one's physical health. One of the most fundamental ways is the potential effect on the duration and quality of sleep.

While sleep deprivation is common and treatable in tweens and teens, there are clear consequences on one's physical, behavioral, mental, and academic health. The desired amount of sleep for an adolescent is eight to ten hours per night, however, Kansagra (2020) recently documented that nearly 73% of middle and high school students reported an average of less than eight hours of sleep on school nights. In particular, Kansagra focused on sleep disorders that affected the quantity of sleep, e.g., poor sleep hygiene, circadian rhythm disorders, and insomnia. In terms of poor sleep hygiene, the author defined it as "the behaviors and environmental factors that can affect sleep" (p. S205). Kansagra continued to describe the importance of avoiding disruptors of sleep, namely light and screen time. A variety of behaviors are described in this article that can lead to sleep disruption, including "increased social media use before bed, sleeping with a mobile device, screen use in the late evening, and the number of devices kept in the bedroom" (S. 205). We cannot stress enough that devices should be out of the bedroom. As described, tweens and teens are spending all too much time with computers, video games, and mobile devices. All technology should be out of their bedroom during designated sleeping times. Like we have mentioned, Kansagra also described how families who utilize a media use plan demonstrate benefits in sleep.

In conjunction with the Adolescent Sleep Working Group and Committee on Adolescence, Owens et al. (2014) presented a technical report in *Pediatrics* which also focused on insufficient sleep in adolescents and young adults. This was an update specifically on causes and consequences of sleep deprivation. In the report, the authors describe chronic sleep deprivation as a "serious threat to the academic success, health and safety of our nation's youth and an important public health issue" (p. e921). In this report the authors review many factors contributing to chronic sleep loss but for the purposes of our discussion, we will review their discussion on electronic media and sleep. Included in the report is a description of Calamaro et al.'s (2009) suburban study which demonstrated that of 100 adolescents: two-thirds had a television in their bedroom, almost one-third had a computer, almost 80% had a digital music player and 90% had a cellular phone in their bedroom. Data revealed that the teenagers engaged simultaneously on their devices in an average of 4 electronic activities after 9pm. This study is over 10 years old and so we can hypothesize that these figures are even higher today, especially with nearly all students relying on a computer to get school work done.

The authors describe how the presence of so many devices impact sleep duration and ultimately sleepiness during the day. Television in the bedroom, for example, lends itself to a later weekday bedtime, longer latency, short sleep time, later wake up time on weekends, and daytime sleepiness. Similar results were found with computer use as well, especially in 2021 when most tweens and teens get their entertainment media from the Internet. In these scenarios, media activities serve as "sleep interfering activities" the mechanisms of which may include sleep displacement as one stays up later using a device. After 9 p.m., Calamaro, Mason, and Ratcliffe discovered that nearly one-third of adolescent participants were text messaging, nearly half were talking on the phone, over half were on the Internet, and a quarter were playing video games after their family had planned for them to be in bed.

Aside from the act of sleep time displacement, there are a few other harmful effects of screen time before bed. Specifically, Owens et al. described the effects of light emission from devices that disrupt circadian rhythms via the suppression of melatonin. Lastly, they discuss media use in its capacity to affect one's arousal. For example, Owen et al. cited a report by Higuchi et al. (2003) which described playing video shooting games and found subjective sleepiness diminished, shorter rapid eye movement (REM) sleep, and longer sleep latency. Open communication will help bring these issues to light, but it won't actually solve anything. The only solution is to have devices charging overnight outside of the bedroom.

PHYSICAL EFFECTS: OBESITY

As a major consequence of poor sleep, a common theme we have mentioned previously with younger age groups is the risk of obesity. Owens et al. described the metabolic effects, including aberrations in insulin, ghrelin, leptin, and cortisol which can lead to "insulin resistance, increased sympathetic nervous system activity, and increased hunger and decreased satiety" (p. e927). Furthermore, decreased sleep can lead to increased calorie consumption and decreased physical activity. The effects of sleep restriction on obesity and concomitantly, the effects of digital media use on sleep lends itself to a broader conversation regarding the effects of digital media use on obesity in this population.

Looking specifically at this, Bickham et al. (2013) investigated the characteristics of screen media use as it was associated with higher BMI in young children. In this research, the authors measured the height and weight of 13–15-year-olds while also obtaining information on their time spent with television, computers, and video games. The participants had a device that signaled to them when they needed to complete on screen questionnaires which required them to report the activities to which they were paying primary, secondary, and tertiary attention. Ultimately, results from the study revealed that primary attention to television had a positive association with increased BMI. The potential mechanisms the authors described included the influences of advertising namely consuming calorically dense foods and the effects of eating while preoccupied with television. We discuss this in more detail in Chapter 4 (page 43).

In addition, in their research into media exposure and obesity in children, Robinson et al. (2017) presented a clear link between screen media exposure and increased risk of obesity. The authors discussed the manners in which media exposure may lead to obesity as well as possible interventions in reducing screen time as it can help minimize weight gain. While we are focusing on tweens and teens in this section, much of this applies to the younger children as well, and we reviewed it in Chapter 5 (page 59). Meanwhile, Robinson et al. were able to narrow possible causes to decreased physical activity, increased energy intake, effects of advertising, and decreased sleep as the key variables. The notion that physical activity is being displaced by screen time as a mechanism of weight gain intuitively makes sense, however, so far, a strong link has not been made to demonstrate this in the research. That said, strong correlations have been found in caloric intake and obesity such that

epidemiologic studies reveal that children who consume more screen media also consume fewer fruits and vegetables and more energy-dense snacks, energy-dense drinks and fast food, receive a higher percentage of their energy from fats and have a higher total energy intake.

(p. S98)

Robinson et al. also described how children consume a large percentage of their daily calories while watching a screen. This is problematic as "the types of high-energy foods and beverages that are consumed while viewing, media acting as a trigger or prompt to eating, media extending the duration of eating, or media distracting from or obscuring feeling of fullness or satiety" (p. S99). Food advertising as it is integrated into children's media plays a role and as discussed above, the impact of inadequate sleep. You can read more about this in Chapter 5 (page 59).

One final question posed with respect to this age group:

When does media cause the most impact?

This is such a difficult question to answer as over the course of this book, one can appreciate a cumulative effect of media exposure from infancy, preschool years, to adolescence with different manifestations. The autonomy of adolescents and the challenges of media supervision in this age group along with exposure to more depth in potential content does make it seem like this demographic is the most affected. However, in our discussions of media effects on younger kids and the critical importance of caregiver engagement, early childhood media experiences and their impact, seem to set a tone for older kids. As every developmental stage is critical, it is very important to adjust and adapt as media influences evolve with a child's development.

REFERENCES

Anderson, C. A., Bushman, B. J., Bartholow, B. D., Cantor, J., Christakis, D., Coyne, S. M., Donnerstein, E., Funk Brockmyer, J., Gentile, D. A., Green, C. S., Huesmann, R., Hummer, T., Krahé, B., Strasburger, V. C., Warburton, W., Wilson, B. J., & Ybarra, M. (2017). Screen violence and youth behavior. *Pediatrics*, 140(Suppl 2), S142–S147. http://doi.org/10.1542/peds.2016-1758T

Bickham, D. S., Blood, E. A., Walls, C. E., Shrier, L. A., & Rich, M. (2013). Characteristics of screen media use associated with higher BMI in young adolescents. *Pediatrics*, 131(5), 935–941. https://doi.org/10.1542/peds.2012-1197

Bickham, D. S., Hswen, Y., & Rich, M. (2015). Media use and depression: Exposure, household rules, and symptoms among young adolescents in the USA. *International Journal of Public Health*, 60(2), 147–155.

Brockmyer, J. F. (2015). Playing violent video games and desensitization to violence. *Child and Adolescent Psychiatric Clinics of North America*, 24(1), 65–77.

Calamaro, C. J., Mason, T. B., & Ratcliffe, S. J. (2009). Adolescents living the 24/7 lifestyle: Effects of caffeine and technology on sleep duration and daytime functioning. *Pediatrics*, 123(6). www.pediatrics.org/cgi/content/full/123/6/e1005

Council on Communications and Media, Strasburger, V. C., Hogan, M. J., Mulligan, D. A., Ameenuddin, N., Christakis, D. A., Cross, C., Fagbuyi, D. B., Hill, D. L., Levine, A. E., McCarthy, C., Moreno, M. A., & Lewis Swanson, W. S. (2013). Children, adolescents, and the media. *Pediatrics*, 132(5), 958–961. http://doi.org/10.1542/peds.2013-2656

Daine, K., Hawton, K., Singaravelu, V., Stewart, A., Simkin, S., & Montgomery, P. (2013). The power of the web: A systematic review of studies of the influence of the internet on self-harm and suicide in young people. *PLoS ONE*, 8(10), e77555.

D'Angelo, J., & Moreno, M. A. (2020). Screening for problematic Internet use. *Pediatrics*, 145(Suppl 2), S181–S185. http://doi.org/10.1542/peds.2019-2056F

Higuchi, S., Motohashi, Y., Liu, Y., Ahara, M., & Kaneko, Y. (2003). Effects of VDT tasks with a bright display at night on melatonin, core temperature, heart rate, and sleepiness. *Journal of Applied Physiology*, 94(5), 1773–1776.

Hoge, E., Bickham, D., & Cantor, J. (2017). Digital media, anxiety, and depression in children. *Pediatrics*, 140(Suppl 2), S76–S80. http://doi.org/10.1542/peds.2016-1758G

Jelenchick, L. A., Eickhoff, J., Christakis, D. A., Brown, R. L., Zhang, C., Benson, M., & Moreno, M. A. (2014). The problematic and risky Internet use screening scale (PRIUSS) for adolescents and young adults: Scale development and refinement. *Computers in Human Behavior*, 35. https://doi.org/10.1016/j.chb.2014.01.035

Kansagra, S. (2020). Sleep disorders in adolescents. *Pediatrics*, 145(Suppl 2), S204–S209. http://doi.org/10.1542/peds.2019-2056I

Lenhart, A. (2012, March 19). *Teens, smartphones & texting*. Washington, DC: Pew Internet and American Life Project. Retrieved August 26, 2013, from http://pewinternet. org/~/media//Files/Reports/2012/PIP_Teens_Smartphones_and_Texting. pdf

Lu, X., Katoh, T., Chen, Z., Nagata, T., & Kitamura, T. (2014). Text messaging: Are dependency and excessive use discretely different for Japanese university students? *Psychiatry Research*, 216(2), 255–262.

Moreno, M. A., Jelenchick, L. A., & Christakis, D. A. (2013). Problematic internet use among older adolescents: A conceptual framework. *Computers in Human Behavior*, 29(4), 1879–1887.

National Campaign to Prevent Teen and Unplanned Pregnancy. (2008). *Sex and tech*. Washington, DC: National Campaign to Prevent Teen and Unplanned Pregnancy.

Owens, J., Adolescent Sleep Working Group, Committee on Adolescence, Au, R., Carskadon, M., Millman, R., Wolfson, A., Braverman, P. K., Adelman, W. P., Breuner, C. C., Levine, D. A., Marcell, A. V., Murray, P. J., & O'Brien, R. F. (2014). Insufficient sleep in adolescents and young adults: An update on causes and consequences. *Pediatrics*, 134(3), e921–e932. http://doi.org/10.1542/peds.2014-1696

Rideout, V. (2010). *Generation M2: Media in the lives of 8- to 18-year-olds*. Kaiser Family Foundation.

Rideout, V., & Robb, M. B. (2019). *The common sense census: Media use by tweens and teens*. www. commonsensemedia.org/sites/default/files/uploads/research/2019-census-8-to-18-full-report-updated.pdf

Robinson, T. N., Banda, J. A., Hale, L., Shirong Lu, A., Fleming-Milici, F., Calvert, S. L., & Wartella, E. (2017). Screen media exposure and obesity in children and adolescents. *Pediatrics*, 140(Suppl 2), S97–S101. http://doi.org/10.1542/peds.2016-1758K

9

When researching this chapter, we found ourselves very weary of any research published before 2020. When thinking of learning in a digital age, as a nation we did it! We survived it! And now we are left to question: What just happened? How did that go? Did children and teens learn anything? What were the positives and the negatives of this forced experiment? We wrote this book in the summer and fall of 2021 and so there is no way for us to truly understand the weight of many of the world's children being removed from the classroom at the same time in 2020. That said, we can offer insight into the learning process and how digital learning is different from in-person learning in a way that is hopefully more than the obvious. In this chapter we will explore facts about learning in a digital age, review the literature, analyze, and answer questions practitioners had from their time seeing kids who were doing school online. We will answer the questions: *Isn't it good for children and teens to learn to navigate all this technology? For their future? How is media affecting reading and literacy rates among kids? In quarantine my client (12) is using media as school avoidance. Her parents are worried that this may move into other elements of her life* and *Are virtual school hours considered screen time?*

Researchers are still investigating the effects of this new "post-pandemic" normal, and there have been some positive and negative outcomes from the new face of learning being in digital formats. Stepping back to credit the fact that digital learning is not new, it was just put through the ringer in 2020 and 2021. To begin our dive into this subject, Jacob (2016) explained that digital learning has the potential to create equal opportunities for children. With the Internet expanding worldwide, the connectivity allows children to open resources that were once unobtainable to them. These open resources can contribute to early literacy and numeracy skills, according to the author. Children now have the opportunity to learn at their own pace and through their preferred choice of learning style

DOI: 10.4324/9781003223412-9

at very young ages (Jacob, 2016). Along these same lines, Loveless (2020) was quick to point out that digital learning is not limited to the classroom. In their research, Loveless demonstrated that the use of educational apps both in and outside of the classroom promotes preparation for future interaction with technology, individualized learning, and fewer barriers for children with special needs. Given these developments in understanding, there is a huge push in technology sectors right now to capitalize on the benefits of digital learning. The latest technology being applied to digital learning is virtual reality (VR). According to a study by Allcoat et al. (2021), not only does learning improve from VR, but there is frequently higher engagement and positive emotions when this technology is utilized. Students in Allcoat et al.'s study looking into the effectiveness of VR in the classroom were more engaged and experienced higher immersion in material. Adapting VR learning will allow students to participate in simulated activities like laboratories, and very importantly, VR can be useful if kids are not able to attend school and miss out on important interactive learning activities. If given the VR technology, students would be able to do those in-class activities from home. Connect this research to Loveless (2020) and we have a new element of control over learning. Specifically, Loveless was interested in educational applications targeted specifically for children and teens. The authors were able to demonstrate that these technologies allowed for students to take control of their learning and in many cases increase and improve academic performance (Loveless, 2020).

But this control over technology comes with a price. Since the integration of digital learning, some schools and teachers have become dependent on the virtual learning space and curriculum and found it to be lacking. Looking again at Jacob (2016), as children enter into new grade levels, research shows that some students lack the "basic skills" to continue advancing to the next grade due to the technology dependency that was created within the classroom setting and the insufficient ways in which some topics are being taught. In 2018, Gillihan described that the implementation of technology within the classroom disengages students. Gillihan's research focused on how young children entering the education system are stimulated through social interaction when it comes to learning new concepts and grasping information, and that this key feature is missing through much of the available digital learning. The author advises that with the implementation of digital learning, classroom engagement and collaborative investigation are important to a student's academic journey. Unfortunately, these have not been widely implemented (Gillihan, 2018). Each of us who witnessed a young person in school in 2020 saw this — glazed eyes, bored stares, and perhaps behavioral issues from children and teens who were not engaged. In 2020, many of the luckier students in more privileged school districts across the country were given what Gillihan advises — simultaneous instruction that encouraged interaction, engagement, and collaboration even while the kids were safely at home. This, however, hinged on the student's willingness to participate without the in-person pressure to do so, the family's involvement, the student's environment, other responsibilities, etc. Regardless of what side of the argument you fall on, however, there are undeniable differences to learning through technology and learning "the old-fashioned way" in a classroom. There are also undeniable effects to spending the whole day in front of a screen. We start to review that below.

TECHNOLOGY EFFECTS ON COGNITION AND EMOTION

Isn't it good for children and teens to learn to navigate all this technology? For their future?

As demonstrated above, technology within the classroom has positive and negative outcomes that researchers are still actively studying, never more urgently than right now. In trying to get a full view of how learning in a digital age affects our youth, it is important to see all technology variables. Stepping aside from the classroom setting, researchers have determined that being exposed to technology for long hours of the day for a young child negatively affects their cognitive and emotional development (page 43). When my first son was born, I was in my third year of my PhD program and spending all my days studying media literacy. It was also the year that the iPad came out, and I wanted one. My husband and I decided that, taking advice from the American Academy of Pediatrics (AAP), our children would all be screen-free until two years old, and I knew enough as a mother to know that anything that was mine would become his and I delayed getting an iPad. Then, when he was around

18-months old, he became enamored with animals – farm animals, domestic animals, zoo animals, anything, he loved them. We would spend hours reading board books with pictures of animals and my husband and I would devotedly say "moo" and "baa" until we just couldn't any longer. Around that time, I attended a media literacy conference in Connecticut where I was privileged to meet some of the top researchers in the field. As a young mother, I immediately told them about my animal-loving kid. I then asked about the iPad. "Surely," I said, "pointing to a live picture of a cow and hearing it say 'moo' was better than any of my attempts!" "No," they replied quite matter of fact. Anything I could do was better than what a screen could do.

The research is quite clear – screens are a poor substitute for learning, whether it be social, emotional, or academic, there is no replacement for interpersonal instruction. Early research by Parish-Morris et al. (2013) introduces this topic in their examination of reading in the digital era. The research cites how early experiences with books is known to foretell later reading success, and previous research all agreed that interactive shared reading, often called "dialogic reading," is especially beneficial to developing literacy in young children. Parish-Morris et al.'s research focused on the efficacy of electronic console (EC) books, CD-ROM books, and e-book applications on literacy skills and comprehension. The authors noted that companies had created these technologies and applications to teach preschoolers pre-literacy skills, but until 2012, research had yet to systematically explore the impact of these types of books on established predictors of positive literacy outcomes. Using 165 parent-child dyads, the authors had parent-child pairs read battery-operated, touch-sensitive children's electronic console books (experimental group) or traditional books (control group). Results demonstrated that parent – child dialogic reading and children's story comprehension were both negatively affected when the pair used any of the electronic options. This research brought to light that there is so much more to reading and learning than simply hearing the words. When the children were being read to by their parents they felt the vibrations of their body, saw their mouth contort to make the shapes, had opportunities to ask questions and be asked questions ("can you say 'moo' after me?"). These features are all missing from the electronic resources. In the end, taking from cognitive development theories, and this research, it became clear that for toddlers and all preliterate children, the predominant contribution to their comprehension is not the accuracy of the sounds, but the holistic experience. Needless to say, after returning home from the conference I had a new appreciation for my own animal sound-making abilities and I did not buy an iPad for a few more years.

How is media affecting reading and literacy rates among kids?

Interest in the impact of the mass media on language and literacy development started as early as the late 1970s (Vulchanova, 2017). Since then, research, like the study explained above, has focused on how and if exposure exclusively to mass media differs from typical language acquisition through interaction with care-givers and peers. Decades of research indicate that profuse exposure to media input can have adverse effects, especially for toddlers (page 47). In a longitudinal study on media effects on cognitive development and literacy, Zimmerman and Christakis (2005) discovered that early television exposure in children younger than three years of age was positively correlated to adverse effects on cognitive development. These damaging effects included not reading at age seven. In a similar study, Tanimura et al. (2007) examined 18-month-old infants (n = 1,900) and revealed that participants who watched a lot of television (classified as more than four hours per day), even when watching with a parent who was talking (i.e., co-viewing (page 25)), had delayed language development/speech production (in terms of meaningful words). As discussed in chapter one, 18-months is a critical time in a child's life to acknowledge and address neurodevelopmental delays especially with respect to speech (page 5). Research showing effects of language development at this time is significant.

Also investigating these age groups, Madigan et al. (2019) did a deep dive into the role of increased technology on children aged 24–60 months. In a longitudinal study (spanning from 24–60 months of age), the authors tested the relationship between screen time and children's development, as assessed by a children's developmental screening tests. Conclusions of the report explained that of the 2,441 mothers and children in the study, the children with the higher amounts of screen time between ages 24 and 36 months were connected to poor performance on a screening measure assessing children's achievement of development milestones at 36 and 60 months, respectively (Madigan et al., 2019) (page 50).

The evidence is clear that screen time leads to decreased literacy among the children with the highest levels of screen time. The only studies to disagree with this research are the *Sesame Street* studies cited in Chapter 4 (page 39). This research showed that specifically watching *Sesame Street* predicted greater prosocial skills and academic achievement. When trying to understand the stark differences in the results of these studies, it is important to note that no other child program has been able to replicate the effects that *Sesame Street* had. For most children, screen time will not hurt them or delay them by a noticeable amount, but screen time will never help them. No matter what the marketing says, screens will never teach children to read. This was shown on a national level during the Baby Einstein debates (page 54). For some, the screen time they are given will reinforce the literacy skills that their parents and teachers are already working on, but it will never be a main contributor to learning.

DIGITAL LEARNING

What does this mean for digital learning? If children are using technology for educational purposes, does it still hold a threat to children's development? In June 2019, when the pandemic was not even conceivable to one's wildest imaginations, the Reboot Foundation asked the question: Does educational technology help students learn? Even in 2019 technology in classrooms was becoming much more common and school districts all over the country were pumping money into tablets and laptops. The Reboot Foundation's research started with a discussion on how some scholars in educational research have argued that educational technology impairs student learning. These scholars referenced data that showed technology as a distraction to students, harmful to their social development, and caused attention issues in some students. To this point, a number of studies have shown that technology-infused learning can lead to negative student outcomes, and in one recent analysis, middle school students who took online classes scored far lower than their peers in standardized tests. More on that to come. Meanwhile, proponents of technology in classrooms advocate for how devices can tailor learning experiences, structure classroom time more effectively, and facilitate more active learning. These scholars support a notable collection of research, including recent studies on computer-based tutoring that demonstrate that some educational software can be just as effective as a human tutor.

It is clear from just this introduction to digital learning that the debate over educational technology isn't black and white. The Reboot Foundation report makes specific note of context, and how the condition of the student and the technology makes a huge difference. Students can use technology, such as a tablet, Chromebook, or the Internet, in myriad ways that it is hard to make a blanket statement regarding whether it will, or will not, improve learning for school-aged children. Questions to ask are: Are students using devices to perform research? take notes? play games? engage in a virtual reality-based simulation? In this way, learning technologies are tools and, as such, they can be used effectively or ineffectively.

So, in looking at how technology is used as an academic tool, Moon and Hofferth (2018) investigated the role of technology on mathematics. The findings suggested that children who had access to a computer during the early elementary school years demonstrated increased mathematics test scores later in their school life (Moon & Hofferth, 2018). Those without computers, the research states, were already in a disadvantaged position from the very beginning of their school life.

While Moon and Hofferth's research is very positive and points to the importance of all students having access to technology, the Reboot report explains that there is actually an insufficient link between technology and outcomes in current scholarship. Specifically, the report from a meta-analysis discovered little support for a positive relationship between student performance on standardized tests and their self-reported use of technology, and some evidence of a negative impact. The report explains that typically students who reported low-to-moderate use of school technology tended to score higher on standardized tests than non-users. Meanwhile, students who reported a high use of technology tended to score lower than their peers who reported low or no use of technology (Lee Bouygue, 2019). All this back and forth of positive and negative outcomes of online learning point to the fact that it is not a black and white issue. There are many variables that go into the success of learning – on and off the screen.

To contribute to this understanding, Sage et al. (2019) conducted research on reading comprehension of college students. For their study, the authors did an experiment where half of their participants read a research report printed out on paper and the other half read the same study on a computer. The authors then evaluated the college students' learning from, and perceptions of, print versus digital readings. The goal of the research was to provide a recommendation regarding best approaches for reading assignments. In their study, students read the article and then completed a comprehension quiz and answered self-report questions questioning the student's cognitive load, perceived control, satisfaction, confidence, knowledge gain, and general preferences for paper versus digital medium. Results were very positive. Students in the study were observed spending similar amounts of time with the article and reported learning equally well from either version. In addition, self-perceptions of their learning were also reported similarly. The authors explained that the student participants said they preferred print over digital resources, but also attested to using digital resources exclusively outside of the study (Sage et al., 2019). Ultimately, the research provides support in illustrating that print and digital readings are equally viable options for students to use while reading. This, however, was a study conducted using college students and so should only be used to understand the effects on older teenagers and not their elementary-aged counterparts.

In addition, this data on preferences and comprehension is nuanced. In some cases, the Reboot Foundation report uncovered favorable outcomes, most specifically when students used computers for research, which had a positive relationship with reading performance. That said, for students using a computer to practice spelling or grammar, there was little evidence of a positive relationship. In addition, evidence was also found for a "technology ceiling effect." This was explained as in some areas, low technology usage correlated to a positive relationship, while high usage showed a negative relationship. One example of this was found concerning tablet use in fourth-grade classes. The data showed a clear negative relationship with testing outcomes for fourth-graders who testified to using their tablet in "all or almost all" classes. These students scored 14 points lower on the reading exam than students who reported "never" using classroom tablets. This difference in scores is the equivalent of a full grade level, or a year's worth of learning. Again, the tablets here are a variable, and in the study, nearly replaced the role of the teacher.

AGE VARIABLE

INFANTS AND TODDLERS

As explained in the early chapters of this book, technology affects children in various developmental stages differently. Specially, Chapter 4 discussed the harmful effects of technology on our youngest kids and how more positive benefits can be seen in older kids (page 43). Learning in a digital age follows that trend as well – we see the most harmful effects on the younger kids. As these kids age and mature, digital learning (like VR for example), can start to offer things that traditional in-classroom learning cannot. Taking a moment to discuss the youngest learners, Lehrl et al. (2021) looked into the role of digital learning for children's socio-emotional and academic outcomes. In an experiment with 4,914 children aged zero to five years, Lehrl et al. demonstrated that an analog home learning environment is most beneficial for toddlers since it is associated with better socio-emotional outcomes and practical life skills and play (Lehrl et al., 2021). The reason being is that young children need to have more interactions (page 44). If most of children's learning is done digitally it decreases verbal communication with parents, but if screen time is not an option, parents are more likely and able to engage with their child. One solution Lehrl et al. (2021) found is that children are less negatively affected if their parents or caregivers are more active during digital learning. If the parent interacts and participates with the child during digital learning it will increase their speaking and social skills because there is more interaction, which has been shown to be paramount to learning.

SCHOOL-AGED CHILDREN

Moving next to school-aged children, Zosh et al. (2016) wrote about my situation with the farm animals and explained that

> children can watch a lion in an actual habitat rather than read about
> it or see a static picture. Children can interact with letters and words

by dragging letters around the screen and hearing how sounds work. Concurrently, these technological enhancements have the potential to distract children from learning and developers from the educational goal.

(p. 2)

While one of the most attractive features of tablets for adults is the fact that children can use devices independently, from very early ages, research has repeatedly shown that these devices are missing the critical element of social interaction. Zosh et al. explain that applications need to support, rather than replace, social interaction in learning. Take the fourth graders for example. Those in the experimental condition were sent off with their devices to learn and take their exams, while the control condition was able to stay in the classroom with the teachers, white board, and opportunity to raise their hands to ask a question. The good news is that we are beginning to see a hybrid solution. Increasingly, app developers are promoting off-screen, or hybrid experiences, where children play an app together or parents are included in the app experience. We saw this also in the change of instruction during quarantine in 2020 and 2021. After they had the summer to plan, a majority of school districts across the country implemented a hybrid/synchronous learning model for the fall of 2021. For the young school-aged children, this seems to be the best solution — in-person teacher, and online material to advance as they are able.

TWEENS AND TEENS

When doing this research, I was reminded of a sociology study I read about in college. In the study, researchers went to schools in inner city areas of Los Angeles and tried to get an understanding for the high dropout rates and low graduation rates at the high schools. The research highlighted the poor quality of the school buildings, the broken desks, lack of books for each student, and overall neglect of the physical space. The authors then interviewed students who had dropped out of high school and a few of them had joined a gang and were wearing expensive clothing (especially the shoes). The teens told the researchers that their main goal in life was money and street life was going to get them there, not school. The teens also expressed that if the school wasn't willing to invest in enough books, desks, and other resources into them, why would they invest their resources into it. Public school districts all over the country faced some of these same issues in 2020 when going virtual. Schools have never invested in their digital platforms, the teachers are undervalued and under trained, and many students lack the digital tools or space to learn effectively online. Lack of efficient WiFi, computers that were too old, and teachers who were untrained in digital learning, were the new broken desks and tattered books. Time will tell, but precedent says our underserved kids will be even more underserved in the new digital evolution of learning.

In quarantine my client (12) started using media as school avoidance. Her parents are worried that this may move into other elements of her life.

In the midst of the COVID-19 quarantine, Loveless (2020) explained that technology in any capacity causes overstimulation, creates possible distraction, and learning imbalances that limits children's development. So the person who wrote this question was not alone! If you Google "distance learning" millions of links pop up talking about distracted kids. Droves of parents fled to virtual community groups to talk about how their kids are bored, unmotivated, distracted, and self-soothing with the internet during school hours. Soon after virtual learning started for many students in April 2020, Johns Hopkins School of Education published a paper titled "8 Tips to Help Your Child Focus and Stay Engaged During Distance Learning" (Carling, 2020). In the article, Linda Carling shares with parents eight tips to help children and teens stay focused during virtual learning. The tips were: (1) understand the expectation for distance learning; (2) determine what type of activities work best for your child; (3) encourage movement; (4) reduce distractions; (5) adjust your schedule as needed; (6) use a checklist for focus; (7) give your child (and yourself) a break; and (8) provide immediate positive feedback. This is a great list full of very useful tips that can be applied to virtual learning, and also to other elements of life like screen time rules and in-person learning.

What the article, and most articles, do not talk about is access. Our students were on computers for up to eight hours per day. In that time, the lucky few had parents or caregivers present with them keeping an eye on assignments and distractions, but most of the kids were on their own with their computer and the understanding that they were with their teacher, or doing what was expected of them. As we've discussed in this chapter and many others, kids are brilliant when it comes to media and finding what they want. They are also digital natives so seamlessly moving in and out of websites and browsers is easy. Finally, boredom, fatigue, monotony, lack of engagement, depression, all make us seek stimulation from somewhere. The good and the bad was that for millions of kids, they got the distraction they were looking for online. Anecdotal reports will speak to kids being on social media or even watching pornography during class time, therefore, missing valuable information and learning, no doubt contributing to drop in academic achievement across the county. It is not surprising that kids took this behavior into other elements of their lives.

The AAP reported that in 2020–2021 depression rates for female adolescents increased 24% (Mayne et al., 2021). Media use among this demographic also skyrocketed as all entertainment, education, and socialization suddenly became screen-based. It is reasonable to surmise that the reliance on screen time is self-propagating. As tweens and teens are isolated, they can become depressed, which in turn can make them more isolated. This then starts the cycle all over again.

The best way to reduce this unwanted behavior of teens using the media to avoid life is media literacy. Talk with them about what they get from the media that they don't get in real life, ask them about the draw to the screen, or about what will happen if they don't check social media for an hour (I once asked a college student this question after she told me it was "unreasonable" of me to expect her to not check her Instagram account during our 80-minute class. She was dumbfounded by the very notion). Next, set rules. The rules can be anything that works for your family – no screens during dinner, no screens until all the homework is done, you can only check Instagram three times per day, etc. There are so many examples of screen rules that it is overwhelming to even search for. Our advice is to focus on the big picture goals and dive deeper in order to achieve them. For example, if nothing works to get a teen off of YouTube during school hours, google sells a device called a "pause button" that allows you to have manual control over the Internet. Or if punishment is not your style, for many teens, media literacy and "reality checking" works for many to get them off of social media. Have them do some research into photoshopping and face tune, and then turn to Carling's list.

Are virtual school hours considered screen time?

The final question we were asked regarding the subject of learning in a digital age was about screen time and if virtual school counted as screen time. I think the simplest answer to this question is, yes, screen time is screen time and if school is on a screen, then that is screen time. Now that we have all read that sentence, we know that this is actually not a simple question at all. In my own home we had strict entertainment screen time rules before the pandemic (one hour a day on Friday, Saturday, and Sunday). Then the pandemic hit and my kids were stuck in a house with two full-time working parents. Screen time rules changed from "only" to "until." Instead of only on Friday, Saturday, and Sunday, the kids didn't get entertainment screen time until they finished their school work, cleaned their room, played in the yard, etc. The world became about survival instead of best practices. Now we are at a precipice of change once again we must acknowledge that technology as tools for education are here to stay. While we outlined many of the negative effects of virtual school, as children get older, the positive effects increase. Technology is also affordable and adaptable and so we must learn how to get along with it instead of continuing to fight against it and we have more difficult decisions to make.

When thinking about screen time, quality versus quantity must be weighed. Is virtual school time quality time on a screen? Yes. Is that time better spent than another activity? Hopefully also yes. Because attending a virtual class is the best use of the child or teen's time at that moment, then it is the right thing for them to do and should therefore be prioritized, even if no screen-time is a priority. That being said, if that educational screen time is well-spent but then you notice a behavior change in the child when they immediately go from virtual class to video games, then the child has reached their screen time limit and needs to take a break to rest their eyes and brains from the constantly moving screen.

REFERENCES

Allcoat, D., Hatchard, T., Azmat, F., Stansfield, K., Watson, D., & von Mühlenen, A. (2021). Education in the digital age: Learning experience in virtual and mixed realities. *Journal of Educational Computing Research*, 59(5), 795–816. https://doi.org/10.1177/0735633120985120

Carling. (2020). *8 tips to help your child focus and stay engaged during distance learning*. https://education.jhu.edu/2020/04/8tipsforfocus/

Gillihan, S. J. (2018, August 13). Does technology in the classroom help or harm students? *Psychologytoday.com*. www.psychologytoday.com/us/blog/think-act-be/201808/does-technology-in-the-classroom-help-or-harm-students

Jacob, B. A. (2016, July 28). The opportunities and challenges of digital learning. *Brookings*. www.brookings.edu/research/the-opportunities-and-challenges-of-digital-learning/

Lee Bouygues, H. (2019). *Does educational technology help students learn?* https://reboot-foundation.org/does-educational-technology-help-students-learn/

Lehrl, S., Linberg, A., Niklas, F., & Kuger, S. (2021). The home learning environment in the digital age – Associations between self-reported "analog" and "digital" home learning environment and children's socio-emotional and academic outcomes. *Frontiers in Psychology*, 12, 355. http://doi.org/10.3389/fpsyg.2021.592513

Loveless, B. (2020). Are learning apps helping or hurting education? *educationcorner.com*. www.educationcorner.com/learning-apps-helping-hurting-education.html

Madigan, S., Browne, D., Racine, N., Mori, C., & Tough, S. (2019). Association between screen time and children's performance on a developmental screening test. *JAMA Pediatrics*, 173(3), 244–250. http://doi.org/10.1001/jamapediatrics.2018.5056

Mayne, S. L., Hannan, C., Davis, M., Young, J. F., Kelly, M. K., Powell, M., Dalembert, G., McPeak, K. E., Jenssen, B. P., & Fiks, A. G. (2021). COVID-19 and adolescent depression and suicide risk screening outcomes. *Pediatrics*, 148(3), 1–11. http://doi.org/10.1542/peds.2021-051507

Moon, U. J., & Hofferth, S. (2018). Change in computer access and the academic achievement of immigrant children. *Teachers College Record*, 120(4). Retrieved September 14, 2020, from www.learntechlib.org/p/189293/

Parish-Morris, J., Mahajan, N., Hirsh-Pasek, K., Michnick Golinkoff, R., & Fuller Collins, M. (2013). Once upon a time: Parent – Child dialogue and storybook reading in the electronic era. *Mind, Brain, and Education*, 7(3), 200–211. https://doi.org/10.1111/mbe.12028

Sage, K., Augustine, H., Shand, H. et al. (2019). Reading from print, computer, and tablet: Equivalent learning in the digital age. *Education and Information Technologies*, 24, 2477–2502. https://doi.org/10.1007/s10639-019-09887-2

Tanimura, M., Okuma, K., & Kyishima, K. (2007). Television viewing, reduced parental utterance and delayed speech development in infants and young children. *Archives of Pediatrics and Adolescent Medicine*, 161, 618–619. http://doi.org/10.1001/archpedi.161.6.618-b

Vulchanova, M., Baggio, G., Cangelosi, A., & Smith, L. (2017). Editorial: Language development in the digital age. *Frontiers in Human Neuroscience*, 11. https://doi.org/10.3389/fnhum.2017.00447

Zimmerman, F. J., & Christakis, D. A. (2005). Children's television viewing and cognitive outcomes: A longitudinal analysis of national data. *Archives of Pediatrics and Adolescent Medicine, 159,* 619–625. http://doi.org/10.1001/archpedi.159.7.619

Zosh, J. M., Hirsh-Pasek, K., Golinkoff, R. M., & Morris, J. P. (2016). Learning in the digital age: Putting education back in educational apps for young children. *Technology in early childhood education.* Encyclopedia on Early Childhood Development. www.child-encyclopedia.com/technology-early-childhood-education/according-experts/learning-digital-age-putting-education-back

10

We don't need to tell you about the horrific rates of children and teens suffering from some type of disordered eating behavior (DEB) (e.g., anorexia nervosa, bulimia nervosa) and how these issues have resulted in increased research efforts and concern in American culture. It was reported in 2021 the total number of admissions for disordered eating among adolescents (ages 10–23) during the first 12 months of the COVID-19 pandemic was more than double the rates of the previous year (Otto et al., 2021). Not only have DEBs proven to be common, but also increasingly severe, and it is well documented how much more prevalent these issues become every year. In this chapter, we review research on how the media is involved in perpetuating body dysmorphia and eating disorders among American youth, what social media is currently doing to combat these issues, and how these issues were exacerbated in the 2020 COVID-19 pandemic. We end the chapter answering the questions: *Will social media inevitably teach people to hate their body? How do the roles and appearances of male versus female characters in shows geared toward young children affect their body image? Disordered eating among teenagers is on the rise, what is the media's role?* and *What is my client seeing that is contributing to her body dysmorphia?* We have already discussed the role of the parent.

MEDIA IMAGERY AND DISORDERED EATING BEHAVIORS

Claiming that the media plays a role in body image issues and disordered eating behavior is not a new concept. However, it may sometimes be overlooked for being so pervasive. Countless studies over the last few decades have examined the main effects of mass media images of the "thin ideal," as well as the many ways in which the media makes body image problems worse or more serious (Harrison & Cantor, 1997; Harrison, 2000; Field et al., 2008). Because it was so on point with

DOI: 10.4324/9781003223412-10

what this chapter will be about, we are going to start with one of the questions we received:

Disordered eating among teenagers is on the rise, what is the media's role? What is my client seeing that is contributing to her body dysmorphia?

In 2001, Groesz et al. completed a meta-analysis of 25 studies that explored the effect of thin media images on body satisfaction. Results from their examination showed that body image was considerably more negative after viewing thin media images than after seeing images of average-size models, plus-size models, or inanimate objects (Groesz et al., 2001). Additionally, the authors reported that these effects were stronger for participants less than 19 years old and those who were more likely to activate a "thinness schema" (Groesz et al. p. 1). We start with this research because it included 25 studies, spanned years of research, and concluded with something that is fairly basic – when we are forced to define "beautiful" as something unattainable, it makes us feel terrible about our own appearance. As adults we understand this, but I am ashamed to say that I didn't learn until my 30s that I couldn't make my body look like someone else's if I tried hard enough. I was in my 30s before I realized that diet and exercise were never going to be enough. I was also fortunate to grow up before social media so the only "beautiful" people I saw in the media were paid models and actors. Teens today have models, actors, and the "regular" people on social media who show off their body, share their diet and workout plans, and are "real." If these people on the screen are real, then it pushes the issue of "why doesn't my body look like that?" to a new extreme.

MALE[1] BODY IMAGE

The bulk of research on ideal body image has been focused on females. However, in 2004, Agliata and Tantleff-Dunn began investigating the impact of media exposure on a male's body image, and started what would become a very popular research topic. To discover the effects

---

1. The majority of research in mass communication has focused on the gender binary of male/ female. While we agree that gender is a spectrum and is non-binary, we use those terms here as an extension of the literature and intend them as social constructs and not biological.

Media, the Body, and Disordered Eating

of media images on the male body image, the researchers exposed 158 males to television advertisements containing either ideal male images or neutral images that were woven between segments of a television program. Their findings revealed that participants who had been exposed to the ideal images became appreciably more dejected and had higher levels of muscle dissatisfaction when compared to the men shown the neutral commercials (Agliata & Tantleff-Dunn, 2004).

More recently, Sumter et al. (2021) researched the effects of muscular and sexualized images of men on Instagram. In their research, the authors explained how stereotypical gender beliefs play a role in the low self-esteem among men. The article pointed to the primary reason for this being that it "refers to a societal pattern in which stereotypically male traits are idealized as the masculine cultural ideal, explaining how and why men maintain dominant social roles over women and other groups considered to be feminine" (p. 4). This demonstrates that when men live up to hypermasculine gendered norms, there is self- and societal pressure to conform to how a man should be. Thanks to this research, we now understand that media impacts the body image of males and females alike and we can talk about teen and age effects instead of gendered effects.

Researchers looking at ideal body images have also investigated the causes of the perpetuation of these images. One example of why these thin ideal images are so widely perpetuated is peer pressure (Stanford & McCabe, 2002). Research has shown that both men and women are culturally bound to appeal to both their same-sex and opposite-sex peers. Females, for example, believe that men prefer very thin women, and often alter men's preferences to bring them more in line with their own opinions (Stanford & McCabe, 2002). Meanwhile, males believe that women desire larger, stronger men, and will distort women's opinions to be more in line with this ideal body type. With men and women believing that the opposite sex desire a body shape unlike their own, there is pressure for both sexes to achieve this standard. This misperception is exacerbated by the media. Typically, male characters are attracted to the thin female characters and the female characters are attracted to the stronger, more muscular men. As we learned from social learning theory (page 8), viewers actively learn from television, therefore, a viewer learns that if they want to attract a man like the one on television, they must look like the women that that man dates on television (Bandura, 2009). The same reasoning is true for men. While our society has been talking about how harmful these images are on body image and self-esteem for some time, little, if any, has been done to change the representation of body image on the screen.

How do the roles and appearances of male versus female characters in shows geared toward young children affect their body image?

According to Common Sense Media (2015), body image is developed very early in childhood and nearly 33% of children between the ages of five and six would choose an ideal body size that is smaller than their current perceived size (Hayes & Tantleff-Dunn, 2010). Research into five-year-olds specifically have found that children this age understand, and even recommend, diet culture (no candy, smaller meal sizes) when asked (Lowes & Tiggemann, 2003). In the past, research has focused on this age group because their toys, specifically dolls and action figures, which are based off of media characters, are stereotypical in nature. Research by Klein and Shiffman (2007) indicated that children's cartoons already portray thinness positively and this trickles down to merchandise and also attitude and understanding. Furthermore, while children are absolutely picking up on diet culture and relationships with food and body image from their interpersonal relationships, predominantly parents and siblings, the media is also a source where body image is learned (Common Sense Media, 2015). Traditional media, in particular, are constantly showing children unrealistic, idealized, and stereotypical images of body types. According to a study completed by the Geena Davis Institute on Gender in Media and the University of Southern California, female characters in family programming are almost two times as likely to have an unnaturally small waist size compared to their male counterparts (Smith et al., 2013). In addition, results of a content analysis explain that female characters with larger body types are dramatically underrepresented in mainstream television programming (Smith et al., 2013). The same can be said for male characters.

In the end, a majority of the research supports the statement that "at best, we can conclude that consumption of mainstream, traditional media (with its stereotypical portrayals) puts children and teens at risk for developing an unhealthy body image" (Common Sense Media, p. 7).

LGBTQIA+

When looking at research focused on the LGBTQIA+ community and body image, the results are even more distressing as body dissatisfaction is even more common among sexual minorities (Blashill et al., 2016). For example, in their research examining body appreciation and sexual orientation, Alleva et al. (2018) learned that body appreciation is inversely related to conformity to masculine norms and positively correlated with physical activity. In effect, the more masculine your body is, the more you appreciate it. Furthermore, the study revealed that body appreciation was lower among sexual minorities compared to heterosexual men. Finally, Alleva et al. (2018) contributed to past research by also demonstrating that body appreciation was "positively correlated with body satisfaction, and inversely correlated with perceived appearance pressures from media and eating pathology" (p. 169). This translates to: the more you appreciate your body, the more satisfied you are with how you look. If you are satisfied with how you look, you are less easily pressured by media images. Simple enough to logically understand, but very difficult to convince someone of when they are already dissatisfied with how they look and suffering from years of mediated thin-ideal messages.

Related to this, in their 2016 study on body satisfaction, sexual health, and depression, Blashill et al. conducted longitudinal research on homosexual and bisexual males. Results from the study uncovered that body dissatisfaction significantly predicted depressive symptoms, lowered sexual drive and occurrence, and elevated sexual anxiety among all participants. Finally, in their research investigating women and body dissatisfaction, Koff et al. (2010) concluded that regardless of sexual orientation, there is a strong risk for body dissatisfaction when the media is involved.

Put all together, regardless of sex, sexual orientation, or even age, the media contributes to feelings of body dissatisfaction which has innumerable negative effects on everything from self-esteem and self-confidence, to depression and loss of sexual drive.

TIME ON SOCIAL MEDIA

Getting more specific into the different types of media children and teens are engaging with that leads to body image issues, we start with social media. A substantial body of research exists that links the use of social media, specifically Facebook and Instagram, to poorer body image among women, particularly those under the age of 25 (Schreiber, 2017). The data will come from TikTok and Snapchat eventually, but since they are newer media, the data is not yet widely available. Nearly all young people who are on social media report using it regularly. Following cultivation theory (page 27), this regular use of the media leads to the risk of experiencing a dip in body image satisfaction (and potentially feeling inclined towards disordered eating behavior or compulsive exercise as a result) remains high for many consumers. Exposure to thin and/or fit ideals that (intentionally or not) encourage the pursuit of a body type different from that which one possesses has been found to lower self-esteem and darken the moods of viewers. Taking from cultivation theory, the more time we spend with media and media-ideal images, the more our view of reality is curated. The magic number with cultivation theory is four hours per day and most of the teenagers in our lives are spending at least four hours a day on social media and observing the thin-ideal.

One culprit of this is the "influencer." A social media influencer is defined as a popular and influential person with a distinguishable number of followers who works to promote and influence a brand's products and/or services to their specific audience demographic (Odynokova, 2019). What makes social media influencers unique is that they expand across various "types" and they have the impact and authority to influence an individual's purchasing habits (Odynokova, 2019). With a job that exists purely with the objective of promoting and influencing a brand's product or service to their audience, influencers almost always post items that highlight the product and themselves in a positive light. With the high reach that influencers carry, taking from social learning theory (page 8), this can be dangerous when viewing products that promote health, fitness, and a certain body image. Leighton (2019) looked into this phenomenon in their research and discovered 47% of surveyed influencers believe that their job has an impact on their mental health. Additionally, Leighton (2019) detailed that 32% of influencers believe that their job has given them a negative view on their own body image. If a high number of influencers feel the effect of negative body image due to their profession, the large following they carry is likely to feel the same, if not more, impact. The additional variable here is that influencers take a different role in the viewer's lives than models or actors. Influencers are real people living their lives and their viewers follow them, not purely because of fame, but because of some personal connection. In today's society, influencers are able to be "authentic" to their viewers in a way that models and celebrities in magazines or on billboards never can. In that way, influencers have considerably more influence over subtle areas in viewers' lives because they are not seen as having commercial motives.

In a recent article published by King University (2020), it was explained that social media posts have the influence to negatively affect an individual's perception of their body and body image. Further, the article investigated a nonprofit organization named Project Know that provided insight that social media posts have the capacity to trigger or worsen eating disorders and psychological predispositions. From expanding the possibility of eating disorders, the article also states that women increase their body image comparisons to the posts they see on social media the longer they spend their time exploring posts (this is in line cultivation theory – the longer time you spend with a familiar mediated image, the more real it becomes). Finally, the article emphasized that social media has become the new vessel for users to actively compare their appearance and body image to what they see online (King University Online, 2020).

FACE TUNE

The good and the bad of social media is that it gives the person who is posting full control over what kind of image they want to show to the world. With technology it is easy to filter away pimples, color-correct uneven skin tone, and photoshop a couple of inches away from the waist. When the audience sees the photos, it depends on their media literacy skills (among other things, including age) whether or not they can recognize the image is altered. Without a critical eye reminding you that what you are seeing on the screen has been modified, exposure to pictures of underweight air-brushed bodies can be extremely detrimental and has been linked to unhealthy eating habits and decreased self-esteem (MacCallum & Widdows, 2018). In the United Kingdom, they are trying to get rid of this issue. Specifically, the Health and Social Care Committee has drawn a bill to force social media users to label images that have been digitally altered. According to the committee, edited photos on social media are fueling a mental health crisis and creating a warped view of beauty (Laws, 2020). This proposal would help educate viewers on image tuning and inform kids and teens, even adults, who cannot recognize a digitally altered image, that images that seem flawless and perfect don't exist without retouching. We have to share, even as adults who understand that images are doctored, we still fall into the trap of comparison. An actual message to viewers that images have been edited would have a huge impact.

Additional research conducted in the United Kingdom by Be Real found that 79% of children between 11 and 16 said looks are important to them. Fifty-two percent of the kids said they often worry about how they look, and 40% of participants said that images they see on social media have caused them to worry about their body image (Mental Health Foundation UK, n.d.). Social media allows children to compare their bodies to others', sometimes without realizing how the images they see have been altered. This in turn cultivates a negative body image which can lead to severe consequences, including depression and eating disorders, like anorexia or bulimia.

SOCIAL MEDIA, DISORDERED EATING, AND THE PANDEMIC

During the COVID-19 quarantine we unfortunately saw an increase in disordered eating among adolescents in the United States. Unsurprisingly, when isolated from everyone outside of their immediate family, teens reported that many of the support systems that typically aid in someone's recovery were not there. This will not be surprising or new information to you. What may be, however, is the new role of social media in this epidemic. During the 2020 quarantine, teens were living their lives online – their social lives now fit perfectly on a rectangle screen. From this came increased social comparison, and also new communities. One such community that popped up was from the hashtag "'quarantine 15," which then translated into a meme and was on every social media platform. These memes helped to perpetuate fat-phobia and anxiety about weight being related to COVID risks. Research into this "quarantine 15" revealed that it was primarily males who were following, reposting, and joining in this current iteration of "fitspiration." In this example, we were able to see that what started as a fitness routine to help fill time or even boost moods, snowballed into something much more serious and negative when there was not much else for the followers to do. Here it is easy to see where the media can be a very slippery slope – what started as positive and healthy eating, became an overblown obsession with working out and being fit for many teens.

INSTAGRAM 2021

In fall 2021, data from an internal Facebook research report was leaked by the *Wall Street Journal*. The report described many ways in which Instagram is physically and emotionally harmful to as many as 20% of teenage girls using the app. This comes with news that young users are a key to Instagram's success with more than 40% of Instagram's users under the age of 23. The *Wall Street Journal* also reported that Instagram "can increase anxieties about physical attractiveness, social image, and money, and even increase suicide risk," and all of this is according to Facebook's own internal research (np). The article took data from an internal slide presentation and presented the following facts:

- "Thirty-two percent of teen girls said that when they felt bad about their bodies, Instagram made them feel worse";
- "Comparisons on Instagram can change how young women view and describe themselves";
- "We make body image issues worse for one in three teen girls";
- "Teens blame Instagram for increases in the rate of anxiety and depression";
- "This reaction was unprompted and consistent across all groups";
- "Among teens who reported suicidal thoughts, 13% of British users and 6% of American users traced the desire to kill themselves to Instagram, one presentation showed."

Naturally, Facebook had a response to this. In a blog article posted to their website, Facebook wrote:

> It is simply not accurate that this research demonstrates Instagram is "toxic" for teen girls. The research actually demonstrated that many teens we heard from feel that using Instagram helps them when they are struggling with the kinds of hard moments and issues teenagers have always faced.

In fact, in 11 of 12 areas on the slide referenced by the Journal –
including serious areas like loneliness, anxiety, sadness and eating
issues – more teenage girls who said they struggled with that issue
also said that Instagram made those difficult times better rather than
worse.

Body image was the only area where teen girls who reported
struggling with the issue said Instagram made it worse as compared
to the other 11 areas. But here also, the majority of teenage girls who
experienced body image issues still reported Instagram either made it
better or had no impact.

(Raychoudhury, 2021)

These arguments deserve some analysis and break down. First, it is
important to note how positive it is that Facebook is conducting their
own research. They are doing this both to attract new teenage users
(less good), but they are also the only social media source currently
putting up safeguards for teens and attempting to protect them. The
social media giant has an understanding of how harmful their product
is for young people, and instead of changing the product, they are
adding in band aids, but it is still more than any other site is doing. For
example, Facebook has created resources to support those struggling
with body image issues and has a dedicated reporting option for
eating disorder-related content. In addition, the company has taken
steps to remove "all graphic content related to suicide" and recently
launched Restrict, an anti-bullying movement that allows users to protect themselves from online bullying. These resources are all available
on the app. It would be interesting to learn how many teenagers know
about or use these services, but they are available and explained on
their blog.

Moving on to the analysis of the data. Facebook interviewed
teenagers about 12 items related to their social media use. These
included anxiety, depression, body image, social comparison, sleep
issues, fear of missing out (FOMO), family issues, loneliness, sadness,
school, stress, and problematic use. While the company did not release
the data or the interview questions, with a glance at the variables it is
clear that most of these items are manifest, and not latent, variables.
Manifest variables are something that cannot be directly measured,
you need to break each manifest variable into a set of latent variables,

things that can be directly measured. The best example of a mani-fest variable is self-esteem. Self-esteem is something that is incred-ibly important and yet you cannot go up to someone and ask "How is your self-esteem today?" as you would if it were a latent variable such as "How old are you?" I've tried asking people how their self-esteem is, most of the time the response is "fine" and I know no more than I did before I asked the question. Manifest variables are not only impossible to ask, they are impossible to answer, for anyone, let alone a vulnerable teenager. If someone asked me how my self-esteem was, I would likely think about how my clothes currently fit on my body, if I exercised that day, and what my chocolate to real food ratio was that day. If I ask someone else, they may think about the last time they spoke to their mom on the phone, the last time someone told them they looked good, or the time on their last mile race. Manifest variables often mean different things to different people and it is up to the researcher to define the variable into latent terms. For example, I can define self-esteem as confidence in one's own abilities, self-respect, or something related to their self-image. Once I have my definition, the only way to properly measure it is to break the definition down into a set of questions that gets at the larger variable I want to know about but can't directly ask.

Turning back to the Facebook study. If you were to ask "How does Instagram affect your anxiety?" or "Do you think your Instagram use is problematic?" or even, "Does Instagram make you feel better or worse about your body?" these are all exceptionally difficult questions for a teenager to answer because they are loaded with so many other things. They also require a level of personal insight missing in most teenagers and adults. When answering these questions myself, I want to say that Instagram has no effect on my body image but most of that is because I want it to be true, or I want the researcher to think it is true of me, or because I think that I am stronger than to allow an image to effect the way I think about myself. Unfortunately, none of these are accurate and from decades of research, we know that mediated images influ-ence our self-image.

In the end, we hope that this article by the *Wall Street Journal* is the first step in ending the dependence teenagers have on social media. As we have already presented from years of data, social media has a nega-tive influence on teenagers and their body image. We are pleased that

Facebook is taking steps to create safer environments online and also that a few days after the *Wall Street Journal* article was posted, Facebook released a press release saying that they were putting a hold on their Instagram for Children app that was in development.

DOOM SCROLLING

Looking specifically at the social comparison that we all do when scrolling through Instagram, McComb and Mills (2021) surveyed women on their physical confidence, appearance, and weight satisfaction both before and after doom scrolling on Instagram. Data was unsurprising, and yet still notable. In their research McComb and Mills (2021) found that appearance comparison is a natural occurrence when on social media and that effects of comparing oneself to the models on the screen led to decreased confidence and increased appearance and weight dissatisfaction. Results also demonstrated that "high trait physical appearance perfectionism" foretold increased weight dissatisfaction and decreased confidence and appearance dissatisfaction. These relationships between comparison and depressed feelings were mediated by what the authors called "engagement in rumination and catastrophizing" (p. 48).

WE PREDICT A MORE POSITIVE FUTURE

Will social media inevitably teach people to hate their body?

To date, nearly all of the research on media and body image is troubling. We have social comparison, unrealistic expectations, thin ideals, etc. In addition, when we were young it was predominantly models and actors on glossy pages setting these delusory expectations of what our bodies should look like to be beautiful. Now children and teenagers have models, actors, influencers, YouTube, Instagram, TikTok, filters, face tune, editing apps, you name it, every image they see has been doctored and beautified, not just the images from the big studios. All that being said, we think we are on the precipice of a change. Young people are demanding more. Thankfully, young people today have parents who went through their lives feeling terrible about their body and they want to raise a generation who doesn't. When writing this chapter, we asked a 13-year-old what she thought of this phenomenon and she explained that she knows some of her friends compare their bodies to the actors in their favorite shows, but she personally knows that those actors are "27 trying to play a 13-year-old and have actual muscles." Because many kids were taught at a young age that the actors on the screen weren't real, they have a much stronger foundation for this understanding.

Because of the demand for more realistic proportions, there has been a global campaign promoting self-love and it is utilizing the power of social media. Now, more and more people are being recognized for their courage and beauty without being made to feel like they are not enough. Not only did social media allow for a community, but it also promoted different lifestyles that can potentially inspire people to be happy in their body.

In her article on how social media can improve body image, Schreiber (2017) says that people are becoming more and more aware of "self-compassion" which "involves adopting a more accepting view of oneself with an understanding that so-called flaws or mistakes are natural and inevitable aspects of being human" (np). Because of social media, there is now an inclusive space for different body types being able to freely express themselves with the different platforms.

Harkening back to the alarming disordered eating statistics at the top of the chapter, Instagram has the ability to empower users because the platform has made eating disorder-specific keywords or hashtags unsearchable. When these search terms are excluded, people can focus on healthier representations of bodies on social media. Additionally, through the use of social media, there are many pages that endorse healthy eating while still being body positive with the hashtags #bodypositive, #edwarrior, and #recovery, that helps the community. Young people often develop eating disorders in order to maintain or achieve "the perfect body," however, there is now a large community of healthy living and self-compassion. An organization called Eating Disorder Hope launched a campaign called Pro-Recovery Movement in order to "combat pro-eating disorder websites while providing a similar sense of community and understanding, instead promoting body positivity, among other important pro-recovery topics" (McGuire & McGuire, 2019, np). In February 2016 they launched Project HEAL with the hashtag #WhatMakesMeBeautiful to encourage women to love and celebrate themselves for everything that makes them beautiful. This campaign opened a new perspective by displaying the importance of celebrating self-love on social media and seeing beauty in a new light.

Despite all the harm social media has done, little by little it has the potential to get better. Wanting to end this chapter on a somewhat higher note, there has been an uptick in recent research on the body positivity movement. Early evidence, as explained by Cohen et al. (2021) show potential benefits from engaging with body-positive content on social media. Early research shows a positive correlation between body-positive content and positive body image. The only thing necessary for this is to see an actual increase in body-positive content.

REFERENCES

Agliata, D., & Tantleff-Dunn, S. (2004). The impact of media exposure on males' body image. *Journal of Social and Clinical Psychology, 23*, 7–22.

Alleva, J. M., Paraskeva, N., Craddock, N., & Diedrichs, P. C. (2018). Body appreciation in British men: Correlates and variation across sexual orientation. *Body Image, 27*, 169–178. https://doi.org/10.1016/j.bodyim.2018.09.004

Bandura, A. (2009). Social cognitive theory of mass communication. In J. Bryant & M. B. Oliver (Eds.), *Media effects: Advances in theory and research* (pp. 94–124). Routledge.

Blashill, A. J., Tomassilli, J., Biello, K., O'Cleirigh, C., Safren, S. A., & Mayer, K. H. (2016). Body dissatisfaction among sexual minority men: Psychological and sexual health outcomes. *Archives of Sexual Behavior, 45*(5), 1241–1247. https://doi.org/10.1007/s10508-015-0683-1

Cohen, R., Newton-John, T., & Slater, A. (2021). The case for body positivity on social media: Perspectives on current advances and future directions. *Journal of Health Psychology, 26*(13), 2365–2373. https://doi.org/10.1177/1359105320912450

Common Sense Media. (2015). Children, teens, media, and body image. *A common sense media research brief*. www.commonsensemedia.org

Facebook. (2021, September). *What our research actually says about teen well-being and Instagram*. https://about.fb.com/news/2021/09/research-teen-well-being-and-instagram/

Field, A. E., Javaras, K. N., Aneja, P., Kitos, N., Camargo, C. A., Taylor, C. B., & Laird, N. M. (2008). Family, peer, and media predictors of becoming eating disordered. *Archives of Pediatric & Adolescent Medicine, 162*(6), 574–579.

Groesz, L. M., Levine, M. P., & Murnen, S. K. (2001). The effect of experimental presentation of thin media images on body satisfaction: A meta-analytic review. *International Journal of Eating Disorders, 31*(1), 1–16.

Harrison, K. M. (2000). The body electric: Thin-ideal media and eating disorders in adolescents. *Journal of Communication, 50*.

Harrison, K. M., & Cantor, J. (1997). The relationship between media consumption and eating disorders. *Journal of Communication, 47*, 40–67.

Hayes, S., & Tantleff-Dunn, S. (2010). Am I too fat to be a princess? Examining the effects of popular children's media on young girls' body image. *British Journal of Developmental Psychology, 28*(2), 413–426.

King University Online. (2020, May 15). *Link between social media & body image.* Retrieved August 2021, from https://online.king.edu/news/social-media-and-body-image/

Klein, H., & Shiffman, K. (2007). Messages about physical attractiveness in animated cartoons. *Body image, 3,* 353–363. https://doi.org/10.1016/j.bodyim.2006.08.001.

Koff, E., Lucas, M., Migliorini, R., & Grossmith, S. (2010). Women and body dissatisfaction: Does sexual orientation make a difference? *Body Image, 7*(3), 255–258. https://doi.org/10.1016/j.bodyim.2010.03.001

Laws, C. (2020, September 4). *This is why people are backing a law for enhanced photos on social media to come with a label.* Glamour. www.glamourmagazine.co.uk/article/law-for-enhanced-photos-on-social-media-to-be-labelled

Leighton, H. (2019). Influencers admit that Instagram is bad for body image, mental health, study shows. *Forbes.* Retrieved December 13, 2019, from https://www.forbes.com/sites/heatherleighton/2019/12/13/is-instagram-bad-for-your-mental-health-body-image/?sh=6bec1dd31e55

Lowes, J., & Tiggemann, M. (2003). Body dissatisfaction, dieting awareness and the impact of parental influence in young children. *The British Psychological Society, 8,* 135–147.

MacCallum, F., & Widdows, H. (2018). Altered images: Understanding the influence of unrealistic images and beauty aspirations. *Health Care Analysis, 26*(3), 235–245. http://doi.org/10.1007/s10728-016-0327-1

Mental Health Foundation UK (n.d.). https://www.mentalhealth.org.uk

McComb, S. E., & Mills, J. S. (2021). Young women's body image following upwards comparison to Instagram models: The role of physical appearance perfectionism and cognitive emotion regulation. *Body Image, 38,* 49–62. https://doi.org/10.1016/j.bodyim.2021.03.012

McGuire, J., & McGuire, J. (2019, April 16). Positive uses of social media in body image advocacy. *Eating Disorder Hope.* Retrieved August 2021, from www.eatingdisorderhope.com/blog/positive-social-media-body-image

Odynokova, T. (2019, July 17). What is a social media influencer? *PromoRepublic.* https://promorepublic.com/en/blog/glossary/what-is-social-media-influencer/

Otto, A. L., Jary, J. M., Sturza, J., Miller, C. A., Prohaska, N., Bravender, T., & Van Huysse, J. (2021). Medical admissions among adolescents with eating disorders during the COVID-19 pandemic. *Pediatrics, 148*(4), e2021052201. http://doi.org/10.1542/peds.2021-052201

Raychoudhury, P. (2021, September). *What our research really says about teen well-being and Instagram.* https://about.fb.com/news/2021/09/research-teen-well-being-and-instagram/

Schreiber, K. (2017, October 21). How social media can actually improve body image. *Recovery.org.* www.recovery.org/pro/articles/how-social-media-can-actually-improve-body-image/

Smith, S. L., Choueti, M., Prescott, A., & Pieper, K. (2013). *Gender roles and occupations: A look at character attributes and job-related aspirations in film and television.* Annenberg School of Communication & Journalism, University of Southern California & the Geena Davis Institute on Gender in Media.

Stanford, J. N., & McCabe, M. P. (2002). Sociocultural influences on adolescent boys' body image and body change strategies. *Body Image, 2,* 105–113.

Sumter, S. R., Cingel, D., & Hollander, L. (2021). Navigating a muscular and sexualized Instagram feed: An experimental study examining how Instagram affects both heterosexual and nonheterosexual men's body image. *Psychology of Popular Media.* Advance online publication. https://doi.org/10.1037/ppm0000355

Wall Street Journal. (2021, September). *Facebook knows Instagram is toxic for teen girls, company documents show.* www.wsj.com/articles/facebook-knows-instagram-is-toxic-for-teen-girls-company-documents-show-11631620739

To say that the media plays a big role in children's understanding of ideals about sex, gender, and sexuality, is a huge understatement. To say that the media helps to *create* our idea of gender and sexuality is much more reasonable. Harking back to our theoretical foundations (page 8), the performance of our own gender and sexuality is shaped through behavior modeling and information processing. In this chapter we will focus on gender and sexuality, and the role that media plays in child and teenage development. We also focus on different types of media, including music. It is critical to note that traditional media portrays gender as a binary – boy/girl, male/female. With the introduction of social media and new online communities, this is changing for new media, but the binary still exists and is being ingrained into our children and youth. We will discuss the research on how children are taught this binary thinking, and then also offer insight into the future. At the end of the chapter, we respond to the questions: *My client is a 17-year-old boy who recently came out to his family as gay. His family disapproves and he says that he has no one in his life who understands. What is the media showing kids about sexuality?* and *This new generation of young people are discussing sexuality in a way I never did. What does the research say about classification?*

Starting at a very young age, children explore cues about gender[1] – what they should play, whom they should play with, and how they should act while they play – from the people closest to them, for example, their families or preschool friends. From the immense variety of gendered cues in their social world, children quickly learn how to behave and what their role is given the social norms. At first,

1. When we use the terms "boy" and "girl" or "female" and "male" these are social constructions and refer only to how the person identifies and so it is meant to include the trans and non-binary communities.

DOI: 10.4324/9781003223412-11

research into the socialization of children focused solely on interpersonal communication channels. In this framework, roles and norms for behavior are first learned through the observation of a child's own family and then later by observing peers and adding exposure through lived experiences. In the last 30 years, however, this view of development has been expanded to also include the effects of media (e.g., Meyer et al., 1991; Hoffner, 2008). Furthermore, gendered identities are much more open to discussion, interpretation, and remediation via new technologies in today's society. It would be wrong to conclude that traditional views of gender have been totally expunged, there is no doubt that as individuals we are much more aware and understanding of the issues that gender and sexuality bring into our lives. We would also argue that this generation of teenagers is leading the charge of exploration and acceptance of gender and sexuality, but they aren't doing it alone. Media plays a critical role in their consideration of gender and sexuality. This big shift from traditional gendered roles to a spectrum of roles comes as teens are in charge of their media and are the content creators, rather than simply viewers.

Dating back nearly 15 years, Hust and Brown (2008) explain that the media presents children with a window into the larger world as soon as they are old enough to sit in front of a television screen. Moreover, Hoffner (2008) argued that the media is not only another influence, but a critical one to a child's development of certain characteristics. The author explained that although children form their first and most important relationships with their parents, at increasingly young ages, children often spend a great deal of time with various media outlets (page 23). The critical nature of exploring gender and sexuality adds additional weight to the claim that children spend an exorbitant amount of time with the media and the effects. Because of this, it is argued that this time is spent learning from television characters and being influenced by the images that they see.

GENDER SCHEMA THEORY

Adding to our collection of theories in this book, let us add gender schema theory (Bem, 1983). This theory, penned by Bem (1983), outlines the cognitive and social process a child goes through when encoding and organizing information regarding themselves, in tandem with cultural definitions of male and female. Like cognitive development theories, Bem's gender schema theory explains that a child's cognitive processes, including developmental limitations, mediate the formation of their conceptual frameworks of gender. This cognitive development process involves a motivation toward self-categorization (Bem, 1983). Piaget's theory (page 12) explains that young children are limited in their cognitive thinking and therefore exhibit a natural inclination to group similar objects and traits together or be easily persuaded by media portrayals of gender stereotypes. Gender schema theory expands on this idea in explaining that these cognitive limitations are what arbitrates the development of gender schemas and forms a child's gendered behavior.

While gender schema theory proposes that sex typing is mediated by a child's cognitive and developmental limitations, it also assumes that sex typing and stereotyping are social phenomena, and part of a process of a greater social community, as in social learning theory (page 8). Thus, gender schema theory shows how a constant depiction of female housewives and male breadwinners can influence a viewer's opinion of gender roles in our society. This is an important element to the theory as it implies that, as a learned phenomenon, sex typing is neither inevitable, nor unchangeable (Bem, 1983). However, it may be the case that, due to their cognitive limitations, preoperational children may be more prone to accepting the stereotyped portrayals of gender seen in the media. Because the media shows children and teens more images and "realities" than their interpersonal relationships can, it can be argued that it plays a large role in the development of a person's gender.

GENDER DEVELOPMENT

Gender development is an ongoing process. Maccoby (1998) estimates that children make the largest advancements during preschool and early elementary school years. In their research from 1998, Maccoby explains that at this age, children's understanding of male and female gender roles is still in a more fluid state and yet it impacts whom the child chooses as a friend and what roles they each play in the relationship (Maccoby, 1998). Meyer et al. (1991) expand on Maccoby's narrower view of social interaction as the primary contributor to gender identity and offer the insight that children spend more time watching television than all other activities besides sleep. In explaining the many influences on gender-identity, the authors state, "even if the family didn't influence the development of gender-differentiated behavior in children, the media would suffice" (p. 537).

Combining all of the above, these facts point to the necessity of researching the media's role in gender development at the age when children first enter school. Martin and Ruble (2004) investigated this more closely in their research on preschool students and gender identity. Specifically, the authors explain, "young children search for cues about gender – who should or should not do a particular activity, who can play with whom, and why girls and boys are different" (p. 67). This research relates to a cognitive theory of gender development in that it discusses a cognitive perspective in which gender development assumes that children are actively searching for ways to find meaning in and make sense of the social world that surrounds them. In order for them to do so, children use the gender cues provided by society to help them interpret what they see and hear. When children are young, they start to observe the world around them, especially the people around them. An example of a gender cue, a child might come to a conclusion to would be a young child seeing his mother and another woman ordering a salad and his father eating a pizza. Naturally, the young child might come to the conclusion that women eat salad and men do not; the same can be said for the more obvious conclusions about dresses, heels, and painted nails. As Martin states,

> By the age of 5, children develop an impressive constellation of stereotypes about gender (often amusing and incorrect) that they apply to themselves and others. They use these stereotypes to form impressions of others, to help guide their own behavior, to direct their attention, and to organize their memories.
>
> (p. 67)

These conclusions children come to is just how they assume boys and girls are until they reach a certain age in which they understand gender and sexuality.

MEDIA AND GENDER IN EARLY CHILDHOOD

While the most salient examples of learned gendered behavior are interpersonal, it is important to recognize how the media is a catalyst for spreading mass amounts of gendered information, especially focusing on the ways that they model messages towards young kids. Disney princesses are introduced to most girls when they are children – mesmerized by each of their unique stories and the beautiful gowns they wear, wanting nothing more than to emulate those looks themselves. Disney princesses are not just characters on a screen, instead they are very powerful figures that girls aspire to be like. To understand what kind of effect images of Disney princesses have on girls' ideas of femininity, Golden and Jacoby (2017) investigated how children would reinvent themselves as princesses and examine whether or not gender stereotypes were shown in Disney media. There were four main themes that resulted from princess play. These included paying attention to beauty; focusing on clothing and accessories; specific body movements; and excluding boys. The research explained, "The reappearance of these four themes across all classes, combined with the girls' near formulaic assessment of the princesses in their interviews, suggests that princess play confines girls to preset and gendered narratives in their play" (Golden & Jacoby, 2017, p. 309). There was definitely a pressure for girls to conform to feminine stereotypes of being thin, soft spoken, and caring because the messages displayed by Disney princesses highlighted those exact themes. Additionally, girls learn that their worth is determined based on physical attractiveness and if there is any hope of finding their "Prince Charming," they must be prim and proper. And of course, they are indoctrinated to believe that Prince Charming is worth finding in the first place. To their credit, Disney has done a lot to reshape the female image in their most recent films, but because children typically watch all Disney movies, the effects of the older films are still being felt today.

As the topic of gender play was mentioned above, dissecting how girls and boys perform their identity can illustrate the different skills they have adopted. Gender stereotypes in children's programming act as a crutch that prevents them from authentic self-expression, which is why we have to refrain from spreading those messages and allow kids to be who they want as opposed to following a set of gender rules. Once kids begin preschool, they are already engaging in gender segregated behaviors. Boys are more inclined to spend time with other boys and participate in rough games. In contrast, girls prefer to play with other girls and are more cooperative than their male counterparts. Additionally, there are multiple factors that contribute to gendered interest in toys such as biology, social agents, and advertisements. A couple of ways to reduce children's gender stereotypes are, "explaining to children what gender stereotypes – and related concepts such as gender discrimination – are [. . .] and increasing the complexity of gender categories by demonstrating gender diversity in children's toys and play" (Weisgram, 2019, p. 82). By implementing these strategies, children are less likely to be swayed by gendered messages. The sooner we take away the labels that come with being a boy or a girl, the easier it will be for children to simply exist without being constrained by masculine and feminine norms. Thus, children should learn about gender stereotypes early on – sending them down a path where they are aware of how the media is trying to influence their behaviors.

Until this point, we have distinguished between "boy" and "girl" behavior significantly, and that is because the media does. To date, in traditional media there lives two genders – that of boy and that of girl in children's programming. As stated in the note at the top of the chapter, we refer to these words as social constructions and not a biological imperative. Young children are working these things out, but in all of the research child participants choose to act like a boy or a girl. This may change by the day for gender fluid children or non-binary children, but at the end of each day, children's understanding of what it means to be male or female is deepened by what they are seeing on the screen.

To conclude, gender stereotypes in media are prominent in early childhood and can leave a lasting impression on kids throughout the rest of their lives. The media frequently tells children how they should behave according to their assigned sex, reiterating the message that girls should be feminine and frail, while boys should be masculine and strong. If there is a child who embodies any characteristics or traits that do not align with their gender, they immediately have a target placed on their back – facing a lot of backlash for not fitting into society's definition of a boy or girl. In order to reduce gender stereotypes, children must be taught that the stereotypes seen in the media should be given context and perspective in order to encourage them to express themselves however they feel comfortable doing so. Things like the Disney princess movies may not be disappearing due to their cultural impacts, but we can assure kids that those behaviors do not have to be replicated.

TEENS AND GENDER

So far, we have spent a lot of time in this chapter discussing gender and young children because the development of gender is critical in a person's understanding of their own gender, however, the questions we received for this chapter all concern older kids, which leads us to believe that those are the issues you are dealing with. Adolescence is a period of development characterized by psychophysical maturation processes in addition to obvious advancements in physical development (page 106). These changes can be particularly difficult for those in the transgender community as physical changes may be counter to their gender identity. The Internet and social media represent a tool to discover and explore human sexuality without restriction.

In their research looking at gender displays on Instagram, Butkowski et al. (2019) investigated how young women display feminine cues through selfies online. Drawing from an expanding body of research which suggests that young women tend to replicate normative feminine cues through selfies, the authors completed a content analysis to investigate gender display on Instagram selfies and the feedback the images receive (likes and comments). Results from the analysis uncovered that stereotypical gender display is indeed widespread on Instagram. Also unsurprising is the fact that teens who posted stereotypically feminine images also received more feedback. With this, the authors conclude that gender stereotyping in selfies and the subsequent reinforcing feedback work to perpetuate gender performance in user-generated content.

Mahon and Hevey (2021) take this research one step further in arguing that increased social media use, especially engaging in appearance-related behaviors, may be a potential risk factor for body dissatisfaction in adolescents. This was found to be less severe in participants who identified as male. We talk about this in more depth in our conversation of Facebook, media and body image (page 139).

SEXUALITY AND TEENS

In my Children and Media class last spring, I asked my students to discuss the role of the media in their own story of sexuality. One student wrote this:

> Growing up, I was very sheltered. I was only able to see certain things and was taught right from wrong based on religion. As I got older, I

got curious and began to play and experiment with my gender and my sexuality. I relied on social media, and the media in general to help me learn about myself, to help me see what I liked and what I wanted to be. It is crazy how much the media can influence your choices when it comes to your sexuality and gender. I was forbidden from seeing all these LGBTQ+ shows and now as I am older and seeing them for the first time I realized a lot about LGBTQ+ portrayal in the media and how different Hollywood portrays LGBTQ+ youth. How much stereotypes live within these popular shows.

This student is not alone – for millions of teens the media is the only outlet they have for self-expression. The student finished with

As a current college student, I have grown to accept myself as a non-binary person. The way I chose to identify was not because of the media. But because of social media. I think social media has a stronger effect when it comes to our lesbian, gay, bisexual, trans, queer, and other sexual and/or gender minority (LGBTQ+) youth than the media does and it is sad. All around the world we have people who are afraid to come out still and they resort to social media to get that inspiration.

I think it is fascinating that the student wrote, "I chose to identify was not because of the media. But because of social media." To them, they are aware enough to NOT be influenced by the media, and yet also aware enough to admit to being influenced by social media. One explanation is that teens have a relationship with social media – the people they follow and engage with are real and they are their friends. In this way, it is not the media that is helping them construct their gender, but the people they learn from on social media. Obviously, we argue that it is all the same thing, but the power social media has over them is worth exploring.

NON-BINARY

One amazing thing that this generation of young people are doing is redefining sexuality, what it is, and how we talk about it. As written above, mainstream media is still stuck in the past – it now shows male, female, hetero and homosexual, but it has not caught up to the myriad LBGTQIA+ that this generation has embraced. Because of that, most adolescents are turning to social media to create, transform, and reimagine their sexual identity. Research by Steinke et al. (2017) showed that LGBTQIA+ youth spend significantly more time online as compared to their heterosexual counterparts. At the same time, Fox and Ralston's (2016) work demonstrated that social media is an informal learning platform for LGBTQIA+ youth during their identity exploration processes. As LGBTQIA+ identities remain highly disparaged in our offline communities, social media provides adolescents with important resources to explore, label, and practice disclosing their identity. Social media also affords users control and opportunity to rehearse their social interactions, as well as access identity-specific resources (we discuss this again in the pornography chapter (page 170))(Craig et al., 2021).

In their research specifically into the benefits of social media for LGBTQIA+ youth, Craig at al. (2021) developed a social media benefits scale (SMBS) in order to determine the five most used social media sites and what benefits (e.g., feeling connected, gaining information) were derived from the sites in order to understand and classify the potential to enhance well-being from each site. According to the research, social media sites offer critical opportunities for lesbian, gay, bisexual, trans, queer, and other sexual and/or gender minority youth to enhance well-being through exploring their identities, accessing resources, and connecting with peers. Through an exploratory factor analysis, the authors determined a four-factor solution that measured participants' use of social media for (1) emotional support and development; (2) general educational purposes; (3) entertainment; and (4) acquiring LGBTQIA+-specific information. This research showed the importance of social media participation for LGBTQIA+ youth and relied on the uses and gratifications (page 80) framework that we can build off of.

While that is all very positive and we want to make sure to highlight the good with the bad, like all other topics in this book, there is usually a negative element as well. De Ridder (2017) specifically looked into how heterosexual teenagers between the ages of 14–19 used social media to make sense of sexuality. Through the use of 14 focus groups, DeRidder concluded that teens are, in fact, making strong value judgments about sexuality on social media. Specifically, the research created a strong demarcation between "good" and "bad" sexual practices as expressed online. This hierarchical system points to a conservatism driven by social media's role in culture and society. DeRidder argues that social media have become a crucial battleground for sexual politics and that we should never downplay the importance of social media as a key area in the production of values and norms about sexuality. Furthermore, the author argues that we should not lose sight of the fact that social media is critical in deciding what kind of sexualities are supported, repressed, or disciplined. We continue this conversation in our pornography chapter.

MUSIC

While the Internet and social media are a tool for teens to learn about and form their identity, they are not the only way. For decades music has also contributed to our understanding of gender and sexuality. From classical to modern era, the lyrics within the songs show the audience- primarily the young demographic, that a woman's qualities should revolve around being passive, avoiding problems, and finding life fulfillment through the love and marriage of a man (Hughes, 2016).

As children grow up and expand their music scope, the lyrics in modern music share the Disney songs' standard message. The only difference is that modern songs made for adolescents and adults promote women's sexualization- other than that, patriarchy ideals and the negative gender stereotypes are still being promoted. As Milling (2015) states, the lyrics within modern songs represent women as sexual objects who carry no depth besides "boobs and backsides." The article continues by saying that the spread of these messages, especially in pop and hip-hop/rap music, promotes the patriarchy idea found within song lyrics, that women are the property of men. An example, as Lipana (2018) states in her article, are songs such as "Gold Digger" by Kanye West, "Talk Dirty" by Jason Derulo, and "No Limit" by G-Eazy. These songs suggest that women rank below men, and therefore women must rely on men. Songs like these explain that women are incapable without a strong, super-masculine man.

The symbolism within song lyrics is dangerous due to the lasting message spread from the very beginning when the child first interacts with music as a source of entertainment. The verses signal a negative stereotypical image of women; it teaches teenage girls the ideal behaviors and characteristics they should uphold. As Milling (2015) states, music lyrics are this way due to our society's misogynistic nature. The author says that when individuals are young, they are taught what is right and what is wrong, but through song lyrics, it introduces a different agenda than initially believed (Milling, 2015). This causes individuals to act and believe in particular views that are highlighted in song lyrics. With music, especially those found in Disney movies, being paired with the visuals representing a message of women being submissive to men, it teaches and promotes that idea. In this way, the research makes the argument that children move from Disney movies where gender is defined in one very clear way, to music where those rigid definitions are enforced and more colorful and adult. Many times, when listening to music, individuals are more involved with the catchy chorus or beats. But when analyzing the lyrics, it is seen that songs teach a message passed down from when individuals were young. Social media and media literacy seem to be our solutions out of this pattern. Through social media, individuals are able to express themselves in communities that are similar and supportive. Teens can learn that there are people out there "like them." Furthermore, as has been the case in nearly every chapter, media literacy is the key to children not taking messages from the media as fact, and more as one single representation.

QUESTIONS

My client is a 17-year-old boy who recently came out to his family as gay. His family disapproves and he says that he has no one in his life who understands. What is the media showing kids about sexuality?

The media representation of gender and sexuality is changing every day, and changing for the better. Numerous times while writing this book I have wanted to report a content analysis on media representation of gender, sexuality, race, and age, but such reports are now impossible. It wasn't that long ago when broadcast and cable were the media options and Ellen was the only self-identified queer person on the screen. Thankfully with streaming services, YouTube, and social media the media options are endless and so are the representations on the screen. What really hasn't changed so much is the formula. Disney movies taught us that everyone always lives happily ever after. Before it was the male and female, now it can be two women, two men, two non-binary people, but at the end of the movie, show, season, etc., the protagonists are always happy, or if not happy, at least resolved. Speaking specifically to this question, in every show about teens and sexuality, by the end of the season the friends and parents have come around to acceptance and everyone loves each other again. I'm reminded of the Hulu show *Love, Victor* which came out in 2020. In the show, Victor is a straight-A, Catholic, basketball playing attractive teenager in high school. Throughout the course of the first season, he slowly comes out to himself and his peers as being gay. At first his devout Catholic parents reject him, especially his mother who rattles off many reasons why this "choice" is not ok. By the next episode his dad has come around out of love for his son and not wanting to lose him, and a few awkward and painful episodes later, his mom stands up to her priest in defense of her gay son. This sends a very clear message to the viewer – if I come out to my parents, they will eventually accept me. As we know, this isn't always true in real life and is another way that the media is setting up unrealistic expectations. It is incredible that the media is an outlet for LGBTQIA+ teens, online kids can join networks and social groups for people who are like them, but when you turn to scripted programming the script is always the same. When this doesn't play out in real life the individual is left to think that they must be the problem, and not that the media is written to make money and the happy ending is what people want. Media literacy can help dissect this, and so can joining in these communities.

This new generation of young people are discussing sexuality in a way I never did. What does the research say about classification?

A growing number of young people are identifying as part of the LGBTQIA+ community, and many are challenging the preexisting binaries that were once held in gender and sexual identity in order to move forward toward a broader spectrum beyond man or woman and gay or straight. To start, let's make sure we have the acronyms in order. LGBTQ2S+, LGBTQ*, LGBTQ+, GLBT, LGBTTQ, LGBTQ2, and LGBTQIA refer to the array of sexual and gender identities that are not cisgender and heterosexual. They include lesbian, gay, bisexual, transgender, two-spirit, queer, questioning, intersex, and asexual. The asterisk (*) or plus sign (+) indicates there are other identities included that aren't in the acronym. Additional terms we have heard this year include pansexual and omnisexual.

Surprisingly, little research has been conducted that directly examines the use of identity labels or the identity development process among adolescents. According to Hammack et al. (2021) who set out to rectify this, the majority of extant research on this population has examined the social and psychological experiences of being a gender or sexual minority. In their research into understanding adolescent sexual and gender identity, Hammack et al. (2021) investigated the ways adolescents engaged with varying conceptions of identity. In their report the authors explain:

> While labels like "gay," "lesbian," and "bisexual" were once the only common options for sexual minorities and "man" or "woman" the only common options for gender identity, today new taxonomies have emerged or become more widespread and have challenged the notion that either sexual or gender identity are inherently binary. A distinction is now commonly made between *monosexual* identity labels such as "gay," "lesbian," or "straight," which signify a singular direction in which one's sexual attractions are oriented, and *plurisexual* identity labels such as "bisexual," "pansexual," and "queer," which typically signify attraction to multiple genders when referring to sexual identity. The label "queer" may signify attraction to multiple genders but also may signify a gender identity or a political or cultural identity intended to challenge sexual or gender normativity.
>
> (p. 7)

Through both survey data and interviews, Hammack et al. (2021) discovered a prolific and positive change in sexual classification. Specifically, the authors noted that the new vocabulary used by teens to describe gender and sexual identity challenges the prehistoric binary conceptions as well as normative ideas about sexuality and gender. This change has allowed adolescents to discuss variability in sexual desire and romantic attraction, as well as have more opportunity to understand themselves and their identity.

We have spent a lot of time talking about this issue lately and ultimately it is our opinion that the language young people are using to describe their own sexual identity is finally evolving to represent the actual diversity of experience that exists. This is a signal that teens have a more extensive vocabulary than previous generations and are able to express themselves in ways previous generations were unable to.

REFERENCES

Bem, S. (1983). Gender schema theory and its implications for child development: Raising gender-aschematic children in a gender-schematic society. *Signs, 4*, 598–616.

Butkowski, C. P., Dixon, T. L., Weeks, K. R., & Smith, M. A. (2019). Quantifying the feminine self(ie): Gender display and social media feedback in young women's Instagram selfies. *New Media & Society, 22*(5), 817–837. https://doi.org/10.1177/1461444819871669

Craig, S. L., Eaton, A. D., McInroy, L. B., Leung, V. W.Y., & Krishnan, S. (2021). Can social media participation enhance LGBTQ+ youth well-being? Development of the social media benefits scale. *Social Media + Society, 7*(1). https://doi.org/10.1177/2056305121988931

De Ridder, S. (2017). Social media and young people's sexualities: Values, norms, and battlegrounds. *Social Media + Society, 3*(4). https://doi.org/10.1177/2056305117738992

Fox, J., & Ralston, R. (2016). Queer identity online: Informal learning and teaching experiences of LGBTQ+ individuals on social media. *Computers in Human Behavior, 65*, 635–642. https://doi.org/10.1016/j.chb.2016.06.009

Golden, J. C., & Jacoby, J. W. (2017). Playing princess: Preschool girls' interpretations of gender stereotypes in Disney Princess media. *Sex Roles: A Journal of Research, 79*(5–6), 299–313. https://doi.org/10.1007/s11199-017-0773-8

Hammack, P. L., Hughes, S. D., Atwood, J. M., Cohen, E. M., & Clark, R. C. (2021). Gender and sexual identity in adolescence: A mixed-methods study of labeling in diverse community settings. *Journal of Adolescent Research, 37*(2). https://doi.org/10.1177/07435584211000315

Hoffner, C. (2008). Parasocial and online social relationships. In S. L. Calvert & B. J. Wilson (Eds.), *The handbook of children, media, and development* (pp. 309–333). Blackwell.

Hughes, L. (2016). Someday my Prince will come: How are gender roles enabled and constrained in Disney music, during classic Disney, the Disney renaissance, and modern Disney? *Honors Theses, 572.* https://egrove.olemiss.edu/hon_thesis/572

Hust, S. J., & Brown, J. D. (2008). Gender, media use, and effects. In S. L. Calvert & B. J. Wilson (Eds.), *The handbook of children, media, and development* (pp. 98–120). Blackwell Publishing.

Lipana, D. (2018, April 4). Gender stereotypes in music industry. *Medium.* https://medium.com/@dianalipana16/gender-stereotypes-in-music-industry-632a91666536

Maccoby, E. (1998). *The two sexes: Growing up apart, coming together.* Harvard University Press.

Mahon, C., & Hevey, D. (2021). Processing body image on social media: Gender differences in adolescent boys' and girls' agency and active coping. *Frontiers in*

Psychology, NA. https://link.gale.com/apps/doc/A662534466/AONE?u=calstate& sid=bookmark-AONE&xid=2b6b8012

Martin, C. L., & Ruble, D. (2004). Children's search for gender cues: Cognitive perspectives on gender development. *Current Directions in Psychological Science*, 13(2), 67–70. https://doi.org/10.1111/j.0963-7214.2004.00276.x

Meyer, S. L., Murphy, C. M., Cascardi, M., & Birns, B. (1991). Gender and relationships: Beyond peer group. *The American Psychologist*, 46(5), 537–539.

Milling, S. (2015, April 8). Popular music may represent women negatively. *Women's Matters Matter*. https://capitalcurrent.ca/archive/capitalnews/women-in-canada/2015/03/27/mainstream-music-is-representing-women-in-a-damaging-way/

Steinke, J., Root-Bowman, M., Estabrook, S., Levine, D. S., & Kantor, L. M. (2017). Meeting the needs of sexual and gender minority youth: Formative research on potential digital health interventions. *Journal of Adolescent Health*, 60(5), 541–548. https://doi.org/10.1016/j.jadohealth.2016.11.023

Weisgram, E. S. (2019). Reducing gender stereotypes in toys and play for smarter, stronger, and kinder kids. *American Journal of Play*, 12(1), 74–88. https://link.gale.com/apps/doc/A623444948/AONE?u=calstate&sid=AONE&xid=ea1cfbd8

Pornography

12

We feel compelled to start with an omission that neither of us had ever researched pornography before writing this book. We then spent what felt like years rummaging through the research, talking to professionals, listening to podcasts, and emerged no longer wondering why we have received so many questions surrounding pornography. It is a big topic with lots to uncover. Pornography is a black hole of media effects research. There is so much dense knowledge and most of it is terrifying. It is also inevitable. As a communication researcher, one of the reasons why I started studying media and media effects is because it is everywhere and affects everyone, and yet, very few people own up to the effects screen time is having on them. Pornography is much the same. The staggering statistics we will share in this chapter highlight the pervasive effects of pornography, and yet, it is often not discussed outside of professional settings. In this chapter we talk about nothing else. Questions that we answer include: *What are they seeing? What is porn these days? Why does this matter? What's the problem with exposure to pornography? Are there any benefits to children and teens watching pornography? I have a client who says her son is addicted to violent pornography. What should I say to her about it?*

The average age of a child the first time they see internet pornography is 11 years old (Rothman et al., 2020). Kids don't have to be looking for pornography; it is programmed to find them and because of this, online pornography was declared a public health crisis in the United States in 2016 (Rothman et al., 2020). A study by Livingstone and Helsper (2008) revealed that 44% of 12–17 year-olds had seen pop-up ads for pornography while doing something else, 41% of these tweens and teens visited a porn site accidentally when looking for something else, 28% received pornographic junk mail, nine percent had been sent pornography from someone they know, nine percent visited a porn site on purpose, and three percent had been sent porn from someone they met online. An additional study from 2007

DOI: 10.4324/9781003223412-12

reported that of children and teens who had been exposed to online pornography, 66% reported that all of their exposure was unwanted, leaving 44% to have sought it out (Wolak et al., 2007). Furthermore, 74% of young people from the same study said that adults should be very or extremely concerned about the problem of young people being exposed to Internet pornography (Mitchell et al., 2007). Updating some of this data in 2019, Putri et al. reported that highschoolers, specifically, viewed pornography about 12 times a week. It is apparent that children and adolescents' exposure to Internet pornography, whether purposeful or not, is increasingly common. The purpose of this chapter is to explain the research in pornography, answer frequently asked questions around the subject, and then offer tangible solutions to approaching these issues with teenagers.

NOT "ALL BAD" NOR "ALL GOOD"

In a 2020 report it was discovered that parents of 16- and 17-year-olds were either in denial or largely unaware of what their child viewed online, with the parents of teenage girls the most likely to be unaware their children were watching pornography (Waterson, 2020). The research, conducted as part of the United Kingdom's interest in introducing age-verification services for online pornography, found that pre-teens were often disturbed by being accidentally exposed to material. However, the report also found that online pornography provided a significant way for older gay, lesbian, and bisexual teenagers to understand their sexuality. It is in this way that pornography is not "all bad" nor "all good." For the most part, watching pornography before being cognitively or developmentally prepared for the content is jarring and comes with negative repercussions (e.g., adoption of aggressive sexual expectations and decreased sexual satisfaction), but it can also be used as a tool for sexual education under the right circumstances. It is up to the adult in the child's life to set the stage. Specifically, Waterson (2020) noted that "viewing pornography has been normalized among children from their mid-teens onwards, with more encountering it on networks such as Snapchat and WhatsApp than on dedicated pornography sites" (np). The study, which combined a survey of secondary school-age children with in-depth interviews and focus groups with parents, found that adult material was a prominent feature in British childhood. Almost half of teenagers aged 16 and 17 said they had recently seen pornography. However, it is believed that this figure is substantially lower than the true statistics because of respondents' awkwardness when faced with the question. Meanwhile, of the children who told researchers they had watched pornography, 75% of parents did not believe their children would have watched the adult material (Waterson, 2020).

What are they seeing? What is porn these days?

According to a recent content analysis, Fritz et al. (2020) coded 4,009 heterosexual scenes from two major free pornographic tube sites, Pornhub and Xvideos. The authors concluded:

> Overall, 45 percent of Pornhub scenes included at least one act of physical aggression, while 35% of scenes from Xvideos contained aggression. Spanking, gagging, slapping, hair pulling, and choking were the five most common forms of physical aggression. Women were the target of the aggression in 97% of the scenes, and their response to aggression was either neutral or positive and rarely negative. Men were the perpetrators of aggression against women in 76% of scenes. Finally, examining the 10 most populous categories, the Amateur and Teen categories in Xvideos and the Amateur category in Pornhub had significantly less aggression, while the Xvideos Hardcore category had significantly more physical aggression against women. This study suggests aggression is common against women in online pornography, while repercussions to this aggression are rarely portrayed.
>
> (p. 3041)

Why does this matter? What's the problem with exposure to pornography?

There are three main problems with children and adolescents being exposed to pornography. First, once we see and learn information, we cannot unsee or unlearn it. We are now responsible for that information and many young people are not yet ready to process what they see or reason it in their mind. Second, adolescents' exposure to Internet pornography is related to attitudes consistent with gender objectification, such as attitudes that support violence against women and the notion that women are sex objects. Third, many studies over the years have demonstrated a strong positive correlation between pornography consumption and sexual dissatisfaction (Perry, 2017). We will now review those each in more detail:

Sexualized Youth

Today, children are being sexualized earlier and earlier, in part because they are exposed to sexual material in movies, television, music and other media earlier than ever.

Even if young children can't understand sex or its role in relationships, the images they see can leave a lasting impression. It is a basic premise of marketing that what we watch, read, and direct our attention toward influences our behavior (see theoretical considerations (page 8) for more detailed information. And, as any marketer knows, sex sells. That's why we see products and services that have nothing to do with sex being marketed in increasingly sexualized ways (que the image of the supermodel in a bikini eating a Carl's Jr. burger on the hood of a car). If a child happens upon penetrative sex for the first time in a pornography before they have had an opportunity to discuss it with an adult, their understanding of that sex act will forever be influenced by what they saw on the screen. As a professional, you are more aware than anyone of the harmful effects of witnessing something before you are able to understand it. This can cause harmful or fearful associations, it can also lead to unrealistic expectations or understanding of "normal." It doesn't end there, ethnographical research explains that children will then share their new information about sex with their peers, thus potentially informing more children about sex before they are ready.

In a 2021 interview, Glennon Doyle, a famous author and wife of Abby Wambach, an equally famous soccer player, were answering questions about sex. Glennon has been open with the public about her sexuality and how she was married to a man for many years and has three children with him. She then met and married Abby and now refers to herself as a lesbian. She was discussing her first sexual encounter with Abby and was asked, "How did you know what to do?" Her response was brilliant and hinged on the idea that the only reason someone would ask her this question is because heterosexual sex is presumed to be "normal" and that we all know how to do it. She then spoke about learning how to have heterosexual sex from movies, shows, and pornography. Pornography is a lead teacher in sex and sex positions.

Gender Objectification and Women as Sex Objects

Most pornography is written and directed with the male gaze in mind. A meta-analysis of pornography's effect on attitudes toward gender revealed a significant positive association between pornography use and attitudes supporting violence against women (Hald et al., 2010). Exposure to Internet pornography primes and reinforces the idea that some women deserve, or enjoy, being harassed, sexually maltreated, or raped (Berkel et al., 2004). Additionally, exposure to Internet pornography is associated with the notion of women as sex objects by both adolescent girls and boys (Peter & Valkenburg, 2009). These views of women as sex objects minimize women to only their physical appearance as sexual playthings desperate to fulfill the desires of males (Peter & Valkenburg, 2009). Furthermore, pornography exacerbates aggressive behavior and negative attitudes toward women, especially among those predisposed for aggression (Allen & D'Allessio, 1995). Research consistently reinforces previously held understandings that exposure to sexual content increased the notion that women enjoy sexual aggression and rape (Brown & L'Engle, 2009). For many young people, pornography has become the default sex educator, meaning both male and female adolescents are being taught about male dominance and female submissiveness. As you can imagine, this is equally detrimental to boys and girls as they form their first sexual opinions and plans.

Furthermore, pornography teaches sexist and sexually objectifying understandings of gender and sexuality. For instance, in an experimental study among young men in Denmark, exposure to even non-violent pornography led to less egalitarian attitudes and higher levels of hostile sexism (Hald et al., 2013). And in a longitudinal study among US adolescents, increased use of pornography predicted more sexist attitudes toward girls two years later (Brown & L'Engle, 2009). What's more, numerous meta-analyses from 2000 and 2015 have found associations between watching pornography and actual violent behaviors (Malamuth et al., 2002; Wright et al., 2019). Aggression, largely by males and overwhelmingly against females, is common in pornography. Men who watch pornography often are more likely to practice, or desire, dominant, degrading practices, such as gagging and choking (Bridges et al., 2016). And women who watch pornography are more likely to practice, or desire, submissive practices (Sun et al., 2017). In fact, longitudinal studies among adolescents find watching pornography is linked to sexually violent behavior later in life. In a US study, people who watched violent pornography were more than six times as likely to engage in sexually aggressive behavior (Ybarra et al., 2011). As previously mentioned, this increased aggressive behavior of frequent sexual harassment has been found up to two years later.

Sexual Dissatisfaction

This third point is the least socially concerning of the three but the research is clear and so it is worth mentioning. Watching pornography sets up unrealistic expectations of sexual intercourse – whether that be in relation to time, size, your partner's reactions, dialogue, results, you name it, the porn that young people are watching is not frequently replicated in their bedroom. Wright et al. (2019) continued a long line of research investigating the influence of pornography on sexual health outcomes. Guided by sexual script theory and social comparison theory, Wright et al.'s study of heterosexual adults tested a conceptual model linking more frequent pornography consumption to reduced sexual satisfaction via the perception that pornography is a primary source of sexual information, a preference for pornographic over partnered sexual excitement, and the devaluation of sexual communication. The model was supported by the data for both men and women (Wright et al., 2019). It was discovered that pornography consumption frequency was associated with perceiving pornography as a primary source of sexual information, which was then linked to a preference for pornographic over partnered sexual excitement and the devaluation of sexual communication. Finally, results of the study indicated that preferring pornographic, to partnered, sexual excitement and devaluing sexual communication were both associated with less sexual satisfaction.

On the same coin of sexual dissatisfaction are unrealistic sexual expectations. Morelli et al. (2016) explain that with overconsumption of pornography, there is also a high instance of sexting behavior and alcohol consumption by young people. When investigating sexting, alcohol consumption, and other risky behaviors in relation to pornography consumption, the data indicated that young pornography consumers had a desire to reenact the plotlines viewed on pornography websites. The authors went further to explain that these desires appear to be expedited by the effects of alcohol consumption. One common behavior uncovered by the research were teens engaging in sexting behaviors with other young people (Morelli et al., 2016).

Furthermore, in their research on the effects of pornography, Maas et al. (2019) discovered a strong positive correlation between an increase in pornography viewing and adolescents engaging in more unprotected oral sex with all types of partners. Specifically, "pornography use among female adolescents and emerging adults specifically, has been linked with outcomes such as a higher likelihood of engaging in sex at a younger age, a higher number of sex partners, and a lower likelihood of using contraception" (p. 838). These are a direct connection between pornography consumption and the theoretical foundations we explained in Chapter 3 (page 36). Young people are watching pornography, learning from the behaviors they are seeing, especially if the actors appear to be satisfied, and they are then both expecting that reality and feel the expectation to perform.

SOCIAL LEARNING THEORY IN PORNOGRAPHY RESEARCH

Learning from media is to be expected but we are not alone in thinking that parents should be wary about their children and adolescents learning from pornography. Later in the chapter we will discuss the positive effects of viewing porn at an appropriate age and also what parents can do to mediate these effects, however, we have to go over a few more things first. To start, as we think is clear, learning from the more negative and harmful attributes of pornography is the biggest issue for children and teens. Using a social learning theory lens (page 8), Quadara et al. (2017) state that the idea of permissive sexual views (ex. premarital sex, casual sex) increases the likelihood that children and teens will engage in their "first time" sexual experiences at an earlier rate and age. With children and teens getting their sex education from pornography, it promotes unsafe "sexual health practices" like not using protection or unsafe anal or vaginal sex (Quadara et al., 2017). This means that with a lack of safe sexual education, it allows for children and teens to have a distorted view of sexuality, individuals having more sexual partners within their lifetime, and an increased risk of STDs and STIs.

In the most recent study of pornography effects that we could find, Maheux et al. (2021) examined the associations between adolescents' pornography consumption and their self-objectification, body comparison, and body shame. Here the researchers looked at how viewing pornography altered their self-image, and not simply the image of others. Responses to the survey were in line with what we see with the effects of viewing others. Results from a sample of over 200 mixed-gender sample of high school students, Maheux reported that both males and females were susceptible to pornography-related body concerns. This included high levels of self-objectification and body comparison, but not body shame. This brings us to our next question:

Could there be any benefits to adolescents watching pornography?

In order to present a fair argument, we must also introduce the two benefits the literature has described regarding pornography exposure. Paula Hall, author of *Sexual Diversity and Sexual Offending* explains that there are two positive benefits for individuals viewing pornography. Hall breaks these into two categories: education and entertainment. If viewed under the correct circumstances, pornography can function as education. Research by Litsou et al. (2021) also examined pornography use for sexual learning. Results from their meta-analysis revealed five key themes about "porn education." The themes were: learning the mechanics of sex; learning concerning sexual identities and sexualities; inadequate information through pornography; wrong lessons from pornography; and a need for more relevant sex education (Litsou et al., 2021). The authors concluded that "according to this dataset, pornography use can offer useful information about the mechanics of sex, and this is particularly pertinent for young gay men" (Litsou et al., 2021, p. 250). Following the study by Litsou et al., Rothman et al. (2021) collected data from over 1,000 individuals aged 14–24 years old on what sources of information from the past year they considered to be the most helpful about how to have sex (n = 600 adolescents aged 14–17 years old, and n = 666 young adults aged 18–24 years old). Results revealed that more males than females, and more self-identified bi-sexuals than heterosexuals, felt that pornography was better education tool than other sources they had available. Finally, results of the large national study showed that one-quarter of US young adults say that pornography is a helpful source of information about how to have sex and what they think that they are learning from it (Rothman et al., 2021). These findings are critical for professionals working with adolescents as it shows that teens feel they are learning more from pornography than from sex education classes taught in schools or from adults in their lives. The results from the study also bring us to Paula Hall's next category: entertainment.

In a very specific study Wallmyr and Welin (2006) asked 876 Swedish young people aged 15–25 years (555 females and 321 males) exactly why they watch pornography. The results from a year-long study revealed that although most had seen pornographic movies, the youngest boys reported viewing the most pornography. The male participants reported that the most common reason they viewed pornography was to get aroused and to masturbate, whereas the female participants stated that they viewed pornography out of curiosity. Whereas in the absence of pornography, the most frequent source of information about sexuality was peers (Wallmyr & Welin, 2006). These results point to the necessity of sex education to educate youth about sex and sexuality in order to counteract the messages they are receiving through pornography.

One of the most important things to know is that watching pornography is ubiquitous. However, in America talking about such issues like pornography are taboo. Not talking about porn makes it secretive, wrong, something to be ashamed of, etc., and as with all difficult subjects, open dialogue should be encouraged. When consumers are viewing consensual and ethical pornography for the purposes of education, research shows that there can be positive outcomes.

I have a client who says her son is addicted to violent pornography. What should I say to her about it?

Violent pornography is out there and in extreme cases, violent sex can be fetishized, and in those cases, violence must be present to have a satisfying sexual encounter. This is related to the main problems with children and adolescents being exposed to pornography discussed above (page 170). In essence, violent pornography exacerbates all of the worst qualities of the porn industry but is exciting and dangerous, and therefore, very attractive to some. What the question is asking is about mediation. The child is already watching violent pornography, so what now?

Mediation, either by a parent, therapist, caregiver, etc., has been shown to be effective at reducing the negative effects of television exposure on children (Chakroff & Nathanson, 2008). Scholars have also tested different strategies of mediation of online material, with varying levels of success. The three types of mediation, most frequently assessed by parental mediation, are – active, restrictive, and co-viewing. Each strategy has been shown to provide some level of benefit, and recently, this has been applied to exposure to pornography. For example, active mediation is active discussion of media content with a child. Restrictive mediation would be when parents set rules about their child's time spent online only after they catch the child visiting an inappropriate website, and co-viewing meditation is when the parent or caregiver watches the program with the child (Livingstone & Helsper, 2008). It is reasonable to suggest that the method of meditation taken by the parent/caregiver would alter the child or teens responses to pornography over someone who had not be restricted. Likewise, it is reasonable to suggest that children whose parents discuss the negative effects of online pornography exposure before the child is exposed to such content would differ in their objectification of women than children whose parents had the same discussion after they caught their child viewing inappropriate material online. Looking specifically at mediation effects, Smahelova et al. (2017) tested which approach (active, restrictive, or co-viewing) was the best method for reducing further pornography viewing. The study illustrated how the timing of parental mediation was a crucial element in the effectiveness of parental mediation. The study determined "children viewed less online pornography when they received active mediation *before* their first exposure to Internet pornography than when they received active mediation after their parents found out about their use of Internet pornography" (Smahelova et al., p. 15). Similarly, parental mediation research seems to substantiate the argument that active mediation is generally more effective than restrictive mediation (Livingstone & Helsper, 2008). While Smahelova et al. found that active discussion was best before the child or teen started watching pornography, they still found the active strategy to be better than the restrictive strategy which leaves the door open for continued mediation. As a communication scholar, I always view communication as the best strategy!

Other resources that may be useful are knowing about ethical pornography sites that are available. For example, Bellesa.co is a porn company run by women. According to the website:

> At Bellesa, we believe that sexuality on the internet should depict women as we truly are- as subjects of pleasure, not objects of conquest. Bellesa is a platform on which community members can find free and ethically sourced porn videos, read intimate erotic stories, explore sexual health articles on the Collective, shop for sex toys at BBoutique and watch the most authentic, pleasure-filled hd porn by Bellesa Films/Bellesa House.
>
> (np)

Providing an outlet for pornography that is void of the negative elements discussed above might be a good active mediation tool. There are also articles on the website that may be interesting to you if you are planning a mediation as they will give you information about ethical pornography.

As a final note regarding addiction to pornography, we have spent a lot of time discussing this and the research is all happening right now, which is exciting. The previous understanding in communication research used to be that we cannot be addicted to the media but we can be dependent. The definition of addiction is one of a physical reliance, while a dependency can be mental or emotional. This opinion has changed with the union of medical research into media areas. Earlier we talked about the dopamine effect on the brain in regards to video game addiction (page 56). We believe that the same logic can be extended to pornography. This is especially true when you consider that as increased levels of dopamine are pumped into your system from watching pornography can lead to a physical and painful withdrawal when that dopamine is reduced. This is also in line with the research to show that increased pornography consumption leads to decreased sexual encounters with a partner because you are not getting the same method of dopamine transfer that your body has come to rely on.

REFERENCES

Allen, M., & D'Allessio, D. (1995). A meta-analysis summarizing the effects of pornography II: Aggression after exposure. *Human Communication Research*, 22, 258–283.

Bellesa.co. www.bellesa.co

Berkel, L., Vandiver, B., & Bahner, A. (2004). Gender role attitudes, religion, and spirituality as predictors of domestic violence attitudes in white college students. *Journal of College Student Development*, 45, 119–131.

Bridges, A. J., Sun, C. F., Ezzell, M. B., & Johnson, J. (2016). Sexual scripts and the sexual behavior of men and women who use pornography. *Sexualization, Media, & Society*, 2(4). https://doi.org/10.1177/2374623816668275

Brown, J., & L'Engle, K. (2009). X-rated: Sexual attitudes and behaviors associated with U.S. early adolescents' exposure to sexually explicit media. *Communication Research*, 36(1), 129–151.

Chakroff, J. L., & Nathanson, A. I. (2008). Parent and school interventions: Mediation and media literacy. *The Handbook of Children, Media, and Development*, 552–576.

Fritz, N., Malic, V., Paul, B., & Zhou, Y. (2020). A descriptive analysis of the types, targets, and relative frequency of aggression in mainstream pornography. *Archives of Sexual Behavior*, 49, 3041–3053. https://doi.org/10.1007/s10508-020-01773-0

Hald, G. M., Malamuth, N. N., & Lange, T. (2013). Pornography and sexist attitudes among heterosexuals. *Journal of Communications*, 63, 638–660. https://doi.org/10.1111/jcom.12037

Hald, G. M., Malamuth, N. N., & Yuen, C. (2010). Pornography and attitudes supporting violence against women: Revisiting the relationship in nonexperimental studies. *Aggressive Behavior*, 36, 14–20.

Hall, P. (2014). *The pleasure, the power, and the perils of Internet pornography*. Published in Sexual Diversity and Sexual Offending, Routledge Press. www.taylorfrancis.com/chapters/edit/10.4324/9780429480034-10/pleasure-power-perils-internet-pornography-paula-hall

Litsou, K., Byron, P., McKee, A., & Ingham, R. (2021). Learning from pornography: Results of a mixed methods systematic review. *Sex Education*, 21(2), 236–252. http://doi.org/10.1080/14681811.2020.1786362

Livingstone, S., & Helsper, E. (2008). Parental mediation of children's internet use. *Journal of Broadcasting & Electronic Media*, 52(4), 581–599.

Maas, M. K., Bray, B. C., & Noll, J. G. (2019). Online sexual experiences predict subsequent sexual health and victimization outcomes among female adolescents: A latent class analysis. *Journal of Youth & Adolescence*, 48(5), 837–849. http://doi.org/10.1007/s10964-019-00995-3

Maheux, A. J., Roberts, S. R., Evans, R., Widman, L., & Choukas-Bradley, S. (2021). Associations between adolescents' pornography consumption and self-objectification, body comparison, and body shame. *Body Image*, 37, 89–93.

Malamuth, N. M., Addison, T., & Koss, M. (2002). Pornography and sexual aggression: Are there reliable effects and can we understand them? *Annual Review of Sex Research*, 11(1), 26–91. http://doi.org/10.1080/10532528.2000.10559784

Mitchell, K. J., Wolak, J. D., & Finkelhor, D. (2007). Trends in youth reports of sexual solicitations, harassment and unwanted exposure to pornography on the Internet. *Journal of Adolescent Health*, 20, 116–126.

Morelli, M., Bianchi, D., Baiocco, R., Pezzuti, L., & Chirumbolo, A. (2016). Sexting behaviors and cyber pornography addiction among adolescents: The moderating role of alcohol consumption. *Sexuality Research & Social Policy*, 14(2), 113–121.

Perry, S. L. (2017). Does viewing pornography reduce marital quality over time? Evidence from longitudinal data. *Archives of Sexual Behavior*, 46(2), 549–559. http://doi.org/10.1007/s10508-016-0770-y

Peter, J., & Valkenburg, P. (2009). Adolescents' exposure to sexually explicit internet material and notions of women as sex objects: Assessing causality and underlying processes. *Journal of Communication*, 59, 407–433.

Putri, G. A., Mulyadi, A., & Jupri. (2019). The phenomenon of social diversion related to teenagers interest in pornography sites. *International Journal Pedagogy of Social Studies*, 4(2), 45–52. https://ejournal.upi.edu/index.php/pips/article/view/19814

Quadara, A., El-Murr, A., & Latham, J. (2017, December 6). The effects of pornography on children and young people. *Australian Institute of Family Studies*. https://aifs.gov.au/publications/effects-pornography-children-and-young-people-snapshot

Rothman, E. F., Beckmeyer, J. J., Herbenick, D., Fu, T. C., Dodge, B., & Fortenberry, J. D. (2021). The prevalence of using pornography for information about how to have sex: Findings from a nationally representative survey of U.S. adolescents and young adults. *Archives of Sexual Behavior*, 50(2), 629–646. http://doi.org/10.1007/s10508-020-01877-7

Rothman, E. F., Daley, N., & Alder, J. (2020). A pornography literacy program for adolescents. *American Journal of Public Health*, 110(2), 154–156. http://doi.org/10.2105/AJPH.2019.305468

Smahelova, M., Juhová, D., Cermak, I., & Smahel, D. (2017). Mediation of young children's digital technology use: The parents' perspective. *Cyberpsychology: Journal of Psychosocial Research on Cyberspace*, 11(3). https://doi.org/10.5817/CP2017-3-4

Sun, C. F., Wright, P., & Steffen, N. (2017). German heterosexual women's pornography consumption and sexual behavior. *Sexualization, Media, & Society*, 3(1). https://doi.org/10.1177/2374623817698113

Wallmyr, G., & Welin, C. (2006). Young people, pornography, and sexuality: Sources and attitudes. *The Journal of School Nursing*, 22(5), 290–295. https://doi.org/10.1177/10598405060220050801

Waterson, J. (2020). *Porn survey reveals extent of UK teenagers' viewing habits*. Retrieved August 2021, from www.theguardian.com/culture/2020/jan/31/porn-survey-uk-teenagers-viewing-habits-bbfc

Wolak, J., Mitchell, K., & Finkelhor, D. (2007). Unwanted and wanted exposure to online pornography in a national sample of youth internet users. *Pediatrics*, 119, 247–257.

Wright, P. J., Sun, C., Steffen, N. J., & Tokunaga, R. S. (2019). Associative pathways between pornography consumption and reduced sexual satisfaction. *Sexual and Relationship Therapy*, 34(4), 422–439. http://doi.org/10.1080/14681994.2017.13 23076

Ybarra, M. L., Mitchell, K. J., Hamburger, M., Diener-West, M., & Leaf, P. J. (2011). X-rated material and perpetration of sexually aggressive behavior among children and adolescents: Is there a link? *Aggressive Behavior*, 37, 1–18. https://doi.org/10.1002/ab.20367

Risky Behaviors Around Sex, Drugs, and Alcohol

13

For our final chapter we are focusing on the issues that impact the oldest set of "kids" – the late teenagers. Since its inception media has glamourized sex, drugs, and rock and roll. The media has taught us how to drink, how to do drugs, when and why to do both of those, how often we should do them, and how drinking and drug use often leads to sex. In this book we have spent a lot of time introducing the concept that the media creates scripts for us to follow and how we learn our behavior by modeling what we see (page 8). Sex, drugs, and alcohol are prolific in mediated images, and it only pays to show the glamour. With recent technologies, buying drugs and alcohol have never been easier. In this chapter we review the literature on media and alcohol, prescription drugs, recreational drugs, e-cigarettes, music, and end with a discussion on the media as a "super peer." Specifically, we answer the questions: *Can it affect kids to hear their favorite artists promoting drug use?* and *Do people who listen to these songs are more likely to use drugs, especially the easily influenced kids and teens?* and *The media has always glamorized issues of sex, drugs, and rock and roll, but my clients seem so much more effected by the peer pressure of it all. I have heard that media is a "super peer," what does that mean in actionable terms?*

The National Center on Addiction and Substance Abuse conducted a recent study among teenagers and found that 70% of teens use social media every day. Meanwhile, teenagers who use social media are five times more likely to buy cigarettes, three times more likely to drink, and two times as likely to use marijuana than those who don't use social media (Hilliard, 2019). As we know, Facebook, Instagram, Snapchat, TikTok, and most other social media allow teens to share photos of their day-to-day life. What we don't always think about is that frequently, this is an unsupervised space where teens feel the behavior their parents would disapprove of can be freely shared (Moreno, 2014). Teens who are more active on social media and following each

DOI: 10.4324/9781003223412-13

other can see the posted content and what they are seeing becomes reality. In communication research, we call this the "cultivation effect" as part of the cultivation theory (page 27).

Applying this theory to social media has been happening for some time. For example, back in Myspace days, and more recently, on Facebook, Instagram, and Twitter, countless research hours have been dedicated to understanding how risky behaviors are being perpetuated. Several studies have shown that teens frequently contend with health-risk behaviors related to alcohol, drugs, and sexual behavior (Moreno, 2014). This includes texts, photos, and links to companies that sell alcohol. Moreno (2014) found a connection between high-risk behavior online and offline. In the study, teens who posted content about sex, drugs, or alcohol were more likely to engage in those substances offline as well. What makes this problematic is that the teens are not sharing the consequences (including hangover, feeling embarrassment, or getting a DUI), so the viewers see only the good and "cool" behavior (Moreno, 2014). This brings us back to social learning theory (page 8). As you will recall, we learn by watching, and we create, or cultivate, a perception of reality from the media. Social learning theory dictates that we learn more readily from positively endorsed behaviors and not when we are witness to a consequence. When teens only show the fun parts of drinking and parties and none of the repercussions, their viewers are led to believe that it is all positive and they too should choose those behaviors. Since this chapter is on various risky behaviors, we will now dive into each subject on its own.

ALCOHOL

Fortunately, we have laws against advertising drugs to consumers, but alcohol is not considered a drug by those who control the media. While it is technically illegal to advertise alcohol to persons under the age of 21, try keeping a 16-year-old off of social media! Just like all other companies, alcohol brands are getting bigger and bigger in digital marketing – they go where the customers are. Alcohol companies are not only posting ads; they are posting fun and creative videos that are easily shareable, have creative content, and include giveaways. Recently Keller (2020) reported that the content brands are posting on social media is normalizing daily drinking and binge drinking. Research completed by the Center on Alcohol Marketing and Youth (CAMY) at Johns Hopkins Bloomberg School of Public Health found that for each dollar the alcohol industry spends on youth advertising, young people drink three percent more each month. This knowledge is not new, back in 2006 Snyder et al. published a report explaining that the more alcohol advertising young people see, the more alcohol they consume, and that was mostly cable television! Thankfully, TikTok has banned all alcohol ads, and Instagram, Twitter, Snapchat, and YouTube are prohibiting alcohol ads directed at minors or advertisements that imply that drinking is somehow healthy. However, many advertising campaigns are still visible, and teens can mark their age higher when creating social media accounts (Suciu, 2020). In addition, not all alcohol related content teens are seeing on social media is paid advertising, in fact most of it is not. The social media companies are taking a stand against advertising, which is commendable, but the harmful effects of seeing influencers drinking is still available to young viewers.

When individuals scroll through social media, they are faced with constant exposure to alcohol-related content. As Keller (2020) described, individuals will post a photo of them drinking, friends gathering for a photo at a bar, all for a well-known alcoholic beverage company advertising their new product. With the increased casual production of alcohol-based content on social media, it brings a unique perception to the public. Seen through this media, and certainly through the eyes of a teenager, the content may be deemed as harmless, but according to research, it is evident that the posting of alcohol related content on social media sites increases the risk of alcohol "consumption, craving, and alcohol addiction" (Keller, np). Further, research has shown a positive correlation between posting images that contain alcohol from friends and alcohol beverage companies, and how much alcohol is consumed with a positive emotion behind the action (Keller, 2020). And as teens are circulating the social media scene at a high rate, researchers have identified that when teens follow a peer who posts themselves consuming alcohol, they are more motivated to "mimic" the behavior they see on social media (Keller, 2020).

To show this in action, Alhabash et al. (2016) conducted an experiment where researchers selected a group of individuals who were exposed to both bottled water ads and alcoholic beverage ads. At the end of the experiment the participants were each offered to choose a gift card to a bar or a coffee shop. Results showed that those who viewed the alcoholic beverage ads were 73% more inclined to choose the gift card to the bar over the 55% who opted to receive the coffee shop gift card. This research shows that through content on social media, an individual is more likely to get the urge to consume alcohol or choose alcohol as their preferred beverage choice (Ellis, 2019).

Adding to the impact of the media, because images shown in the media always glorify alcohol consumption, it gives viewers a false idea of what consuming alcohol is like – content creators never go into detail or show the reality of what the afterward and consequences may be like. In a study conducted by Lui et al. (2020), the authors investigated how the glorification adolescents give to alcohol follows them towards adulthood and into college. Looking specifically at alcohol and ethnicity, the authors learned that Asian Americans were most at risk for high levels of alcohol use due to their college beliefs from a young age being centered on alcohol in order to truly experience a college lifestyle. The study also showed that Asian Americans have increasingly high rates of contracting alcohol induced diseases due to the normalization of drinking in their own homes, their friend groups, and through media impact. The story doesn't end here. We will discuss other ethnic and racial groups as we get into the impact of music on drinking and drug use later in the chapter.

Wanting to understand exactly what alcohol content these young people are seeing on Instagram, Hendriks et al. (2020) conducted a content analysis of alcohol posts by Instagram influencers. The study focused on how Instagram influencers normally (63% of the time) post alcohol related posts, whether it includes active drinking or a bottle in the photo. These types of posts always have positive feedback and large amounts of young Instagram users are able to see it. Unfortunately, there is no regulation on these types of posts, making younger followers more susceptible to thinking that drinking is all fun and games. There is also no type of legislature against what age groups can view these posts, and the influencers are using their own private accounts to promote substance consumption to people of a vulnerable age, not the alcohol companies themselves, so there is no one to regulate. Recently, Instagram has been trying to change this and started requiring influencers to hashtag that it is an ad and attach the company to the post; but no one is paying attention to that, especially young people. Specifically, comments from underage viewers asked, 'What drink is that?' and when is it their turn to try it or post a photo just like it. The final results from Hendricks et al.'s study revealed that the posts that disclosed sponsorship information gained fewer likes and comments than the posts without disclosures. In their paper, the authors issue a warning explaining that "there is a lot to be concerned about in this context, especially since many minors can be exposed to influencers' alcohol posts, potentially leading to increased drinking among this vulnerable age group" (Hendricks et al., p. 1).

With adolescents joining social media at younger and younger ages, kids are likely to see a photo of alcohol or drug use before they reach 15 years old (Fitzgerald, 2020). In a student paper on the subject in one of my classes on children and media, the student wrote:

> This research made me think about how many times I was exposed to alcohol by the media when I was a teenager. I remember watching Teen Television shows and seeing them drink beer and I thought to myself I don't drink, I'm not that cool . . . When I was a teenager I used to think that drinking was very cool and it showed maturity. I remember watching That 70's Show where all the characters who are teens would drink beer. I wanted to be cool like them. I felt I was missing out.

We will let you connect the dots connecting viewing these images and mental health, but the point of this chapter was to get in writing how ubiquitous alcohol images are to teens and the overwhelming effects these images have on their choices.

DRUGS

Moving on from alcohol to drugs, and the image is still grim. It is now easier than ever for young teenagers to get their hands on illegal substances. The media plays a huge role in influencing adolescents to know about, pursue, and purchase drugs. Social media has created a loophole for teenagers, or almost anyone, to purchase illegal drugs under the radar. The pop culture scene is not shy about their use of drugs as they push it onto their audience, which makes it the norm. Prior to social media, and because drugs in our country are illegal, consumers would rarely see drugs in the media and it was difficult to purchase them. Now, every time a teenager turns to their social media apps there are people posting about drugs and alcohol. It is everywhere and society has accepted it.

Hilliard (2019) states that 75% of teens today are regularly exposed to drug related content (including smoking marijuana) on social media. Further, the author explained that when exposed to drugs in the media, the messages encourage teens to experiment the same way they see in through their screens. Social media posts related to drug use and drinking alcohol advertises a false perception to teens that partaking in these types of activities is exciting and positive, especially if they see friends and family having "fun" (Hilliard, 2019). Because the images are everywhere, teens have become desensitized to the harsh reality of drug use due to their personal media content, constant exposure, and witnessing their friends and family having a good time while engaging in drug activities online. With this type of content being normalized, it glamorizes such behavior and allows teens to think that this behavior is appropriate and safe (Hilliard, 2019).

According to the American Addiction Center, it is quite easy for people to purchase illegal drugs on the Internet. The center explains that drug use is no longer something that is limited to celebrities and strangers; now, friends and even family members can share a picture of a joint of marijuana, or even harder and more dangerous drugs with hundreds of contacts, all at the click of a button (American Addiction Center, 2020). In addition, a survey was conducted to see a correlation between social media use and drug use. Given what we already know about the relationship between social media and alcohol, it will come as no surprise that teenagers who use social media regularly are more likely to consume drugs as compared to teenagers who do not use, or simply spend less time, on social media. The research sheds light on the online drug trading world. The American Addiction Center calls this, the "digital underground," where the possibilities of buying drugs are limitless. With marijuana and ecstasy being the most popular party drugs, social media makes it easy to target young teens. Dealers have turned social media into a tool and use special symbols to sell and market their product. The American Addiction Center states, "dealers simply have images of their products as well as symbols (emojis) that, at a glance, convey the quality, purity, amount, and cost of the product, which ranges from weed to ecstasy" (np). This is a method dealers use to communicate secretly with clients, after a transaction is made, accounts are deleted to erase their tracks.

E-CIGARETTES

E-cigarettes, also known as vaping, are disposable or battery powered devices that are filled with flavored liquid that heats up and becomes vapor. Smoking, or vaping, has become so popular they earned their own section in the book! Vaping became popular in 2010 after on-the-go-size vape pens started coming out along with new flavors that would be especially attractive to the younger generations. In a 2019, a national youth tobacco survey found that 55% of teens tried vaping out of curiosity, 30% saw a friend or family use them, 22% enjoyed the availability of flavors such as mint, candy, fruit or chocolate, and 21% wanted to do tricks with them. Because of the amount of advertisements that are on all the social media platforms, seven in ten students are heavily exposed to vape advertisements. Meanwhile, roughly 37% of 12th graders reported vaping in 2018, compared with 28% in 2017. Knowing these statistics, it is not surprising that vaping use percentages have increased among students, especially boys who are twice as likely to use e-cigarettes. Due to limited lived experiences, teens are especially prone to underestimate the risk. When students were asked in a 2019 Centers for Disease Control and Prevention (CDC) National Youth Tobacco Survey which tobacco products they perceived as causing no harm or little harm 28% of respondents said e-cigarettes, compared to 9.5 percent for cigarettes. The CDC notes that many young people report using e-cigarettes because "they think they are less harmful than traditional cigarettes" (np).

Given the gift of hindsight, a student in my children and media class wrote: "I found that as a kid the media tried to push people to stop smoking tobacco and in doing so they turned to other forms of 'non-tobacco' smoking." The student admitted this in a class after reviewing ads that were prevalent in their childhood. After being shocked at the connection, the student discussed how their whole family smoked cigarettes and in elementary school the student learned how bad it was for the body. Thankfully my student never started smoking nicotine but they are part of a dying generation of people saved from nicotine from school programs like DARE and the like. Unfortunately, those programs lost funding, advertisers got more creative, manufacturers got more creative and here we are today with a rise in nicotine addictions and the media has contributed to the normalization and trend of using JUULs/vapes.

The way the media has promoted e-cigarette products is catered to a youthful audience; they intentionally do this to try and get the addictions and curiosity started at a young age. The way it is spoken about in the media further influences this perspective. In a content analysis on JUUL, a popular vape brand, online conversations for young age groups found the "primary reasons for youth use indicate the strong influence of social norms" further providing support that social platforms do indeed impact the perceptions of substance use (Bretat et al., p. 358). The analysis also referred to the conversation of age restrictions, and how it is indeed a barrier but not one that is too hard to go around.

As a communication professor who studies effects on children, I have always found the use of JUULs to be interesting. First, the primary users of JUULs are middle school and young high schoolers. Next, the JUUL is made to look like a flash drive – kids that age don't know what a flash drive is! They are all on the cloud! And therefore, the JUUL is designed for kids to be able to sneak the device past parents, and other adults, who are all too familiar with a flash drive and don't think twice when we see it sticking out of a teen's computer. JUUL flavors are also targeted specifically to children, they are fruity and sweet, and taste nothing like their cigarette ancestors. After I learned about the primary age of JUUL users I went to a 14-year-old to ask about them. The teenager laughed when I asked if they had ever heard of them and explained that JUULs are as common as cell phones in their middle school. Much more common than a physical digital storage device! Next the teen said that in all of their classes, kids are JUULing in class. They said it is a game they play when the teacher's backs are turned – who can JUUL before the teacher turns back around. On the JUUL box there is a surgeon general's warning and a label saying that "you must be 18 to purchase." When I asked the teen how all these 13- and 14-year-olds are getting the JUUL they laughed again. They then explained that "all you have to do is click the 'yes I am 18 years old' box on the website and they send it to you in the mail. No one ever checks." In this way, the media, the companies, and the teens are all working against parents and teachers to deliver e-cigarettes to underage teens.

All this being said, there is good news in 2021 regarding vaping and teens. In October 2021 the CDC reported 11.3% of high school students and less than three percent of middle school students said they recently used e-cigarettes and other vaping products (Park-Lee et al., 2021). According to the Associated Press, these findings indicate that teen vaping use dropped about 40% from 2020 to 2021 (Perrone, 2021). Last year, nearly 20% of high school students and 4.7% of middle schoolers said they'd recently vaped. This is obviously excellent news and is attributed to the pandemic. As the middle schooler explained to me – kids vape in school. If you take away the in-person school and peer pressure, and add in in-person masks, the combination makes vaping during class even harder, therefore, fewer students feel compelled to vape. Time will tell if these behaviors begin again when schools get back to normal.

PRESCRIPTION DRUGS

Moving on to different types of drugs, prescription medication misuse and abuse is a major health problem globally, and a number of recent studies have focused on exploring social media as a key factor (Sarker et al., 2020). Given the high occurrence of discussing drug use online, Kim et al. (2017) used twitter in order to complete their research on drug abuse and addiction. Results highlighted the fact that substance use, and related communication for drug use promotion, is extremely prevalent on social media. We have learned through theoretical explanations (page 7) that the effect of these mentions, lack of consequence, and ease of availability of prescription drugs is a recipe for disaster. Looking specifically into social media and opioid use, Chary et al. (2017) analyzed mentions of misuse of prescription opioids on twitter and found a strong positive correlation between the number of tweets referencing the misuse of prescription opioids with the state-by-state national surveys on drug usage and health estimates of misuse of prescription opioids. This indicates that social media is a mirror for what is happening in society. The Addiction Center explains it well when they say,

> young people experimenting with drugs and alcohol is nothing new; however, social networking sites are offering new and dangerous opportunities for adolescents to be exposed to drugs. Teens are

uniquely vulnerable to the effects of what they see on social media, as this age group is highly susceptible to peer influences and pressure. Sites like Instagram, Facebook, and Snapchat provide an environment where kids are exposed to famous and normal people alike engaging in risky behaviors involving drugs and alcohol.

(Hilliard, np)

Furthermore, research into drug use, media, and teens often come to the same conclusion: FOMO. Teens have a fear of missing out, and prescription drug use is no different than alcohol.

Stepping outside of social media, Fogel and Shlivko (2016) found reality television to be associated with prescription drug misuse among viewers. In their research, the authors concluded that watching a reality television show and identifying with the characters were each related to greater incidences of drug use. Results also demonstrated that following the reality television character on Twitter had an even greater effect on the likelihood of drug misuse. The authors indicated that there was no cultivation effect (page 27) found, which means that these shows were not creating a reality where drug use was "normal," but instead were actively convincing and persuading the viewers to use drugs.

MUSIC

A medium well known to promote both alcohol and drug use of all kinds is music. When adults heard Miley Cyrus singing about drugs in her 2013 comeback hit, "We Can't Stop," they were shocked. That, in fact, if they realized that "dancing with molly" was not a reference to a friend and everyone "trying to get a line in the bathroom" was not referencing the everlasting wait in front of the lady's room. How is Miley Cyrus singing about drugs? Isn't she the girl playing Hannah Montana on the Disney Channel? She, just as her fans, have grown up since the Hannah Montana days, and adults have to face a new reality: *Can it affect kids to hear their favorite artists promoting drug use?*

Miley Cyrus has come a long way from her last party song's "My Tummy's Turnin' and I'm Feelin' Kinda Homesick" to snorting lines in the club's bathroom. But she is not the only one singing about drugs. According to Preidt (2018), 42% of hit songs have references about substance use. In addition, 34% of rap songs on the Billboard Hot 100 list between 2007 and 2017 contained at least one reference to drugs or alcohol (Gonzales, 2020). *Do people who listen to these songs are more likely to use drugs, especially the easily influenced kids and teens?*

It's not quite that simple. Researchers have learned that there is a connection between music and risk-taking behavior. In their work on media exposure and drug and alcohol use among adolescents, Primack et al. (2009) found that high schoolers who listen to four hours or more music a day were significantly more likely to use marijuana than those who listened less than four hours. This is also in line with research into cultivation theory, which proposes four hours a day to be a somewhat magic number in relation to cultivating a new vision of reality (page 27). In addition, Chen et al. (2006) investigated music, substance abuse, and aggression and found that listening to rap music was positively correlated with teens' drug use and aggressive behaviors. The findings suggest substance use and aggressive behaviors are related to the exposure of music containing references to drugs and violence, such that as one increases, so does the other. While it doesn't necessarily mean a child who loves to sing out loud how they are "trying to get a line in the bathroom" will end up doing so, taking from our understanding of social learning theory and cultivation theory, it seems clear that popular culture influences adolescents' choices and behavior and makes these risky behaviors more attractive, consequence free, and normal.

Looking at different genres, Motyka and Al-Imam (2019) found that many genres in today's popular music have drug or alcohol references in their lyrics: nine percent of pop, 14% of rock, 20% of hip hop and R&B, and 77% of rap. It is almost inevitable for adolescents to be exposed to some type of drug reference, especially when it is constantly being promoted. Furthermore, Motyka and Al-Imam (2019) found that certain genres of music perpetuate drug use and culture more than others. In addition, Tettey et al. (2020) specifically looked into how hip-hop lyrics promote drug use and explained the skyrocketing rate of promotion and glamorizing of drug use in hip-hop music. The research went on to explain that while the promotion of drug use can be found in any genre of music, hip-hop comes in at the top. While this on its own is a problem, content analysis of hip-hop music has shown that now musicians are promoting heavier drugs like promethazine, and pills such as

Xanax, in their songs. Things that are once again, easy for young listeners to get their hands on, are things they have heard of, and therefore, have a schema for, and are things young viewers have no idea how dangerous they are. One of the lyrics that was analyzed by Tettey et al. (2020) was written by the rapper Future. The lyrics say: "My ambitions as a rider/Sippin' on lean getting higher/N**** I'm a codeine buyer/No you not a foreign whip driver." A few minutes on the Internet after hearing this music and any teen knows what to buy and how easy it is to get.

As mentioned above, lyrics have the power to move people and when adolescents listen to songs like "10 crack commandments" by The Notorious B.I.G., all they are listening to is how this famous rapper followed these commandments to be successful in drug dealing. These types of lyrics not only mention the use of drugs, but also glorify drug dealing. There are some songs in hip hop and rap that talk about the artist's struggles with addiction but are often misunderstood by young people as something positive because they don't understand the consequences of substance abuse. This is especially dangerous for teens who either haven't experienced, or witnessed, the negative effects of these drugs. While music provides ways for young people to express their feelings and emotions, it can also help them discover their identity, one that the artists are all too happy to involve drugs and alcohol. The problem comes when teen consumers start imitating the artists and imagining they need to do what the artist sings about in their songs. The most troublesome references songs make are glamorizing drug use, talking about suicide as a solution, portraying graphic violence, and using sex to control women or value them based on their looks. All this leads to the conclusion that adults should always pay attention to their child's playlist. If you notice repetitive destructive themes, it's essential to discuss with the child about the song and messages they are getting and how they are encoding those messages.

THE MEDIA AS A "SUPER PEER"

The media has always glamorized issues of sex, drugs, and rock and roll but my clients seem so much more effected by the "peer pressure" of it all. I have heard that media is a "super peer," what does that mean in actionable terms?

As we hope is clear from the chapter, the media is absolutely a "super peer." A review of the literature explained above demonstrates that exposure to alcohol and drug-related advertising, promotion, and social media posts are able to predict both the onset of drinking and increased alcohol and drug consumption among adolescents. In addition, in this chapter we spent a significant amount of time discussing research that found exposure to peers' alcohol and drug-related social media content, such as images and videos of drinking, predicted alcohol and drug consumption both concurrently and prospectively. Elmore et al. (2017) explained it really well when they said,

> although youth have opportunities to observe substance use norms from their own peer group, media messages about substance use offer additional socialization opportunities beyond direct social contacts. When operating as a "super peer", media messages serve as a potentially powerful and influential source of information about alcohol and tobacco use.
>
> (p. 378)

In actionable terms, the media is a conglomerate of all of a teen's friends, acquaintances, role models, people they love, people they hate, people they want to emulate, etc. Taking from theories of communication and psychology, it becomes easy to see that teens look to the media to show them how to behave, think, dress, act, and essentially be as a person. Finally, teens and adolescents spend more time with media than they do in school, with their family, or with their friends and so it is natural that they would place more weight on learning from, and impressing, on social media. Simply put, the media is not a "peer," it is millions of "peers" all sending one very clear message glorifying consumption.

REFERENCES

Alhabash, S., McAlister, A., Kim, W., Lou, C., Cunningham, C., Quilliam, E., & Richards, J. (2016). Saw it on Facebook, drank it at the bar! Effects of exposure to Facebook alcohol ads on alcohol-related behaviors. *Journal of Interactive Advertising*, 16(1), 44-58. https://doi.org/10.1080/15252019.2016.1160330.

American Addiction Center. (2021). Retrieved August 2021, from https://america-naddictioncenters.org

Chary, M., Genes, N., Giraud-Carrier, C., Hanson, C., Nelson, L. S., & Manini, A. F. (2017) Epidemiology from Tweets: Estimating misuse of prescription opioids in the USA from social media. *Journal of Medical Toxicology*, 13, 278–286. https://doi.org/10.1007/s13181-017-0625-5

Chen, M. J., Miller, B. A., Grube, J. W., & Waiters, E. D. (2006). Music, substance use, and aggression. *Journal of Studies on Alcohol*, 67(3), 373–381. https://doi.org/10.15288/jsa.2006.67.373

Ellis, M. E. (2019, October 16). The role social media plays in alcohol addiction. *Alta Mira Recovery*. www.altamirarecovery.com/blog/the-role-social-media-plays-in-alcohol-addiction/

Elmore, K., Scull, T. M., & Kupersmidt, J. B. (2017). Media as a "super peer": How adolescents interpret media messages predicts their perception of alcohol and tobacco use norms. *Journal of Youth and Adolescence*, 46, 376–387. https://doi.org/10.1007/s10964-016-0609-9

Fitzgerald, K. (2020, February 18). The influence of social media on alcohol use. *The Recovery Village*. www.therecoveryvillage.com/alcohol-abuse/social-media-alcohol/

Fogel, J., & Shlivko, A. (2016). Reality television programs are associated with illegal drug use and prescription drug misuse among college students. *Substance Use & Misuse*, 51(1), 62–72. http://doi.org/10.3109/10826084.2015.1082593

Gerbner, G., Gross, L., Morgan, M., & Signorielli, N. (1986). Living with television: The dynamics of the cultivation process. In J. Bryant & D. Zillman (Eds.), *Perspectives on media effects* (pp. 17–40). Lawrence Erlbaum Associates.

Gonzales, M. (2020, March 2). Rap music and substance use: Addiction and mental health. *Drug Rehab*. Retrieved August 2021, from www.drugrehab.com/featured/substance-use-and-rap-music/

Hendriks, H., Wilmsen, D., Dalen, W. V., & Gebhardt, W. A. (2020). Picture me drinking: Alcohol-related posts by Instagram influencers popular among adolescents and young adults. *Frontiers in Psychology*, 10. http://doi.org/10.3389/fpsyg.2019.02991

Hilliard, J. (2019, July 16). The influence of social media on teen drug use. *Addiction Center*. www.addictioncenter.com/community/social-media-teen-drug-use/

Keller, A. (2020, February 28). Social media and alcohol. *Drug Rehab*. www.drugrehab.com/addiction/alcohol/influence-of-social-media/

Kim, S., Marsch, L., Hancock, J., & Das, A. (2017). Scaling up research on drug abuse and addiction through social media big data. *Journal of Medical Internet Research*, 19(10), e353. www.jmir.org/2017/10/e353

Lui, P. P., Berkley, S. R., & Zamboanga, B. L. (2020). College alcohol belief and alcohol use: Testing moderations by cultural orientations and ethnicity. *Journal of Counseling Psychology*, 67(2), 184–194. https://doi.org/10.1037/cou0000374

Moreno, M. A. (2014). *Influence of social media on alcohol use in adolescents and young adults*. www.ncbi.nlm.nih.gov/pmc/articles/PMC4432862/

Motyka, M., & Al-Imam, A. (2019). Musical preference and drug use among youth: An empirical study. *Research and Advances in Psychiatry*, 6(2), 50–57.

Park-Lee, E., Ren, C., & Sawdey, M. D. (2021). Notes from the field: E-cigarette use among middle and high school students – National Youth Tobacco Survey, United

States, 2021. *MMWR Morbidity and Mortality Weekly Report 2021*, 70, 1387–1389. http://doi.org/10.15585/mmwr.mm7039a4

Perrone, M. (2021, September 30). Big drop in US teen vaping seen with COVID school closures. *The Associated Press.* https://apnews.com/article/coronavirus-pandemic-business-science-health-tobacco-industry-regulation-42c74433853293af2ea65caa10e9cb7e

Preidt, R. (2018). 1 in 3 hit songs mentions substance abuse, smoking. *ABC News.* abcnews.go.com/Health/Healthday/story?id=4510327

Primack, B. A., Kraemer, K. L., Fine, M. J., & Dalton, M. A. (2009). Media exposure and marijuana and alcohol use among adolescents. *Substance Use & Misuse*, 44(5), 722–739. https://doi.org/10.1080/10826080802490097

Sarker, A., DeRoos, A., & Perrone, J. (2020). Mining social media for prescription medication abuse monitoring: A review and proposal for a data-centric framework. *Journal of the American Medical Informatics Association*, 27(2), 315–329. https://doi.org/10.1093/jamia/ocz162

Snyder, L. B., Milici, F. F., Slater, M., Sun, H., & Strizhakova, Y. (2006). Effects of alcohol advertising exposure on drinking among youth. *Archives of Pediatrics and Adolescent Medicine*, 160(1), 18–24. http://doi.org/10.1001/archpedi.160.1.18

Suciu, P. (2020, February 6). Alcohol ads on social media could encourage underage drinking. *Forbes.* www.forbes.com/sites/petersuciu/2020/02/06/alcohol-ads-on-social-media-could-encourage-underage-drinking/

Tettey, N., Siddiqui, K., Llamoca, H., & Nagamine, S. (2020). Purple drank, sizurp, and lean: Hip-hop music and codeine use, a call to action for public health educators. *International Journal of Psychological Studies*, 12(11). http://doi.org/10.5539/ijps.v12n1p42

AAP guidelines 23, 36–37, 39–41, 43, 46, 60, 65–66, 70, 75, 107–108
active co-viewing *see* co-viewing
addiction 41, 51–52, 99–100, 110, 180, 184, 186, 191–192, 195
adolescent development 6–7, 30–31, 39–41, 68, 80, 106, 111, 118, 122, 135, 139, 146, 163, 167, 188, 194
Adolescent Sleep Working Group 119
age eight 15–16, 23, 27–28, 30, 61, 73, 107
aggression 17, 20, 29, 31, 95–98, 103–104, 112, 118, 172, 174, 194
aggressive behavior 20, 28, 62, 94–96, 98, 102, 117–118, 174–175, 194
aggressive thoughts 98, 117–118
alcohol use 41, 187, 194
Alicia Kozakiewicz 87, 90
American academy of pediatrics x, 36, 43, 48, 60, 107
American addiction center 189
American Psychological Association 100–101
anorexia *see* disordered eating
antisocial behavior 62
anxiety *see* mental health

baby boomer 75
Baby Einstein 54–55, 129
background television 38, 43–44, 47
bedtime 38, 60, 67–68, 108, 119
behavior health *see* behavior outcomes

behavior outcomes 2–4, 8–10, 15–20, 25, 27–29, 31–32, 37, 40–41, 46, 49–51, 59, 67–68, 84, 94–98, 100, 102, 113–114, 117–118, 135, 160, 173–176, 184
Bellesa 180
bisexual *see* LGBTQIA+
Bobo doll experiment 8, 20, 28, 97
body dysmorphia *see* disordered eating
body image 19, 25, 113, 117, 139–159, 161
body mass index (BMI) 11, 38–39, 52, 64, 67, 120–121
British food commission 65
bulimia *see* disordered eating
bullying 59, 115, 148

Canada's center for media literacy 30
caregiver engagement 41, 122
cell phone *see* smartphone
center for disease control (CDC) 23, 190, 192
Charlotte's Web 55
child development 2, 12–20, 38–40, 44–50, 54–55, 59–62, 106–107, 114, 117, 122, 129, 134, 155–157
civic engagement 69
cognitive development 1, 5–8, 12–13, 20–21, 31, 38–39, 45–50, 61–62, 66, 94, 102, 128, 156–158
cognitive impacts of digital workgroup 47
cognitive processing 13

common sense media 24, 31, 37, 71, 108–109, 142
community building 101
comprehension 39, 48, 61, 127–128, 131
consequences 6, 57, 72, 93, 108, 110, 114, 118–120, 146, 185–187
content 75, 91, 148
content creation 109
cortisol 98, 120
council on communications and media 37, 39–40, 47, 49, 52, 65, 68, 107, 112
COVID-19 pandemic ix, x, 36, 41, 44, 93, 107, 124, 134, 139, 146, 192
co-viewing 25–26, 37, 40, 43, 69, 113, 179
cultivation theory 27–28, 33, 74, 144–145, 185, 194
current events 69, 40
cyberbullying 82–84, 114–116

depression see mental health
desensitization 117–118
developmental screening 1–2, 5
diagnostic and statistical manual (DSM) 99–100
digital books 39
digital footprint 85
digital learning see virtual learning
digital native 30, 135
Discord 89
Disney 29, 158–160, 164–165
disordered eating 11, 117, 139–151
diversity 160, 168
doom scrolling 26, 150
drugs 9, 28, 184

e-cigarettes 184, 190–192, 197
educational programming 37, 39, 43, 48–49
Ellen Degeneres 33, 165
emotional effects 68, 90, 98, 113, 126, 132

emotional emancipation 7
emotional regulation 2, 5, 38, 51, 114
encoding 12–13, 156, 195
e-reading 108–109
executive functioning 39, 46–47, 62–63
extremist groups 88–90

face tune 136, 145, 150
Facebook x, 80–81, 85, 144, 147–150, 152, 154, 161, 184, 185, 19, 196
fake news 24–25
Family Guy, The 9
family media use plan 40, 60, 109, 111, 113
family programming 75, 142
fear of missing out (FOMO) 148, 193
firearms see weapons
first-person shooter game 89, 95, 98
fitspiration 19, 146
flourishing 63
food advertising 9, 41, 52, 65–66, 121
food marketing see food advertising
Future (the rapper) 195

gaming disorders 41, 99–100, 103
gay see LGBTQIA+
gender 7, 155–161, 63, 72–73, 141–142, 152, 155, 167, 174
gender development 157–158
gender objectification 174
gender schema theory 156–157
Generation Z (Gen Z) 75
google classroom see video chat
groomers see grooming
grooming 86–87, 89
guns see weapons

Harry Potter 55
heterosexual 143, 163, 167, 172–175, 177
home life 7, 106, 107, 110, 187
homework 60, 63, 111, 135
homosexual see LGBTQIA+
Hulu 66, 166

imaginary play 3–4, 16, 94
importance of media literacy 24
impulse control 39, 99
increased cognition 101, 103
individual differences 11–12, 74
infant development 1–2, 38–40, 43–50,
    128, 132
information processing theory 12–20, 97
Instagram x, 25–26, 28, 81–83, 85,
    135, 141, 144, 147–151, 161,
    184–187, 193
institute of medicine 65
interactive media 55, 62, 69, 82, 114
interactivity see interactive media
International Compendium of Diseases
    (ICD) 99
internet gaming disorder (IGD) 100,
    103
Internet safety 79
interpersonal relationships 4, 7, 63,
    101, 114, 142, 157
interracial relationships 73
iPad 88, 126–128

JUUL see e-cigarettes

Kanye 164
Kim Kardashian 25

language development 4–5, 38, 47, 128
late adolescence 7
latency phase 59
latent variable 148–149
learning from media 8–11, 16, 25,
    28–29, 33, 37–38, 55, 124, 126–128,
    136, 156–157, 163, 176, 196
learning process 13, 15, 17–20, 124
LeBron James 30
lesbian see LGBTQIA+
LGBTQIA+ 33, 84, 143, 162–163,
    165–168, 171, 173, 177
literacy 3–4, 39, 40, 44, 49–51, 62–63,
    108–109, 124, 127–129, 131–132
long term memory 13–18

loneliness see mental health
Love, Victor 166

manifest variable 148–149
M-CHAT 1–3
mealtime 38, 54, 60, 67
media and young minds see AAP
    guidelines
media literacy 22, 61, 66, 76, 88, 104,
    136, 165–166
mediation 179–182
media violence 15, 95, 112, 117
mental health 31–32, 36, 41, 60–61,
    63–64, 69–70, 86, 95, 99–101, 103,
    106–107, 110–111, 113–118, 135,
    143–149, 188
Messenger Kids 60–69
Michelle Obama 64, 74
middle adolescence 7
middle childhood 5, 7, 24–25, 59–61,
    64, 66, 68, 84, 91, 118, 129,
    191–192, 197
middle school students see middle
    childhood
Miley Cyrus 193
mobile phone see smartphone
modeling behavior 8, 17–18, 32, 97, 155
music 164–165, 173, 193–195

negative outcomes 61–62, 94–95,
    124–126, 129–132, 176
non-binary 152, 160, 162, 166, 168
Notorious B.I.G 195

obesity 9, 11, 21, 31, 38, 41–42, 45,
    48–49, 52–54, 59, 64–67, 120–121
Omegle 85
online citizenship 37, 40
online predator 79–80, 84–86, 89–90
opioid use see prescription drugs

pandemic 36, 41, 44, 70, 107, 124,
    139, 146, 192
parasocial relationships 71

PBS Kids 37
personhood 6
physical activity 2, 11, 37, 40, 45, 52, 60, 63, 65, 75, 99, 109–111, 121, 143
physical effects 62–63, 60–61, 64–65, 93, 98–100, 113, 120–121
physical health 1–2, 6, 32, 36–37, 52, 60–61, 64–65, 99–100, 106–107, 113–114, 118
Piaget 12–13, 61, 94, 156
play 3–4, 8–10, 16, 29, 38–40, 44–48, 53–56, 89–90, 132–133
pornography 170
positive outcomes 29, 49, 61–62, 68–69, 94–95, 124, 127, 130–132, 178
prescription drugs 184, 192–193, 195
prime time 33, 75
problematic internet use 110–112
problem solving 2, 46, 101–102
process model 12–18
prosocial effects 63, 69, 94–95, 101–102, 117
prostituting 90

quarantine 15, 146
queer see LGBTQIA+

race and ethnicity 32–33, 60, 70–74, 103–104
racial identity 72–73
reading see literacy
reality television 11, 193
Reddit 85
resonance see cultivation theory
restrictive co-viewing see co-viewing
risk-taking behaviors 7, 194

safety concerns 41, 82
satiety 53, 65–67, 120, 122
schema theory 28, 156–157
school readiness 3, 5, 46
screen time statistics 23, 31–32, 72, 83–85, 93, 97, 107–112, 119, 147, 170–172, 184, 189

scripts 10–11, 13–15, 17, 19, 28, 74, 184
self-esteem 5–6, 22, 25, 31, 72, 86, 90, 141–145, 149
self-harm 115–116
Sesame Street 37, 39, 48–50, 53–54, 68–69, 95, 128
sex 9–11, 19–21, 28, 41, 84–86, 106, 112, 117, 155, 184
sex education 163, 171, 176–178
sex objects 164, 173–174, 180
sexting 19–20, 175–176
sexual behaviors 9, 15, 41, 176, 185
sexual dissatisfaction 173, 175
sexuality 117, 155, 171–174, 177–180
short term memory 13–14
sleep 1, 37–41, 52–53, 59–60, 67–68, 100, 107, 109, 111, 113–114, 118–122
sleep problems 31, 68, 114
smartphone 32, 47, 50, 83, 10, 112–113, 115, 119, 191
Snapchat 23, 81, 85, 144, 171, 184, 186, 193
social avoidance 114–115
social cognitive theory see social learning theory
social comparison theory 175
social competency 2, 6–7
social development 3–6, 38–40, 44–46, 49, 55, 59, 62, 114, 129, 132, 150, 155–158
social isolation 69, 99–100, 115, 135
social learning theory 8–29, 32–33, 74–76, 97, 141, 176, 185, 194
social media 14–21, 24–29, 40–41, 66, 69–75, 79–81, 83–85, 89–90, 109, 114–119, 136, 139–140, 143–152, 155–165, 184–190, 192–193, 196
social media influencer 14, 71, 109, 144–145, 150, 186–188
stereotype 33, 71–74, 157–160, 162, 164
suicidal ideation 116
suicide 106, 113–116, 147–148, 195
super peer 184, 195–196

support groups 116
support networks 40, 69
surveillance 1, 3, 5, 81, 109

tablet use 23, 30, 43, 47, 50, 52–53,
    129–133
tantrum 51, 57
teens 7–9, 14, 18–20, 23, 25–27, 31,
    33, 64, 79–80, 82–84, 90, 93, 96,
    98–99, 101–102, 107–110, 114–116,
    118–121, 124–126, 133–136,
    139–148, 156–157, 160–168,
    170–171, 176–179, 184–196
TikTok 14, 23, 26, 28, 34, 81, 85, 113,
    116, 144, 150, 184, 186
tobacco 41, 190, 196
toddlers 1, 4, 25, 37, 39, 43–44, 47–48,
    51, 53–54, 128, 132
toys 3, 44, 47, 142, 159–160
traditional media 40, 69, 114, 142,
    155–156, 160
transitions 56–57
tunnel vision 30–31
tweens 31, 64, 86–87, 106, 133, 135, 170
Twitter 81, 85, 185–186, 192–193

uses and gratification theory 61, 79–82,
    90, 112, 115, 163

vape see e-cigarettes
video chat 36–38, 43, 46, 70,
    108–109
video game addiction see addiction
video game benefits 69, 101
video games 24, 41, 67–69, 88–89, 93,
    119–122
violence 8, 15, 94–98, 103–106, 112,
    117–118, 172–174, 178, 194–195
violent content 20, 28–29, 62, 79, 93,
    174, 179
virtual learning 50, 62, 85, 107, 110,
    113, 124–126, 129–136
virtual reality (VR) 125, 130

weapons 96–98
weight gain 39, 66–67, 121
WhatsApp 85, 171
White supremacy 89
World Health Organization (WHO) 65,
    100

Xanax see prescription drugs

YouTube 14, 27–29, 33, 135, 150, 165,
    186

Zoom see video chat

For Product Safety Concerns and Information please contact our EU
representative GPSR@taylorandfrancis.com
Taylor & Francis Verlag GmbH, Kaufingerstraße 24, 80331 München, Germany

www.ingramcontent.com/pod-product-compliance
Lightning Source LLC
Chambersburg PA
CBHW071413290326
41932CB00047B/2818